T0215146

Digital Mediascapes of Transnational Korean Youth Culture

Drawing on vivid ethnographic field studies of youth on the transnational move, across Seoul, Toronto, and Vancouver, this book examines transnational flows of Korean youth and their digital media practices.

This book explores how digital media are integrated into various forms of transnational life and imagination, focusing on young people's engagement with digital media. By combining theoretical discussion and in-depth empirical analysis, the book provides engaging narratives of transnational media fans, sojourners, and migrants. Each chapter illustrates a form of mediascape, in which transnational Korean youth culture and digital media are uniquely articulated. This perceptive research offers new insights into the transnationalization of youth cultural practices, from K-pop fandom to smartphone-driven storytelling.

A transnational and ethnographic focus makes this book the first of its kind, with an interdisciplinary approach that goes beyond the scope of existing digital media studies, youth culture studies, and Asian studies. It will be essential reading for scholars and students in media studies, migration studies, popular culture studies, and Asian studies.

Kyong Yoon is an associate professor of cultural studies at the University of British Columbia Okanagan. He has published widely on digital media, migration, and youth culture in international journals, including *New Media & Society*, *Popular Music & Society*, and *International Journal of Communication*.

Routledge Research in Digital Media and Culture in Asia
Edited by Dal Yong Jin, Simon Fraser University

Digital Mediascapes of Transnational Korean Youth Culture

Kyong Yoon

Routledge
Taylor & Francis Group

NEW YORK AND LONDON

First published 2020
by Routledge
605 Third Avenue, New York, NY 10017

and by Routledge
2 Park Square, Milton Park, Abingdon, Oxon, OX14 4RN

First issued in paperback 2022

Routledge is an imprint of the Taylor & Francis Group, an informa business

Publisher's Note
The publisher has gone to great lengths to ensure the quality of this reprint but points out that some imperfections in the original copies may be apparent.

Library of Congress Cataloging-in-Publication Data
A catalog record for this title has been requested

ISBN 13: 978-1-03-240101-0 (pbk)
ISBN 13: 978-1-138-60300-4 (hbk)
ISBN 13: 978-0-429-46925-1 (ebk)

DOI: 10.4324/9780429469251

Typeset in Sabon
by codeMantra

Contents

Acknowledgments

This monograph was supported by the Academy of Korean Studies Grant (AKS-2018-P06). Early versions of Chapters 5 and 6 appeared as Yoon, K. (2016). The cultural appropriation of smartphones in Korean transnational families. In S. S. Lim (Ed.), *Mobile communication and the family* (pp. 93–108). New York, NY: Springer and Yoon, K. (2016). The migrant lives of the digital generation. *Continuum: Journal of Media & Cultural Studies, 30*(4), 369–380.

Note to Readers

In this book, Korea refers to the Republic of Korea (South Korea) unless otherwise stated. In romanization of Korean sources and names, the Revised Romanization of Korean is used except for already established customs such as a person's name and locations.

1 Introduction

Transnational Youth and Digital Media

In August 2016, Tiffany, a member of the popular Korean pop group Girls' Generation, posted photos on her Instagram with a Japanese flag emoticon and an image of the Rising Sun Flag (known as *ugilgi* in Korean and *kyokujitsuki* in Japanese) to indicate that she was in Tokyo for a concert. The 27-year-old soon realized that her postings caused heated disputes among her Korean fans. Uploaded on August 15th, Korea's annual Liberation Day, which commemorates the country's independence from Japanese colonialism in 1945, the postings triggered public criticism of this Korean American star's ignorance of Korea's colonial history and memory. Consequently, Tiffany posted an apology—a picture of a handwritten note in Korean—on her Instagram page the following day, stating, "I am sorry for causing trouble on such a meaningful day. I am very embarrassed and regretful about my mistake, I will be more considerate next time" (Choi, 2016).

This incident shows how popular culture, digital media, and young people interact with each other in transnational contexts. As a popular figure in Asian youth culture and Korean idol pop music (K-pop)'s intra-Asian cultural traffic, Tiffany was criticized by her Korean fans due to her social media postings that she uploaded in Japan. While digital media enabled her to keep her fans informed about her intra-Asian tour, it also reminded her of existing national borders and her ethnic identity. Perhaps her identity as a Korean American born in California and trained by a major Korean entertainment agency since the age of 12 further complicates the transnational aspect of this incident. The Korean public has maintained an ambivalent attitude toward Western-raised talents of Korean heritage, desiring yet distancing itself from such individuals (Ahn, 2018). The Korean media industry has sought "global talents" (Ahn, 2018; Shin & Choi, 2015); consequently, young foreign-born Koreans—Tiffany, Jay Park, Krystal, and Eric Nam, to name a few—have continuously been introduced to Korean audiences. Due to their transnational experiences and upbringing, these young entertainers/artists have further facilitated the already vibrant Korean media industry. However, as shown in the fans' responses to Tiffany's postings, the globally recruited figures of Korean heritage have conveniently been represented as "us" or "them."

As young people physically or virtually move across national boundaries, they constantly engage with cultural forms that are produced in other countries. Digital media play an integral role in young people's physical and/or imagined border crossings. However, as shown in the Korean fans' dispute over the Japanese imperialist symbols in Tiffany's postings, the nation as an imagined community has not necessarily lost its influence on the seemingly transnationalized landscapes of youth culture. While transnational encounters may provide young people with resources for "possible lives" (Appadurai, 1996), young people's transnational cultural practices are not free of globalization's tensions, contradictions, and obstacles. In this regard, this book address how young people's agency is articulated with existing structural forces, such as resilient national gatekeeping and the hegemonic ideology of neoliberalism.

Korean youth and their culture have increasingly become transnational, especially since the 1990s. Over the past three decades, young Koreans' transnational mobility has been accelerated by the substantial deregulation of overseas tourism and studies abroad, as well as the flourishing national economy and media industry. In particular, since the Kim Young-sam administration's (1993–1998) declaration of globalization as a national policy in the mid-1990s, which consequently opened the country's domestic market based on international trade agreements, Korea has rapidly been incorporated into the global neoliberal system (S. S. Kim, 2000). Furthermore, the popularization of the Internet and the digital revolution have exposed young Koreans to transnational culture and media forms. Thus, for a better understanding of the contemporary youth cultures in and of Korea, it is important to examine the incorporation of digital media into young people's everyday lives.

In recent cultural studies, young people's cultural practices have been examined through global–local interactions (Maira & Soep, 2004; Pilkington & Johnson, 2003; Wise, 2008). These studies have explored how young people use "global resources to deal with local conditions" (Wise, 2008, p. 63). In particular, Maira and Soep (2004) proposed a framework to address how local young people's cultural practices are embedded within the shifts in local, national, and global forces, which is referred to as the "youthscape."

Despite flourishing theoretical and empirical discussions of youth culture in the global context over the past two decades at least, the globalization discourse has often involved the assumption of cores or norms, rather than the exploration of diverse transnational interactions (Lionnet & Shih, 2005). However, due in part to the role of digital media, young people have become increasingly involved in multidirectional transnational flows. The dominant discourse of globalization often assumes "a universal core or norm, which spreads out across the world while pulling into its vortex other forms of culture to be tested by its norm"; however, young people have increasingly engaged with the possibility of cultures "produced and performed without necessary mediation by the center" (Lionnet & Shih, 2005, p. 5). For example, the recent intra-Asian cultural flows have revealed that young people in non-Western regions appropriate various hybrid cultural texts, moving beyond the West–Rest framework. Many young Japanese and other Asians have been enthusiastic about K-pop, and an increasing number of candidates from other Asian countries have participated in auditions to become K-pop idols. The intra-Asian flows of popular culture show that Asian youth who enjoy K-pop may not necessarily consume this Asian cultural genre in relation to its Western counterpart (e.g., as a supplement to or replacement for Western pop music). In particular, the K-pop phenomenon in Japan raises questions regarding how and why Japanese youth enjoy the pop music of a country that was colonized and discriminated against by the Japanese colonial power. That is, recent transnational cultural phenomena have revealed various moments and forces that affect young people's cultural practices and identities.

This chapter provides the theoretical and empirical contexts for the role and meaning of digital media among young Koreans and their culture in transnational contexts, with reference to the post-1990s. It offers a framework for understanding the empirical chapters, and it discusses the process, rationale, and outline of the research on which the book draws. Drawing on media and cultural studies' frameworks and extensive empirical studies, this book examines young people's digital media practices in the transnational context, questioning how they access and appropriate global cultural resources to negotiate their locally specific conditions and identity work. In particular, it analyzes digital media as an increasingly important transnational cultural resource. Existing cultural studies of global youth have paid insufficient attention to the role of digital media in the transnational flows of youth cultural forms. Consequently, it is important to address digital media as integral components of young people's everyday lives.

This book examines how young Koreans and their digital media practices are on the transnational move. Drawing on extensive field studies conducted between 2004 and 2018, this book explores how digital media are integrated into various forms of transnational life and imagination. Through its five case study-based chapters, the book provides engaging narratives that reveal the realities and complexities of young people's digital media practices. The book critically examines the digital generation's lived experiences with transnational media flows by addressing different groups of young people who are virtually and/or physically mobile: transnational popular culture fans, young people in transnational families, overseas sojourners, and young migrants.

The young people examined in this book are not a homogeneous group. However, they can be categorized as the "digital generation" as they share common experiences of digital media evolution to some extent.

That is, the young people under examination in this book may constitute a "media generation [. . .] constructed as collectively produced, shared and processed responses to the availability or pervasiveness of a particular technology" (Vittadini, Siibak, Reifová, & Bilandzic, 2014, p. 66). This digital generation includes young people who might share similar memories about the development of new media, such as the Internet and particular social media, from their childhood, despite potential differences in their social and cultural backgrounds.

By examining a facet of the digital generation, each chapter illustrates a form of mediascape, in which transnational Korean youth culture and digital media are uniquely articulated with each other. In so doing, the book proposes the transnational mediascape framework, by which media are analyzed as a series of imaginations, practices, and negotiations (Appadurai, 1996; Georgiou, 2006). By utilizing the suffix "scape," Appadurai (1996) examined the processes of globalization as

> deeply perspectival constructs, inflected by the historical, linguistic, and political situatedness of different sorts of actors: nation-states, multinationals, diasporic communities, as well as subnational groupings and movements (whether religious, political, or economic), and even intimate face-to-face groups, such as villages, neighborhoods, and families.
>
> (p. 33)

Among other "-scapes", the mediascape refers to "distribution of electronic capabilities," which also involves various inflections, depending on such factors as technological mode, audiences, and media ownership (Appadurai, 1996). By applying the term "mediascape," this book examines how different structural and agentic forces are involved in digital media-driven flows of transnational youth culture.

The book aims to explore how young people's digital media practices are transnationalized and, thus, contribute to redefining their cultural identities. Through an in-depth observation of the digital generation's media practices, the book addresses under-researched questions about the integration of digital media into the transnational lives and cultural imaginations of young people. By examining the movements and traces of digital media and their users throughout and beyond Korea, this book offers a transnational and ethnographic analysis of digital Korea and its youth culture. In so doing, it makes methodological and empirical contributions to the field.

First, the research problematizes pervasive "methodological nationalism," which considers the nation-state as a naturalized unit of analysis (Wimmer & Glick Schiller, 2002). Transnationalism offers a critical perspective that recognizes "the possibilities of networks and communities to surpass national boundaries, as well as the continuing significance of the national borders in partly framing and restricting social actions and their meanings" (Georgiou, 2006, p. 10). This book enriches the digital media scholarship by exploring media practices as transnational and diasporic flows that can be constrained and redirected by the ways in which globalizing and localizing forces are articulated with each other (Georgiou, 2006; Y. Kim, 2011; Madianou & Miller, 2012; Sun & Sinclair, 2016).

Second, the ethnographic research on the transnational traces and movements of digital media and their users offers an insightful cultural investigation of global and local digital mediascapes. This ethnographic research on transnational media flows challenges the top-down approach through which digital media are analyzed as a structural or institutional process. The book makes a contribution by furthering cultural and media studies' methodological scopes, which often focus narrowly on media representation or small groups of audiences (Moores, 2012). By examining various young people's lived cultures and media uses, the ambivalent and complex nature of media in the transnational construction of youth identities can be revealed. In addition, the book's ethnographic research explores how emerging digital media are appropriated in relation to other areas of our daily lives (Moores, 2012) and how newer digital media might remediate and be signified in relation to older media forms (e.g., the television) (Bolter & Grusin, 2000). In so doing, the book examines the role of digital media in young people's transnational lives, in which they negotiate between different digital media forms and cultural identities (Madianou & Miller, 2012).

Evolution of Youth Culture in Korea

Korean popular cultural forms emerged on a global scale in the 21st century. As exemplified by the Korean Wave (i.e., the global diffusion of Korean popular culture) and the global fans of K-pop in particular, global youth have increasingly engaged with cultural forms that have emerged in Korea. This phenomenon is surprising, especially given Korea's recent and short history of deregulation and the liberalization of its cultural industries. Indeed, for three decades between the 1960s and 1980s, the country was ruled by military regimes that strictly regulated the transnational flows of young people and youth cultural forms, and thus, the exposure of Korean youth and their cultures to transnational contexts has been relatively recent.

Until the 1990s, authoritarian regimes imposed the values of anti-communism and patriotism on young people through numerous educational regulations and rituals, such as nationally controlled history textbooks and the Charter for National Education (J. Kang, 2016). The Park Chung-hee regime, which took power through a military coup in 1961 and ended with Park's assassination in 1979, and the next military regime (1980–1988), which was established by the military coup and civilian massacre by Chun Doo-hwan, sought rapid, export-driven development by oppressing any dissident voices (Kim & Shin, 2010). Thus, not surprisingly, young people's transnational imaginations and cultural practices were restricted to a large extent until the 1990s. Due to nationalizing forces that imposed defensive nationalism from above, young people were not significantly exposed to transnational influences under the authoritarian regimes. Under the system of total mobilization for authoritarian development, Koreans were constantly interpellated into *kukmin* (nation-state people) without being allowed to contemplate and seek their identities as individual citizens (Cho Han, 2000). The political liberalization began under the semi-civilian regime (1988–1993), during which the Seoul Olympic Games were hosted in 1988. This event attracted international attention to Korea as one of the emerging Asian economic powers and accelerated its political liberalization and opening up to the world. The social atmosphere during the transition into a post-authoritarian government caused increased transnational flows of young people and cultural content.

While the paternalistic nation-state strictly controlled young people's outbound international mobility regarding tourism and the pursuit of studies overseas, the ban was lifted in 1989. In fact, until 1989, young Koreans under the age of 30 were not legally permitted to go abroad for pleasure, while overseas studies were allowed on some occasions (Son & Choi, 2014).[1] In contrast to the period under the authoritarian regime, when young Koreans' overseas tourism and studies were restricted by government regulations, overseas backpacking and short-term language study abroad have become rites of passage among an increasing number of Korean youth since the 1990s. According to a recent national survey (2013), 13.3% of young Koreans aged between 13 and 24, who are often defined in Korean policy documents as the "youth" (*cheongsonyeon*) group, have taken trips overseas (Statistics Korea, 2014). The pursuit of studies overseas during the early or mid-teens has become a popular option for middle-class families. In comparison, more recently, long-stay overseas travel has emerged as a lifestyle option among Koreans in their twenties and thirties (M. Y. Lee, 2019; K. Yoon, 2014).

In addition to the strict controls on the transnational mobility of young people, transnational cultural forms were tightly regulated until the early 1990s. The importation and domestic circulation of media content were monitored by the government, which allegedly protected not only the national economy but also traditional values (Jung, 2007). Censorship was applied to not only Korean but also foreign content. In particular, politically liberal content tended to be banned or had to be adjusted before its public release. For example, rock music in the 1970s and 1980s was severely monitored and often criminalized by the government (Kim & Shin, 2010). All forms of Japanese popular cultural content were banned until the late 1990s. Consequently, young people's desires to engage with overseas popular culture were oppressed and marginalized. Thus, as will be discussed in Chapter 2, young Koreans often had to bypass national gatekeeping to access foreign popular culture and, in so doing, developed particular subcultures, such as fan groups of Japanese animation (*donghohoe*). Young people's negotiation of the national regulation of popular culture implies that culture is an arena of hegemonic struggles between the dominant and the subordinate (Fiske, 2011).

After decades of the authoritarian nation-state's control, the 1990s ushered in a new phase for youth and their cultures. The interplay of several structural factors such as political liberalization, economic growth, and involvement in the global market economy contributed to the emergence of a new era, which was referred to as "the era of culture" (K. H. Lee, 2007) or "the era of cultural tribes" (D. Y. Lee, 2005). Urban young people's styles, influenced by Western popular culture and the emerging consumer culture, became more visible, as evidenced by the 1990s' "urban tribes" in the Apgujeong area of the Gangnam District (K. H. Lee, 2007). The 1990s marked a radical cultural change that enabled the emergence of numerous subcultures and their incorporation into the mainstream consumer culture.

In the early 1990s, young people who were exposed to the rapidly emerging urban consumer culture, which was influenced by Western youth cultural styles, were often referred to as "the New Generation [*sinsedae*]" (K. H. Lee, 2007). *Sinsedae* extensively appropriated foreign (especially Western) cultural styles and materials, and creatively localized them. For understanding global–local conjunction in the 1990s' Korean youth culture, Seo Taiji (born in 1972) might be one of the most important figures. By adapting and appropriating American hip-hop and rap, his music and performance styles went viral among young Koreans. Seo was not only a best-selling musician but also the most influential musician among young Koreans in the 1990s, and his influences on later generations of Korean pop musician have been significant. Seo creatively reappropriated Afro-American music and fashion, infused with social messages such as criticism of the strict school system and the pursuit of North–South Korean reunification. Seo's musical style and lyrics also affected and reflected the rising individualism among young Koreans (Maliangkay, 2014). His music was particularly influential among young people undergoing the transition to adulthood and thus seeking to distinguish themselves from others. K. H. Lee (2007) argued that "For youth, Seo Taiji's music gave a transitory moment to avoid the dominant structures of feeling by empowering themselves" (p. 63).

The significant growth of young people's transnational mobility and their exposure to global cultural products increased Western influences and the rapid relocalization of the influences in Korean youth culture, which later contributed to the emergence of the Korean Wave. While Western influences on Korean popular music can be traced to Korean performers who imitated American musicians in bars near the US military bases in Korea starting in the 1950s (Shin, 2016), it was not until the 1990s that the new genres of hip-hop and rap were substantially incorporated into Korean popular culture and mainstream media. By incorporating Western influences extensively, the K-pop industry has developed its unique manufacturing system, which is referred to as the "in-house system" (Shin, 2009). In this system, Korean-based entertainment companies combine the contributions of international talents (e.g., composers, producers, and choreographers). For example, major K-pop companies have increasingly recruited non-Korean composers, including American, Swedish, Danish, British, and Norwegian specialists (S. Yoon, 2013).

However, the flourishing cultural discourses and practices of Korean youth in the 1990s did not last beyond that decade but, rather, shifted into other forms. When the Korean national economy was devastated owing to the Asian financial crisis of 1997, the hedonistic and liberal atmosphere of youth culture, drawn from the flourishing consumer economy of the early and mid-1990s, shifted into the neoliberal mode of the competitive, market-oriented youth culture (Cho, 2015). The post-1997 Korean youth, especially those who entered the new job market in and after 1997, were often referred to as "Generation IMF," symbolizing the financial crisis, during which Korea had to rely on an International Monetary Fund (IMF) bailout (J. Kang, 2016). Youth labor markets stagnated, and thus, unemployment rates rose rapidly. The neoliberal economic reform accelerated the influx of global corporations and the competition between domestic workers and global competitors. Accordingly, as J. Kang (2016) pointed out, the IMF generation youth were forced "to equip themselves for global competitiveness—including acquiring English competency and a cosmopolitan sensibility, as well as honing their creativity" (p. 34). In contrast to the era of the authoritarian developmental state or the early 1990s' liberal era, the post-1997 neoliberal economy has facilitated the individual's self-development and ability to fit into and survive the highly flexible labor market (Cho, 2015). This ethos has dominated society and has accordingly influenced youth cultural styles, as evidenced by the rise of K-pop fan culture. G. Kim (2019) argued that, from a political economy perspective, the recent global rise of Korean popular culture (the Korean Wave phenomenon) is a beneficiary of Korea's neoliberal reengineering of the nation-state. As will be further discussed in Chapter 3, K-pop as a recent cultural genre and commodity form emerged in relation to the neoliberal commodification of young, soft dancing bodies through digital platforms and the affective labor of young people (I. Kang, 2014; G. Kim, 2019).

Since its "compressed modernization" (Chang, 2010), led by the authoritarian and developmental state (the 1960s–1980s), followed by the rise of a consumer society in the early 1990s, Korea has rapidly adapted to the neoliberal global economy. Through various forms of Western-influenced media and West-seeking migration, globalization has rapidly been embodied in young Koreans' lived experiences. Korea's transition to the post-developmental state and integration into the neoliberal global economy have provided young Koreans with the momentum to engage with the discourse and practice of global youth culture. That is, young Koreans have become transnationally mobile due to the lifting of the overseas travel ban and the growth of outbound tourism, on the one hand, and they have become culturally mobile due to their extensive exposure to global popular culture, on the other. As Wise (2008) pointed out, global youth and their culture are facilitated by the accelerated transnational mobility of young people and the imaginary flows of popular culture. This emergence of global youth culture is evident in the recent history of young Koreans and their cultural practices. By appropriating different cultural resources, Korean youth and the country's cultural industries have generated a unique form of cultural content and styles, which has become the genesis of the recent Korean Wave.[2]

Since the "era of culture" in the 1990s, popular culture has been deeply incorporated into young Koreans' everyday lives. Since the 2000s, various forms of digital media, which flourished in Korea's highly advanced information technology (IT) environment, have even increased young people's exposure to transnational popular culture. To examine youth audiences' interpretation and negotiation of the transnational flows of popular culture, which will be discussed in detail in Chapters 2 and 3, cultural studies provide an effective toolbox, as the field has explored how cultural consumption engages with the process of resignification and negotiation of social words (e.g., Fiske, 2011; Storey, 2018). In the classical cultural studies tradition (Cohen, 1999; Hall & Jefferson, 1976), young people's consumption of popular culture is considered symbolic resistance. However, by focusing extensively on spectacular working-class youth, the classical youth cultural studies restricted their applicability to a wider range of the young demographic (Clarke, 2005).

Given the limitations of the early youth cultural studies, recent studies have focused more on ordinary young people's engagement with popular culture—digital media in particular—in conjunction with the legacy of (active) audience studies. According to the advocates of active audience studies, while popular cultural forms as products of cultural industries may construct dominant audience positions, audiences may evade and/or resist the dominant ideology inscribed and reproduced through popular cultural texts (Fiske, 2011). The audiences have the ability to construct their "own meanings of self and of social relations" (Fiske, 2011, p. 8). Audiences interpret, respond to, and "poach" the popular cultural text, and they, thus, produce new meanings from different perspectives (Ang, 1990; Jenkins, 1992; Liebes & Katz, 1994). Moreover, a group of youth studies, often referred to as "post-subcultural studies," may provide some insights to young audiences' sociality and thus enhance an understanding of how young people consume popular culture for their sociality and identity work. By questioning the previous youth studies' strict subcultural identity and divisions, this new stream of youth studies suggests that young people engage more flexibly with different micro-groups and reveals that they increasingly navigate from one cultural style to another in the "supermarket of style" (Polhemus, 1997). In particular, the digital media-driven youth culture allows young people to be more individualized and to engage with different forms of transnational and/or translocal popular culture (Bennett & Kahn-Harris, 2004; Hodkinson, 2016).

Audience studies, along with post-subcultural studies, offer an effective theoretical lens through which digital media-driven, flexible, and individualized cultural consumption among young Koreans since the 2000s can be analyzed from a cultural studies perspective. That is, young people's appropriation of transnational popular culture shows that culture is always an arena of power relations in which different identities are imagined, formed, and/or negotiated (Storey, 2018).

Digital Korea and Youth

Digital media have been integral components of young people's everyday lives. In particular, Korea has experienced the unprecedented growth of its digital media technology industry, which also involves a vibrant user culture. In this regard, it is worth reviewing how Korea has evolved as a digital nation and how its user culture, especially among young users, has been analyzed. Furthermore, for a better understanding of young people's digital media practices and their cultural meanings, it is necessary to address relevant theoretical discussions. Thus, this section historically reviews the traces of digital youth culture in Korea and proposes a framework for analyzing the transnational dimension of digitally driven Korean youth culture.

The transnational mobility of young Koreans and their culture has largely benefited from the vibrant growth of the IT industry and its infrastructure. In the late 1990s and early 2000s, Korea experienced the record-breaking penetration of new media technologies. Korea is considered a country that has been affected extensively and intensively by digital technology especially since the 1990s (Jin, 2017; Oh & Larson, 2011). Furthermore, the Korean IT industry and vibrant user culture have continued in the smartphone era, that is, the 2010s (Jin, 2017). Korea has been considered a test bed for cutting-edge technologies (Jin, 2010). As a response to the aftermath of the 1997 financial crisis, the country's IT industry grew rapidly, along with the government's supportive policy.[3] Korean IT corporations, such as Samsung and LG, have quickly caught up with their global giant counterparts in the IT market and, in particular, in relation to the smartphone (Jin, 2017). The state–industry symbiosis, as evidenced by the successful government-led broadband infrastructure plans in the 1990s, accelerated the expansion and development of the IT sector (K. S. Lee, 2012).

In addition to the structural aspect of Korea's IT development, comprising the fast-growing industry and the interventionist government, the country's young media users have played a significant role in constructing "the most connected and Net-addicted country on Earth" and of the future (Taylor, 2006). The digital media-driven youth culture in Korea can be analyzed by examining how young people have responded to different phases of the digital media evolution. Young Koreans have been known as early adopters of digital technologies (Jin, 2017). Especially in the early era of the Internet and social media, the international news media reported on young Koreans as an example of the cutting-edge digital generation (Jin, 2010). Young Koreans' unique user culture and community revolving around the Korean-based Cyworld, one of the world's first social networking sites, are considered an enlightening example that might have prophesied the Facebook phenomenon (E. M. Kim, 2016).[4]

There are ongoing debates about the sociocultural consequences of digital media's rapid penetration into a wide range of social worlds in Korea. For some, digital media technologies accelerate individualism and might, therefore, adversely affect the traditional norms of communication. In particular, mobile phones (2G feature phones) became one of the first personal technology devices to be extensively adopted by young people in Korea in the 1990s and 2000s, and were considered to promote hyper-individualism, thus in turn increasing the dislocation of families and disrupting other social relations (K. Yoon, 2006). In some ways, the enhanced individualization of communication seemed to offer the potential to empower individuals. For example, mobile phones were considered to contribute to young women's social negotiation by enabling an expressive culture (Y. Kim, 2007).

In contrast, some scholars have found that digital media technology is rapidly localized and even "re-traditionalized" in the Korean context. In his study of Korean teenagers using mobile phones in the early 2000s, K. Yoon (2003) found that local sociality, drawing on traditional family-oriented norms, might not have been severely challenged by the new technology but, rather, were incorporated into mobile phone-driven communications without much tension. Similarly, Hjorth (2007) found that emerging digital technologies reinforce existing familial norms. According to her, digital communication technologies in the Korean context contribute to ritualizing existing social relationships and ties. She also stated that "Korea's model of technological innovation has led to far-ranging social consequences that demonstrate the role of 'socio-technologies' in reinforcing localised modes of sociality and identity" (Hjorth, 2007, pp. 398–399). Digital media technologies, some of which may, by design, facilitate individualization (boyd, 2014), may not necessarily shape young people's sociality. By challenging technological determinism, several empirical studies have addressed young Koreans' local sociality in the digital mediascape. For example, different digital media forms such as Cyworld, blogs, and Twitter have been considered to generate digital connections, often in close relation to existing offline sociality (E. M. Kim, 2016; D. H. Lee, 2013). These studies suggest that while resonating with offline, conventional social ties and intimacy, digital media provide "a mediated aural space" in which users negotiate heterogeneous social relations and access different cultural resources (D. H. Lee, 2013).

As indicated in several recent studies, young Koreans' digital connections have extended to the public sphere. For example, empirical studies have examined the roles and meanings of digital media among young Koreans who have participated in massive candlelight vigils against governments and promoted public agendas since the 2000s. For these young people, digital media platforms have been an affective public sphere (Ok, 2011), in which emphatic emotions and feelings are shared and transferred to social movements. By focusing on digital media's mobilization processes among young participants in candlelight vigils, J. Kang (2016) argued that digital media contributed to the "cultural ignition" process, by which technological innovation enabled youth to share content that intrigues them and to form a collective that does not necessarily comprise intentional protesters. According to these studies, digital media have contributed to a "cultural turn in civil resistance" (S. M. Kim, 2015, p. 238), which can be characterized by a diverse range of participants, including teenagers, and mobilization without centralized leadership (J. Kang, 2016).

Overall, the rapid evolution of Korea's digital media and IT industry has undeniably contributed to accelerating the transnational flows of youth cultural forms and imaginations. For example, as will be discussed in Chapter 3, K-pop's incorporation into digital media platforms has attracted overseas fans and encouraged their enthusiastic consumption of and participation in the music. However, the celebrated history of IT growth in Korea also involves a "dark side of Korean IT development," which includes the government's surveillance of online users (K. S. Lee, 2012, p. 5). Indeed, the government and major corporations have attempted to control Korea's digital mediascapes. In 2009, the economic blogger known as Minerva, a 30-year-old unemployed man who criticized the government's economic policy, was charged with spreading false rumors. The arrest of the self-taught economic blogger who questioned the dominant system was an example of how digital mediascapes have been strictly controlled by the government. Another example is the Shutdown law, which forbids anyone under 16 to play online games between midnight and 6 A.M. The law passed in 2011 and, with some revisions, has applied to young online gamers. Apart from the government's policing of digital mediascapes, the extensive commodification of media practices may be an emerging problem for the digital media-driven youth culture in Korea. For several political economic critics, digital media may accelerate the commodification of culture while exploiting young Koreans' free labor (Epstein & Jung, 2011; Hjorth, 2011). Hjorth (2011) argued that the flourishing user-generated content in Korean cyberspace and the celebratory discourse of the participatory culture have, in reality, been repurposed and redirected toward platform-providing corporations.

To examine young people's appropriation of emerging digital technologies, media and cultural studies have explored different approaches. Among others, this book—Chapters 4–6 in particular—engages with the technology domestication approach, which effectively examines the context and agency in the process of technology appropriation. The domestication approach, initially proposed by Silverstone and Hirsch (1992), examines how media technology as a cultural object and a conveyor of meanings is incorporated into the user's everyday contexts and generates meanings. Based on ethnographic evidence, this approach analyzes media in context and in progress and, in so doing, contributes to a nuanced understanding of media practices. For example, a few empirical studies conducted in Korea offered contextual analysis of new media appropriation (Lim 2008; K. Yoon, 2003). In the domestication thesis, the process of domestication does not have to narrowly address home and household contexts (Haddon, 2011). In the ubiquitous media era, the domestication approach has been extended to various moments and locations in which media are used. However, with a few exceptions, the process of technology domestication has been insufficiently addressed in transnational contexts. For example, despite the increasing attention to digital media in Korean youth culture, there is insufficient research on the transnational dimension of young people's digital media practices. A few recent studies have examined young migrants' use of digital media for connection with the homeland and coping with transnational lives (Lee & Ahn, 2019; K. Yoon, 2018). However, these studies focus on remediation of homeland media in diasporic contexts rather than fully explore how and why particular modes of mediated communication develop through transnational digital media. Further research is needed to examine how young people on the transnational move adopt and domesticate a particular digital media form and how such appropriation affects the young people's identity work.

Transnational contexts may further complicate how emerging digital media forms are adopted, appropriated, and resignified. By further articulating the technology domestication framework, Madianou and Miller (2012) claimed that factors such as affordability, availability, and literacy influence the transnational individuals' choices, preferences, and uses of particular forms of technology among a variety of possible media options. They further articulated the technology domestication theory to propose the polymedia theory that explores "how users can overcome the limitations of any particular medium by choosing an alternative in order to achieve their communicative intents and to assume control over their relationships" (Madianou & Miller, 2012, p. 9). That is, polymedia theory focuses on "the social and emotional consequences of choosing between a plurality of media" (p. 8) and is, thus, a particularly effective theoretical tool for understanding transnational youth and their media use. Transnational young people are exposed to different media environments, literacies, and meanings simultaneously in two or more cultural contexts. For example, young migrants' media practices involve not only how they synchronically choose and distinguish between emerging media forms but also how they diachronically relate an emerging media form to previous ones.

Young people have engaged with popular culture and digital media while being on the transnational move. To acquire a comprehensive understanding of the transnational mobility of digitally equipped youth, it is important to examine the contexts of media use. As Hjorth (2009) claimed, "divergent formations informed by linguistic and sociocultural specificities (...) have disrupted any notion of the Internet as homogeneous entity", and "what it means to be 'online'–and its relationship to the offline–are indeed informed by already existing cultural practices and customs" (p. 248). Physical locations, boundaries, and cultural norms continuously inform particular forms of digital media and how they are used. As suggested by Couldry (2004), the exploration of media use as "practice," rather than as narrowly defined "media consumption," challenges "the normal media studies assumption that what audiences do ('audiencing') *is* a distinctive set of practices rather than an artificially chosen 'slice' through daily life" (Couldry, 2004, p. 121). By examining media practices in context and as a process, structural forces and user agency can be comprehensively considered, and the diversities and complications in the emerging digital mediascapes can be effectively explored.

Organization of the Book

This chapter has introduced the background and theoretical frameworks for subsequent chapters. Drawing on field studies conducted in Korea and Canada between 2004 and 2018, the remaining chapters present empirical studies that explore diverse aspects of young people's engagement with digital media in transnational contexts. The empirical analysis comprises two different yet overlapping approaches. The first approach explores the translational flows of popular culture. Chapters 2 and 3, respectively, examine how young Koreans engage with Japanese popular culture and how K-pop is integrated into global mediascapes. The second approach examines the transnational flows of young people equipped with digital media. Chapters 4–6 discuss how young Koreans use digital media in the process of transnational migration. The two approaches serve to capture moments of the digital mediascapes of Korean youth culture. They address transnational cultural practices via digital media (Chapters 2 and 3) and transnational communication via digital media (Chapters 4–6).

Chapter 1 provides the theoretical and empirical contexts for the cultural meanings of digital media in transnational Korean youth culture, with reference to the post-1990s period. Drawing on media and cultural studies' approaches, such as audience studies and technology domestication studies, the chapter discusses the process, rationale, and outline of the research on which this book draws.

Chapter 2 examines young Koreans' subcultural engagement with Japanese popular culture, which was officially banned in Korea for decades. The chapter illustrates that the young fans developed subcultural strategies to bypass national gatekeeping and regulations. It shows that paradoxically the national regulations allowed young Koreans to engage reflexively with postcolonial histories, on the one hand, and to rethink the national, on the other. Moreover, the chapter discusses how young Koreans experimentally appropriated digital media technologies, which might later influence the evolution of the Korean Wave and its participatory fan culture.

Chapter 3 addresses how K-pop as a hybrid popular cultural form created in Korea moves across national borders and is incorporated into the transnational digital mediascape. Drawing on interviews with K-pop fans in Canada, the chapter shows how digital media are integrated into the process of transnational cultural consumption and participatory fan culture. By examining fans' engagement with reaction videos and dance cover videos, the chapter explores how the participatory aspects of media fandom are exercised and articulated with structural forces, such as the media corporations' commodification of fan labor.

Chapter 4 focuses on Korean sojourners in Canada and their use of digital media technologies in their transnational lives. These sojourners, who held nonrenewable one-year working holiday visas, were motivated partly by the dominant discourse that defines the global experience as an important component to become global citizens. While seeking global experiences and personal growth during their overseas gap year, the young sojourners explored particular ways of using digital media in coping with their transnational and transient lives—such as temporary control and disconnection, connection with the homeland media, and digital storytelling.

Chapter 5 explores how different forms of digital media are appropriated in transnational family communication. Drawing on in-depth interviews with young people in transnational Korean families, the chapter reveals that the young people engaged with digital media to negotiate their transnational family relations and to manage different senses of belonging while switching and choosing between different digital media platforms. For the young Koreans who grew up with distant, technologically mediated parenting, the Korean-developed Kakao apps (KakaoTalk and Kakao Story) were often used for virtual family time, while other social media platforms, such as Facebook and Instagram, were appropriated for peer networking.

Chapter 6 examines diasporic young Koreans' media practices. Drawing on interviews with young Koreans who are permanent residents of Canada, the chapter illustrates how young migrants' use of digital media is influenced by their memories and literacies of the earlier media used in their homeland and by their desire to be connected with diasporic ethnic networks. The chapter shows that, while the young Korean migrants were able to omnivorously access and appropriate different new media forms, the ethnically oriented boundaries in their digital media use did not seem to be diluted.

Chapter 7, the concluding chapter, synthesizes the main research findings and identifies the significance of the research. Moreover, future research agendas for transnational media studies are proposed.

Notes

1 The authoritarian regimes did not only control young people's transnational mobility but also policed their everyday mobility. Until the late 1980s, young people—that is, university students and young workers—were policed by the military regimes, which oppressed any dissident voices. Under the radar of the military governments, student activists and labor union participants were reportedly surveilled, and thus, their mobility was limited (Moon, 2005).

2 Since the 1990s, the Korean government's regulations and public attitudes to American popular culture and consumer culture have become relaxed. Until the early 1990s, a trend of anti-Americanism among young people was evident, especially among leftist or student activists who challenged the neo-colonial power of the United States. However, along with neoliberalization of society, American cultural forms and brands have been deeply incorporated into Koreans' everyday lives since the 1990s. Consequently, Koreans' lifestyles have become increasingly hybridized in regard to global brands and commodities. For example, since its arrival in Korea in 1999, Starbucks, which initially represented a high-end global coffee brand, has expanded its franchises to the extent that Seoul holds the record as the city with the largest number of Starbucks stores ($n = 284$ as of 2014), followed by New York City and Shanghai (Yanofsky, 2014).

3 In his study of Korea's online gaming industries and culture, Jin (2010) claimed that the rapid increase in the number of PC *bangs* (Korean-style Internet cafés, equipped with high-end personal computers for online gaming), which played an important role in the flourishing of the online gaming culture

among Korean youth, was first "introduced during the economic crisis by workers who had been laid off from major electronic companies" (p. 24).
4 Cyworld is a Korean-developed social networking site, which was active and popular between 1999 and 2015. For further discussion about the role and meanings of Cyworld in Korean youth culture, please refer to Chapter 5.

References

Ahn, J. (2018). *Mixed-race politics and neoliberal multiculturalism in South Korean media.* New York, NY: Palgrave Macmillan.

Ang, I. (1990). Culture and communication: Towards an ethnographic critique of media consumption in the transnational media system. *European Journal of Communication, 5*(2), 239–260.

Appadurai, A. (1996). *Modernity at large: Cultural dimensions of globalization.* Minneapolis, MN: University of Minnesota Press.

Bennett, A., & Kahn-Harris, K. (Eds.). (2004). *After subculture: Critical studies in contemporary youth culture.* New York, NY: Palgrave.

Bolter, J. D., & Grusin, R. (2000). *Remediation: Understanding new media.* Cambridge, MA: MIT Press.

boyd, d. (2014). *It's complicated: The social lives of networked teens.* New Haven, CT: Yale University Press.

Chang, K. S. (2010). *South Korea under compressed modernity: Familial political economy in transition.* New York, NY: Routledge.

Cho, H. (2015). The spec generation who can't say "No": Overeducated and underemployed youth in contemporary South Korea. *positions: east asia cultures critique, 23*(3), 437–462.

Cho Han, H. (2000). "You are entrapped in an imaginary well": The formation of subjectivity within compressed development-a feminist critique of modernity and Korean culture. *Inter-Asia Cultural Studies, 1*(1), 49–69.

Choi, H. W. (2016, August 16). Tiffany upsets fans with social media blunder. Retrieved from http://kpopherald.koreaherald.com/view.php?ud=201608161438201839354_2

Clarke, G. (2005). Defending ski-jumpers: A critique of theories of youth subculture. In K. Gelder (Ed.), *The subcultures reader* (pp. 169–174). London: Routledge.

Cohen, P. (1999). *Rethinking the youth question; Education, labour and cultural studies.* Durham, NC: Duke University Press.

Couldry, N. (2004). Theorising media as practice. *Social Semiotics, 14*(2), 115–132.

Epstein, S., & Jung, S. (2011). Korean youth netizenship and its discontents. *Media International Australia, 141*(1), 78–86.

Fiske, J. (2011). *Reading the popular* (2nd ed.). London: Routledge.

Georgiou, M. (2006). *Diaspora, identity and the media: Diasporic transnationalism and mediated spatialities.* Cresskill, NJ: Hampton Press.

Haddon, L. (2011). Domestication analysis, objects of study, and the centrality of technologies in everyday life. *Canadian Journal of Communication, 36*(2), 311–323.

Hall, S., & Jefferson, T. (Eds.). (1976). *Resistance through rituals: Youth subcultures in postwar Britain.* London: Hutchinson.

Hjorth, L. (2007). Home and away: A case study of the use of Cyworld mini-hompy by Korean students studying in Australia. *Asian Studies Review, 31*(4), 397–407.

Hjorth, L. (2009). Gifts of presence: A case study of a South Korean virtual community, Cyworld's mini-homphy. In G. Goggin & M. McLelland (Eds.), *Internationalizing internet studies: Beyond anglophone paradigms* (pp. 237–251). London: Routledge.

Hjorth, L. (2011). Locating the online: Creativity and user-created content in Seoul. *Media International Australia, 141*(1), 118–127.

Hodkinson, P. (2016). Youth cultures and the rest of life: Subcultures, post-subcultures and beyond. *Journal of Youth Studies, 19*(5), 629–645.

Jenkins, H. (1992). *Textual poachers: Television fans and participatory culture.* London: Routledge.

Jin, D. Y. (2010). *Korea's online gaming empire.* Cambridge, MA: MIT Press.

Jin, D. Y. (2017). *Smartland Korea: Mobile communication, culture, and society.* Ann Arbor, MI: Michigan University Press.

Jung, Y. (2007). Japan in the eye of the beholder: Its evolution and dilemma. *Japan Space, 2*, 70–91.

Kang, I. (2014). The political economy of idols: South Korea's neoliberal restructuring and its impact on the entertainment labour force. In J. B. Choi & R. Maliangkay (Eds.), *K-pop—The international rise of the Korean music industry* (pp. 63–77). London: Routledge.

Kang, J. (2016). *Igniting the internet: Youth and activism in postauthoritarian South Korea.* Honolulu, HI: University of Hawai'i Press.

Kim, E. M. (2016). Digital media and connected individuals. In Y. Kim (Ed.), *Routledge handbook of Korean culture and society* (pp. 231–242). London: Routledge.

Kim, G. (2019). *From factory girls to K-pop idols girls: Cultural politics of developmentalism, patriarchy, and neoliberalism in South Korea's popular music industry.* Lanham, MD: Lexington Books.

Kim, P. H., & Shin, H. (2010). The birth of "rok": Cultural imperialism, nationalism, and the glocalization of rock music in South Korea, 1964–1975. *positions: east asia cultures critique, 18*(1), 199–230.

Kim, S. M. (2015). *Being surplus in the age of new media: Ing-yeo subjectivity and youth culture in South Korea* (PhD thesis). George Mason University, Fairfax, VA.

Kim, S. S. (2000). Korea and globalization (*segyehwa*): A framework for analysis. In S. S. Kim (Ed), *Korea's globalization* (pp. 1–28). Cambridge: Cambridge University Press.

Kim, Y. (2007). An ethnographer meets the mobile girl. *Feminist Media Studies, 7*(2), 204–209.

Kim, Y. (2011). *Transnational migration, media and identity of Asian women: Diasporic daughters.* New York, NY: Routledge.

Lee, C. S., & Ahn, J. H. (2019). Imagining homeland: New media use among Korean international graduate students in the U.S. In A. Atay & M. U. D'Silva (Eds.), *Mediated intercultural communication in digital age* (pp. 185–203). London: Routledge.

Lee, D. H. (2013). Smartphones, mobile social space, and new sociality in Korea. *Mobile Media & Communication, 1*(3), 269–284.

Lee, D. Y. (2005). *A society of cultural tribes: From hippie to pyein*. Seoul: Chaeksesang.

Lee, K. H. (2007). Looking back at the cultural politics of youth culture in South Korea in the 1990s: On the new generation phenomenon and the emergence of cultural studies. *Korean Journal of Communication Studies, 15*(4), 47–79.

Lee, K. S. (2012). *IT development in Korea: A broadband nirvana?* New York, NY: Routledge.

Lee, M. Y. (2019). "Escape from Hell-Joseon": A study of Korean long-term travelers in India. *Korean Anthropology Review, 3*(19), 45–78.

Liebes, T., & Katz, E. (1994). *The export of meaning: Cross-cultural readings of Dallas*. Oxford: Polity Press.

Lim, S. S. (2008). Technology domestication in the Asian homestead: Comparing the experiences of middle class families in China and South Korea. *East Asian Science, Technology and Society: An International Journal, 2*(2), 189–209.

Lionnet, F., & Shih, S. (2005). Introduction: Thinking through the minor, transnationally. In F. Lionnet & S. Shih (Eds.), *Minor transnationalism* (pp. 1–23). Durham, NC: Duke University Press.

Madianou, M., & Miller, D. (2012). *Migration and new media: Transnational families and polymedia*. New York, NY: Routledge.

Maira, S., & Soep, E. (Eds.). (2004). *Youthscape: The popular, the national, the global*. Philadelphia, PA: University of Pennsylvania Press.

Maliangkay, R. (2014). The popularity of individualism: The Seo Taiji phenomenon in the 1990s. In K. H. Kim & Y. Choe (Eds.), *The Korean popular culture reader* (pp. 296–313). Durham, NC: Duke University Press.

Moon, S. (2005). *Militarized modernity and gendered citizenship in South Korea*. Durham, NC: Duke University Press.

Moores, S. (2012). *Media, place and mobility*. New York, NY: Palgrave Macmillan.

Oh, M., & Larson, J. (2011). *Digital development in Korea: Building an information society*. London: Routledge.

Ok, H. (2011). New media practices in Korea. *International Journal of Communication, 5*, 320–348.

Pilkington, H., & Johnson, R. (2003). Peripheral youth: Relations of identity and power in global/local context. *European Journal of Cultural Studies, 6*(3), 259–283.

Polhemus, T. (1997). In the supermarket of style. In S. Redhead, D. Wynne, & J. O'Connor (Eds.) (1998), *The club cultures reader: Readings in popular cultural studies* (pp. 130–133). Oxford: Wiley-Blackwell.

Shin, G., & Choi, J. N. (2015). *Global talent: Skilled labor as social capital in Korea*. Stanford, CA: Stanford University Press.

Shin, H. (2009). Have you ever seen the Rain? And who'll stop the Rain? The globalizing project of Korean pop (K-pop). *Inter-Asia Cultural Studies, 10*(4), 507–523.

Shin, H. (2013). *Gayo, K-pop, and beyond*. Paju: Dolbaege.

Silverstone, R., & Hirsch, E. (Eds.). (1992). *Consuming technologies: Media and information in domestic spaces*. London: Routledge.

Son, M., & Choi, S. (2014). 25 years since lifting the ban on overseas travel: Then and now. Retrieved from https://news.joins.com/article/13548604

Statistics Korea. (2014). *Statics on youth 2013*. Retrieved from http://kostat. go.kr

Storey, J. (2018). *Cultural theory and popular culture: An introduction* (8th ed.). London: Routledge.

Sun, W., & Sinclair, J. (Eds.). (2016). *Media and communication in the Chinese diaspora: Rethinking transnationalism*. London: Routledge.

Taylor, C. (2006). The future is in South Korea. Retrieved from https://money. cnn.com/2006/06/08/technology/business2_futureboy0608/index.htm

Vittadini, N., Siibak, A., Reifová, I., & Bilandzic, H. (2014). Generations and media: The social construction of generational identity and differences. In N. Carpentier, K. C. Schrøder, & L. Hallett (Eds.), *Audience transformations: Shifting audience positions in late modernity* (pp. 65–88). London: Routledge.

Wimmer, A., & Glick Schiller, N. (2002). Methodological nationalism and beyond: Nation-state building, migration and the social sciences. *Global Networks, 2*(4), 301–334.

Wise, J. M. (2008). *Cultural globalization: A user's guide*. Oxford: Blackwell.

Yanofsky, D. (2014, May 27). *A cartographic guide to Starbucks' global domination*. Retrieved from https://qz.com/208457/a-cartographic-guide-to-starbucks-global-domination

Yoon, K. (2003). Retraditionalizing the mobile: Young people's sociality and mobile phone in Seoul, South Korea. *European Journal of Cultural Studies, 6*(3), 327–343.

Yoon, K. (2006). The making of neo-Confucian cyberkids: Representations of young mobile phone users in South Korea. *New Media & Society, 8*(5), 753–771.

Yoon, K. (2014). Transnational youth mobility in the neoliberal economy of experience. *Journal of Youth Studies, 17*(8), 1014–1028.

Yoon, K. (2018). Multicultural digital media practices of 1.5-generation Korean immigrants in Canada. *Asian and Pacific Migration Journal, 27*(2), 148–165.

Yoon, S. (2013). New Korean Wave and deterritorialization of social network communication in Europe. *Korean Journal of Journalism & Communication Studies, 57*(3), 135–161.

2 Digital Mediascape of the Korean *Otaku*

This book aims to examine transnational young people's media practices. This chapter and the following four present empirical analyses of how digital media have been incorporated into the transnational flows of popular culture and young people. This and the next chapter focus in particular on the transnational flows of popular culture. Popular culture is often a "culture of conflict," as it involves "the struggle to make social meanings that are in the interests of the subordinate and that are not those preferred by the dominant ideology" (Fiske, 2011, p. 2). An analysis of young people who engage with transnational popular culture would reveal how the dominant national culture and identity are questioned through media-driven cultural practices. In this regard, this chapter explores how Japanese popular culture, once strictly regulated and banned in Korea, was consumed by young Koreans through their subcultural engagement with early digital media technologies in the 2000s. In comparison, the next chapter examines how "made-in-Korea" popular culture, often referred to as the Korean Wave or *Hallyu* in Korean, is incorporated into the overseas fans' mediascapes.

Drawing on in-depth interviews with young Korean fans of Japanese popular culture, this chapter discusses how cultural forms are recontextualized and negotiated when they cross national boundaries. How does popular culture move transnationally via digital media technologies? How do young people reimagine the national through their transnational media consumption? To answer these questions, this chapter examines the intra-Asian context of popular cultural flows between Korea and Japan. Japanese popular culture—animation and comics in particular—has penetrated the global market, entailing the emergence of the "*Pokémon* generation," who have grown up watching Japanese animation, such as *Pokémon* and *Dragon Ball Z* (Allison, 2006; Darling-Wolf, 2015). Despite Japan's culture and technology industries, which have stood out among Asian countries (Otmazgin, 2013), Japanese content has not been particularly popular in Korean cultural markets and has, therefore, remained subcultural. The restricted influence of Japanese popular culture on Korean cultural markets is primarily rooted in the two countries' historical backgrounds—that is, Japan's colonization of Korea and Koreans' antagonistic attitudes toward Japan.[1] In this regard, young Koreans' consumption of Japanese popular culture is an intriguing topic that reveals contradictions between historical memories and cultural tastes—that is, what Appadurai (2013) described as "blockages, bumps, and interference" in transnational cultural flows (p. 69).

The long official ban that lasted until 1998 did not allow any type of Japanese popular culture products (e.g., music, film, games, animation, comics, and performance) to be imported and released in Korea. Moreover, the ban was often accompanied by media panic and negative mass media representation of the content of Japanese popular culture as obscene and violent. Consequently, Korean audiences were able to assume moral superiority to the "morally inferior" Japan.[2] However, the censorship and control of Japanese popular culture in Korea have not only blocked transnational flows. Paradoxically, the blockage has also facilitated a unique form of subcultural and grassroots consumption among young people who have rapidly engaged with digital media technologies. Enthusiastic Korean fans of Japanese music, animation, and games have developed cultural tastes for the forbidden cultural content and have explored strategies for accessing, translating, and sharing the content that is otherwise unavailable in official markets. Korean fans' subcultural consumption of Japanese popular culture has contributed to, and benefited from, the emergence of unique cultures in Korea's digital mediascape (H. M. Kim, 2003). In this regard, to acquire a better understanding of the evolution and diversity of Internet-driven youth cultural practices in Korea, it is important to trace how Korean youth negotiated intra-Asian pop cultural flows in the late 1990s and 2000s, during which Japanese popular culture began to be increasingly integrated into Korean youth culture through digital media technologies. This chapter addresses how young Koreans accessed and appropriated Japanese media in the early period of the Internet (i.e., the 2000s)—especially during the pre-social media era.

This chapter analyzes in-depth interviews conducted in Seoul between 2004 and 2007 with 32 young Korean fans of Japanese popular culture. The participants, for whom pseudonyms are used in this chapter, were in their late teens or twenties and self-identified as fans of Japanese television (TV) dramas (J-dramas or *ild* in Korean), popular music (J-pop), and/or animation. The interview participants were recruited through either a Japanese culture-related student club (*dongari*) at a university or a snowballing method. They were primarily longtime fans and were, therefore, able to recollect how their fan activities had evolved over several years. These early digital media fans grew up during the rapid growth of Korea's digital media industry. This early period of digital media integration into cultural consumption occurred in the 2000s and is significant for understanding the transnational flows of youth culture, which has since been accelerated along with the popularization of social media.

This chapter illustrates how these young fans engage in transnational media flows via digital media technologies and how the national is negotiated in the process. In this chapter, the *national* refers to not only a

political or economic entity but also a form of shared memory, imagination, and feeling; thus, it is analyzed as a set of forces that institutionally,
materially, and culturally filter intra-cultural flows. The formation and
circulation of popular cultural texts provide the fans with meaningful
resources not only at the symbolic and semiotic levels but also at the
political level (Fiske, 1992). As cultural studies scholars have claimed,
the youth subculture operates as a collective and symbolic solution to
particular social contradictions (Hall & Jefferson, 1976; Hebdige, 1979)
or as an individual strategy "for surviving the degradation of everyday
life in postmodern society" (Calluori, 1985). The respondents' subcultural engagement with Japanese media appeared to have some political
implications for questioning the national as an institution of cultural
regulation.

Young Koreans adopted digital media extensively for cultural consumption, especially since the 2000s. Subcultural fandom and its strategies, which developed through the digital media-driven and often pirate
consumption of Japanese content in the late 1990s and 2000s, played
an important role in shaping the way in which digital media are incorporated into the Korean youth subculture. Moreover, the Korean Wave,
which will be discussed in Chapter 3, has been influenced partly by the
Korean *otaku*—sometimes referred to as *odeokhu* or, more often, *deokhu*
for short—which refers to the digitally savvy fans of Japanese popular
culture or more widely any type of popular culture.[3] As early adopters
of the emerging digital technologies, the Korean *otaku* pioneered their
extensive use to access and appropriate transnational cultural materials,
which were not widely available in domestic cultural markets. These fans
generated a unique subculture in which the cultural content that was
blocked by the national regulatory powers was shared, translated, and
reworked through digital media—the Internet in particular—throughout
the 2000s. The fan practices may reveal how young people engage with
"transnationalism from below" (Smith & Guarnizo, 1998) by bypass-
ing the national control of transnational cultural flows. However, the
fans might not be entirely free of nationalizing forces with which certain
transnational culture is stereotypically othered.

While negotiating the nationalizing forces, young fans were involved
in the early form of online subcultures. The nascent form of digital
media-driven fan culture has evolved, as observed in recent K-pop fandom in Korea and overseas. By examining the subcultures of the Korean
otaku in the mid-2000s, later transnational flows of Korean youth cultural forms during the recent phase of the Korean Wave, discussed in
Chapter 3, can be better understood. This chapter begins with reviewing
a few key themes salient in the recent studies of intra-Asian cultural flows
by focusing on the circulation of Japanese popular culture. Drawing on
interview data, the chapter examines how young Korean fans bypassed
the national gatekeeping of Japanese media content through exploring
subcultural strategies of consumption. In particular, it addresses how

the national was negotiated and reimagined by the young media fans by looking at how the fans engaged with the nation-state, national audience, and transnational other.

Studying Intra-Asian Cultural Flows

Despite their geographic proximity, the countries of the intra-Asian region have not sufficiently developed their regional markets and audiences until recently. Otmazgin and Ben-Ari (2012) argued that it was not until the 1990s that massive transnational circulation and consumption of popular culture began in East Asia. In this regard, it is not surprising that academic discourse on transnational cultural flows in Asia has been scarce, with the recent exceptions of studies on Japanese and Korean popular culture. According to Fung (2013), transnational flows of Asian popular culture have been examined primarily in terms of (a) the interconnectedness between Asian and Western popular culture and/or (b) the localization of global popular cultures in Asian contexts. That is, discussions of Asian popular cultural flows often involve the ongoing influence of the global cultural center—the West—rather than the exploration of intra-Asian cultural production and consumption. While it is undeniable that some Western cultural and media industries, as represented by the Hollywood film industry, have been globally influential in several cultural realms, this framework of the West versus Asia as the Rest/Other of the West is open to questions. Asian countries' media collaboration and mutual influences have increased over the past two to three decades (Berry, Liscutin, & Mackintosh, 2009; Jin & Su, 2019), thus requiring further consideration of the internal dynamics of Asian cultural industries and audiences. Moreover, the West–Rest framework is open to criticism, as the West and Rest categories are often ambiguous. In this framework, America and a few other Anglophone countries in the Global North are conveniently represented as the West; thus, Asian countries' positions are not sufficiently addressed (Darling-Wolf, 2015). The assumption of the dominant effects of Western cultural industries and texts on Asian audiences and markets, which has been referred to as the cultural imperialism thesis, "cannot explain either the diverse ways of transnational exchange among Asian nations or the complicated process of cultural hybridization occurring at the local site" (D. H. Lee, 2004, p. 272).

Intra-Asian cultural flows involve geopolitical complications that are rooted in the region's histories and international relations. Due to the remaining memories of colonization-involving Japan as the neighboring ex-colonizer, the cultural proximity between East Asian countries and audiences may differ from that of other geocultural regions, such as Latin America, where intra-regional cultural content, such as telenovelas, has attracted culturally similar audiences (Straubhaar, 1991). In particular, the cultural flows of the intra-Asia region have revolved around the tensions between Japan as a media center and other Asian countries that have developed ambivalent attitudes toward—that is, partly resisting and partly desiring—Japan (D. Y. Lee, 2007). Until the 2010s, most empirical studies of intra-Asian cultural flows focused on the influx and consumption of Japanese animation, dramas, and pop music in other Asian countries (e.g., Iwabuchi, 2004). In terms of research areas, studies on the intra-Asian cultural flows of Japanese popular culture addressed primarily texts (e.g., D. H. Lee, 2004) and audiences (e.g., Hu, 2005; Siriyuvasak, 2004), with industry analysis being an exception (Berry et al., 2009).

Until recently, texts of Japanese popular culture—J-dramas in particular—which were widely circulated in Asia were considered to have "indigenized American media culture in its local context and created distinctive cultural trends" (D. H. Lee, 2004, pp. 254–255). The effective and prompt adaptation of foreign culture was often considered a primary characteristic of Japanese cultural industries (D. Y. Lee, 2007). Japanese cultural industries extensively adopted Western cultural content and formats before rapidly re-localizing them, as evidenced by the content and style of Japanese media. The hybridization of Western culture in Asian contexts may potentially challenge the existing Western hegemony, which defines global cultural flows as a unilateral process from the West to the Rest (Ryoo, 2009). However, as Iwabuchi (2002) argued, Japanese popular cultural texts may be a mixture of different styles but may not necessarily involve subversive power; thus, it rather constitutes a pseudo-hybridity that lacks political implications.

The intra-Asian flows of Japanese popular culture have also been examined in terms of audiences' consumption. Some groups of Asian youth enjoyed and appropriated Japanese popular culture as a cultural resource that can be used to articulate "their frustrations and the lack of free expression in a highly paternalistic society" (Siriyuvasak, 2004, p. 196). Studies of Asian youth's consumption of Japanese media have revealed that this media may be consumed as an alternative and pleasurable cultural resource that is relevant to their everyday lives (Davis & Yeh, 2004). Until the early 2000s, Asian audiences actively explored unofficial channels for consuming Japanese media, as exemplified in the growth of illegal video compact disc (CD)—widely known as VCD—markets and online networks in several Asian countries. In this regard, Hu (2005) defined the emerging Asian audiences who appropriated new technologies for illegal consumption as foot soldiers of "guerrilla transnationalism" who generated "a new form of global distribution and consumption with quite different mechanisms of operation from the legally recognized and regulated systems" (p. 224).

The aforementioned studies of Japanese media in the intra-Asian context have empirically addressed how the intra-Asian mediascape has emerged, especially through the popularization of Japanese media content. They have suggested how Japanese media texts are hybridized, how they appeal to Asian audiences, and how they are often circulated outside the official markets. Intra-Asian cultural flows have offered young people in Asia new resources that enable them to consider their cultural identities. By consuming Asian materials, Asian cultural industries and cultural consumers may no longer be necessarily subjected to or reliant on the dominant Western cultural system. Intra-Asian cultural flows facilitate a new perspective of transnationalization that emphasizes hybrid cultural forms that do not necessarily require mediation by the center (Lionnet & Shih, 2005). These findings can be applied to young Korean fans of Japanese popular culture and their digital media practices, which will be discussed in this chapter. In particular, the recent global rise of Korean pop music has provided new insights into transnational cultural flows in Asia and among the Asian diaspora. As discussed in several recent studies, young Asians and young people of Asian descent explore digital media to negotiate their cultural identities and local contexts (Hu, 2016; Yoon & Jin, 2016).

Until recently, there have been few studies of how young people appropriate intra-Asian cultural resource to negotiate local, national, and global forces. Thus, further empirical studies and theorization of the intra-Asian "youthscape" (Maira & Soep, 2004) are needed to understand how young people challenge Western-centric modernity and explore different "possible lives" (Appadurai, 1996).

Regulatory Power and Subculture

One reason that transnational cultural flows are restricted and challenged by nationalizing forces in Korea is the remaining colonial memories. Korea's restrictions on Japanese popular culture are derived from residual colonial memories involving Japan as the colonizer and Korea as the colonized. The effects of these traumatic memories have been evident in postcolonial Korea, where symbolic and practical efforts have persistently been made to avoid cultural content that serves as reminders of the nation's colonial past. The postcolonial nation-state has suppressed the visibility of the former colonizer's cultural legacies while exhibiting an aggressive effort to decolonize and modernize itself. The lingering "national sentiment" (Han, 2001) toward Japan accounted for the long official ban on Japanese popular culture in Korea. It was not until 1998 that the Korean government began lifting the ban on Japanese media content, to a limited extent.

Korea was not the only country that banned the importation of Japanese media content. Several Asian countries have had restrictions or bans on certain if not all Japanese popular cultural products. Japanese media content was banned in Taiwan until the early 1990s, while certain Japanese content, such as animations and comics, was subjected to strict censorship for a while in the Philippines and Malaysia (Otmazgin, 2013, pp. 45–48). Even among the countries whose governments strictly regulated or banned the importation of Japanese popular culture, Korea had strict regulations, especially during the period of the military regimes who wanted to boost blind nationalism (Nam, 2018). In Korea, the de-regulation process (i.e., the lifting of the ban on Japanese popular culture) initiated by the liberal Kim Dae-jung administration in 1998 has been slower than the original plan. In fact, it was not until 2004 that the domestic market was open to Japanese films, music, and games. Accordingly, its impact on the Korean cultural market has been less significant than originally anticipated (Park, 2006). Paradoxically, the de-regulation of Japanese popular culture in Korea appeared to provide Korean cultural industries with a momentum to reach out to Japanese and Asian audiences. Consequently, Korean popular culture industries—music industries in particular—rapidly penetrated Japanese market and boosted the Korean Wave across Asia and globally (H. Kim, 2011).

In the social engineering of decolonization, Koreans have been portrayed and imagined as a homogeneous ethnic nation (*minjok*) and mobilized as patriotic national subjects (*kukmin*) (Cho Han, 2000; Kal, 2011). In particular, the making of *kukmin* has been accompanied by hegemonic practices of creating vicious transnational others—North Korea and Japan. While the former has been demonized on both ideological and political bases, the latter has been "othered" on historical and ethnic bases. This process implies that the production of fear and anxieties about others is strategically rooted in the construction of Korea's postcolonial national identity. However, this is not to suggest that the postcolonial discursive politics of anxieties has had an identical effect on all citizens regardless of their subject positions, derived from attributes such as class, gender, and age (Moon, 2005). For instance, generational differences have played a significant role in Koreans' negotiation of their anxieties about transnational others. In this regard, it is noteworthy that some youth groups have challenged the hegemonic mode of postcolonial nation building by engaging with countercultural or subcultural practice and reimagining the imposed national subjectivity (D. Y. Lee, 2005). Some of the young Koreans who participated in countercultural *minjung* movements in the 1980s rejected the "othering" of North Korea and, thus, attempted to redefine the nation. Further, the young Korean fans of the Japanese media culture began to question the "national sentiment" toward Japan especially in the 1990s and 2000s. In both examples, the hegemonic process of manufacturing transnational others was challenged by young people who grew up in a post-authoritarian society.

The cultural practices of post-authoritarian youth have been especially visible since the early 1990s, when the global consumer culture began to be rapidly incorporated into young Koreans' everyday lives (K. Lee, 2000). In particular, young Koreans' appropriation of Japanese media and popular culture represents an important example of how young people renegotiate post-coloniality and national cultural identity through their transnational imagination and practices. Young Korean fans' engagement with the popular cultural texts of the transnational other reveals how the national is negotiated by post-national subjects who are no longer homogeneously interpellated as *kukmin*, yet are highly detraditionalized (Cho Han, 2000).

The main consumers of Japanese popular media have been "young and subaltern" (Han, 2001). In Korea's dominant cultural economy, in which cultural objects associated with Japan tend to be degraded as "low-quality" (*jeojil*) content that threatens the imagined purity of the Korean national culture, the enjoyment of Japanese cultural resources has been considered taboo (Y. Jung, 2007). Due to this stigmatization, Japanese media content was not readily available in the Korean market until the early 2000s, and Korean fans of Japanese media had to, therefore, develop subcultural strategies and communities to enable access to the forbidden cultural forms. The forbidden nature of Japanese media in Korea was narrated by the respondents in the current study, most of whom recalled their first encounters with Japanese cultural materials in the late 1990s or early 2000s as somewhat "strange experiences." For instance, 19-year-old Jina recollected her first impression of Japanese popular music several years earlier:

> We've often listened to (American) pop songs since childhood, haven't we? (American) pop songs are all around. They are played on TV and pretty much everywhere. They are also recommended by friends. So, I never feel that there's much foreignness about them. However, when I listened to Japanese songs for the first time, I felt quite strange and, so, was sort of repulsed.

The Korean fans' initial repulsion toward Japanese media can be largely explained by the "national sentiments" and strict national control. This control and the "othering" of Japanese culture in postcolonial Korea have consequently minimized the presence of Japan in the dominant cultural economy. Japan's presence in the Korean cultural economy since the 1980s can be divided into three different stages based primarily on changes in the state's regulation of Japanese cultural commodities: the "illegal" presence (1980s–1997), the "transitional" presence (1998–2004), and the "newly sanctioned" presence (since 2004) (E. Y. Jung, 2007). Although this division is, for the most part, a result of structural factors related to national policies on the importation of Japanese media content, it also reflects, to some extent, the alterations in the subcultural economies of Korean fans.

Paradoxically, the alienation of Japanese popular culture in the dominant cultural economy during the period of the "illegal" and "transitional" presence triggered the rise of the subcultural fandom of Japanese media and popular culture in Korea (D. H. Lee, 2006).

The fan subculture has been further expanded during the "newly sanctioned presence" period. In Korea's digital media environment, which is equipped with extensive, high-speed Internet infrastructure, the "digital generation" youth have increasingly accessed Japanese popular media content. Most respondents agreed that the nationwide diffusion of high-speed Internet, rather than the lifting of the ban, paved the way for an increase in the subcultural consumption of Japanese media content in Korea. Young Korean fans' access to Japanese media via the Internet and unofficial channels outside the dominant cultural market initiated the subcultural economy, especially in the early and mid-2000s.

The subcultural economy consisted of interpretive, meaningful, and resistant practices. First, the subcultural economy of fandom involved interpretive processes, as Japanese popular culture was often compared with that of Korea. For some interviewed fans, the initially foreign feelings about Japanese popular culture were transformed into a sense of cultural proximity. They recalled their initial attraction to Japanese media due to its "high quality" and "variety," after which they found some familiarity with its Korean counterpart. Nara, a 20-year-old woman who had been a fan of Japanese popular music for over seven years, noted the following:

> When I listened to songs by Amuro Namie [i.e., a J-pop singer] for the first time, I thought they were so cool. Really! In a way, Japanese music sounded somewhat similar to Korean music. Both might elicit similar feelings, maybe because both are Asian. [Interviewer: Could you tell me more about the similar feelings?] For example, on Japanese TV dramas, there are things that are similar to ours, such as the family structure and eating habits. However, Japanese things actually look better. The characters on Japanese TV are meticulous, modest, and polite. They seem to live cool lives. Things on Japanese TV look better than those on Korean TV.

Consequently, Japanese media content appealed to the Korean fans because it was *foreign*, on the one hand, and *familiar*, on the other. Moreover, like Nara, some young people in the study tended to consider Japanese popular cultural materials as being more advanced than their Korean counterparts in terms of quality. Given that until recently Japanese media industries have affected youth cultural trends in some Asian countries, the quality discourse may not be surprising, at least at the time of interviews (the 2000s).

Second, whether foreign or familiar, the feelings elicited by Japanese media content constituted the Korean fans' economy of meanings. In the subcultural economy of fandom, popular cultural resources were not simply traded as commodities; rather, they were meaningfully rearticulated with fans' everyday lives. As claimed in previous fan studies, the subcultural economy of fandom develops through a process of affective, semiotic, enunciative, and textual production through consumption (Fiske, 1992; Grossberg, 1992). The digitally mediated do-it-yourself culture of subcultural economy allowed young Korean fans to maintain a subcultural economy in which information about transnational celebrities and popular cultural texts are digitized, disseminated, and shared (Darling-Wolf, 2004).

Third, the Korean fans' subcultural economy seemed to involve youthful "resistance through rituals" (Hall & Jefferson, 1976), in which the hegemonic national subjectivity was rethought. While resistance through rituals, styles, and pleasures is not exclusive to Korean fans of Japanese media and may be observed in various other fan cultures, the nature of the dominant culture resisted by the young Korean fans seems somewhat different from that of previous cultural studies of youth. The previous Western-centric studies of youth examined youth subcultures as symbolic struggles of working-class youth who exhibit "spectacular", excessive, cultural styles. Furthermore, the Western-centric fan studies literature (e.g., Duffett, 2013; Gray, Sandvoss, & Harrington, 2007) has focused on media fans mostly in national contexts, and thus failed to effectively explain how the national and transnational are negotiated in the subcultural economy of fandom. In comparison, a few recent Asian-based empirical studies have begun to examine the meanings of the national and transnational in fan subcultures (e.g., Fung, 2009).

The subcultural economy enabled the fans to challenge the dominant representation of Japan and its popular culture in Korea. The cultural logic of the subcultural economy is to simultaneously question and reengage with the national. The Korean fans not only negotiate the nation-state as an institution but also rework the affective dimensions of being Korean in their transnational and subcultural consumption. The young Korean fans' subcultural economy appeared to engage with different yet overlapping aspects of the national. In particular, as will be discussed in the following sections, three aspects of the national–the nation-state, national audience, and transnational other (Japan)–seemed to influence the Korean fans' subcultural identity.

Negotiating the Nation-State

The young Korean fans' subcultural engagement with Japanese popular and media culture concerned the question of who owns the rights to the transnational popular cultural resource within the nation-state. According to the older respondents—those in their mid-twenties—Korean fans accessed the forbidden cultural content through pirated CDs and VCDs during the "illegal" presence period (until 1997). The interviewees recalled that Japanese popular culture fan communities, known as *dong-hohoe*, were a common source of "illegal" Japanese cultural materials among Korean youth until the early 2000s (Yoon, 2014). By sharing their materials and fan knowledge of Japanese comics, animation, TV dramas, films, games, and music, the fans challenged the nation-state as the holder of the legal ownership of Japanese media content. This process resonates with Harrington and Bielby's (1995) observation of media fans' moral and emotional engagement with popular cultural texts; fans tend to have a sense of "moral ownership" over the characters and content of the popular cultural texts with which they engage and challenge the state's legal control over the importation of popular cultural commodities.

Even since 2004, when access to Japanese media is not rigidly restricted in Korea, the fans have not relied on the "legitimate" cultural market, where licensed or imported materials are released, because the market does not meet the fans' needs for unlimited and immediate access to a wide range of Japanese popular cultural content. The study respondents were actively using the Internet, as highly developed fan networks provided almost real-time introduction to and translation of newly released Japanese TV dramas, films, games, and music. The rapid dissemination of Japanese media content in Asia has been facilitated not only by emerging transnational market forces but also by fan practices that are accompanied by technologically mediated piracy (Hu, 2016; Otmazgin, 2013). The substantial increase in file sharing via person-to-person networks or web-hard services since the early 2000s in Korea has contributed to the explosive growth of the subcultural economy of pirated materials, which makes unlicensed Japanese materials widely available for Korean fans at no or little cost. As young Koreans have increasingly appropriated the Internet as a key channel of fan practices, national control of Japanese materials in the official cultural economy has increasingly lost its validity. Ari, a 19-year-old female fan of J-pop and J-dramas, pointed out the decreasing power of the nation-state and the increasing role of the Internet in intra-Asian cultural flows:

> Most of what I know about Japanese popular culture has been learned from the Internet. Without the Internet, I would not have enjoyed Japanese music this much. I feel that it's pointless to ban Japanese culture [in Korea] these days, because the Internet doesn't have national boundaries, and, thus, information easily crosses national boundaries. [National] control might have worked previously, but would never work these days. It seems almost pointless.

The Korean fans' critique of the nation-state's regulation of transnational media content is sometimes extended to a critical perspective on the state's nationalistic rhetoric of globalization. A few young people in the current research commented on the government's and the dominant media's promotion of Korean popular culture (*Hallyu*) in Asia. For instance, Hojin, a 19-year-old male, noted, "The [Korean] mass media tends to speak very highly of Hallyu. Well, Korea does not allow Japanese culture, while actively promoting and exporting our culture to other countries. I think that's so unfair." Consequently, the fans tended to advocate for an open mode of transnational cultural flows, as opposed to the outdated nationalistic regulation. The once exclusive role of the nation-state as the gatekeeper of the allegedly "unsound" foreign culture is now being fundamentally questioned, as fan knowledge about Japanese popular culture has been exponentially accumulated and shared among fans through digital media. Japanese visual and audio texts have increasingly been translated by Korean fans and have been stored on fan communities' online archives, YouTube channels, and low-cost web-hard services. In this early era of digital media, Korean *otaku* seemed to witness the rise of "peer-to-peer networks" (Benkler, 2006), which is based on peer networks, yet challenges the nation-state's and the industry's regulation of cultural production and consumption. Increasing digital media convergence (Jenkins, 2006), through which different media forms can be synergistically produced *and* consumed, facilitated grassroots do-it-yourself media consumption among the young people in the study. By utilizing the Internet extensively to access and reproduce the cultural content that is blocked by national gatekeepers, the young fans question the regulatory power of the nation-state. Indeed, circumventing the official market regulated by the government was considered as a challenge to the nation-state, especially during the official ban on several Japanese media products until the early 2000s. While popular culture texts and practices have political implications, the Korean *otaku*'s practices before and during the 2000s involved clear political meanings: the consumption of Japanese products meant a challenge to the Korean government and the dominant social order of the nation-state.

Negotiating the National Audience

Media fans can be distinguished from mainstream media audiences in terms of how to consume and what to consume (Duffett, 2013). While such distinction is socially constructed, fans also consciously differentiate their cultural tastes, sociality, and identity from those of mainstream audiences. The fans' challenge to the national regulation of transnational cultural flows did not necessarily mean that they welcomed the popularization of Japanese culture in Korea. According to Hana, a 22-year-old female fan who has been a Japanese popular culture enthusiast for nearly 10 years,

> Lately, I have been told that Arashi [i.e., a J-pop band] is going to visit Korea soon. Well, I would like to say to Arashi, "PLEASE don't

come. I will go to Japan [to attend your concert]." If they come to Korea, lots of [Korean] people will know about the band. Then, I will no longer feel like they're *my* Arashi.

The fans anticipated and hoped that Japanese popular culture would remain a fan-based subcultural economy to enable their cultural tastes to be distinguished from those of the "mainstream" national audience. This anticipation was often based on the fans' claims that they were the only ones who possessed the ability to "truly" appreciate Japanese popular cultural texts, as Namwoo, a 19-year-old male fan of J-dramas, noted:

> Japanese animations and TV dramas have sentiments that Koreans cannot easily accept . . . Only those who are in favor of Japanese culture, like me, can *truly* enjoy them. General viewers may not appreciate them. Even if released on terrestrial TV channels, they would hardly succeed, I think.

This attitude resonates with the findings of a recent empirical study indicating that young Korean fans were skeptical about the opening of Japanese popular culture in Korea and, therefore, wished to maintain the subculture economy (S. J. Ha, 2010).

Until recently, the Korean fans of Japanese media have had to negotiate any probable public prejudice against their cultural taste for the forbidden content. Fans' sensibilities, facilitated through the subcultural exchange of pirated materials, have distinguished them from the mainstream audience. The public prejudice against Japanese media in Korea has paradoxically enhanced the solidarity among fans. To be a fan is to enunciate one's cultural taste in more or less collective or subcultural ways and, thus, form an interpretive community (Fiske, 1992). According to the interviewees' recollection, it was not easy to openly admit to being J-pop or J-drama fans in the early 2000s. Each study respondent had been a member of a few online and offline fan communities for a number of years. By assuming a sense of subcultural belonging, the Korean fans attempted to distinguish themselves from the mainstream media consumers, who enjoyed officially approved popular cultural forms, such as domestic TV dramas, dubbed American TV series, and licensed pop songs. The fans in the study were practicing "fan productivity" (Fiske, 1992), by means of which popular cultural texts were transformed into collectively and personally meaningful resources, and were consequently able to have an impact on the official economy.

The distinction between fans in the subcultural economy and the national audience in the dominant cultural economy is not always rigid and visible. Rather, the distinction seems to have gradually become blurred by some fans who are willing to cross the boundaries between different fan communities and even between fans and the national audience. In the 2007 interviews, compared to those conducted in 2004, the fan practices increasingly showed a "post-subcultural" tendency (Bennett & Khan-Harris, 2004), in which the participants' affiliations were no longer limited to one or two fan communities but, rather, were extended to numerous groups and individuals who were interested in Japanese media. While some fans still wanted to remain exclusively within the subcultural economy, others were flexibly exploring different subcultural styles, including those of Korean, Japanese, and Western popular culture. As post-subcultural theorization claims, the sociality of youth subculture increasingly consists of fluid and disjointed formations in a rapidly globalizing and technologically mediated world (Bennett & Kahn-Harris, 2004). This approach can be contrasted with the classical cultural theories of youth subculture, which defined it as a collective and symbolic expression of resistance (Hall & Jefferson, 1976). As digital media technologies evolve and the once-rigid restriction is relaxed, the young Korean fans of Japanese popular culture seemed to gradually enjoy multiple memberships of different fan clubs and to frequently access numerous fan blogs of individuals who solely communicate with each other online. The fans rarely chose to restrict themselves to a single fan club, opting to move continuously from one club to another instead. It was significant that, in this recent phase of fandom, the individual emerged as a unit of fan activities and practices without necessarily relying on the subcultural structure or resources. In the emergence of individualized and flexible fans, the offline-based exchange of fan materials and information decreased, while the boundary between the real and the referent became blurred. In this respect, the recent fans' cultural economy can be defined as a "post-subcultural" economy in which fans are deeply involved in the individualized and mediated consumption of transnational culture. For instance, personal blogs and online discussion boards appeared to play an important role in Korean *otaku*'s fan practices. As 20-year-old Jisong commented on her blog:

> Well, I would say blogs have a huge impact [on the growth of fan activities]. When I come across a cool drama scene while watching a Japanese drama on the Internet, I capture and upload it on my blogs with some comments. I sometimes replace the original dialogues with mine. If my post is interesting, visitors will respond. Blog visitors who haven't seen the drama yet will go watch it and come back with comments. That sort of feedback is common.

In this post-subcultural phase of fandom, the Internet serves to construct flexible fan communities that are based on a virtual and eclectic mode of participation. Compared to their precedents who consumed the forbidden foreign cultural content in the 1990s and early 2000s

(H. M. Kim, 2003), the Korean *otaku*'s fan practice in the current study seemed to more eclectically navigate from one cultural form to another rather than being exclusively dedicated to particular genres of Japanese popular culture.

If fandom is ultimately about how to connect with others (Bury, 2005), the subcultural economy in the current study primarily involves two modes of sociality—communicating with other fans and distancing oneself from the mainstream national audience and its mass consumer culture. However, as revealed in the 2007 interviews, the fans increasingly sought to move freely between different subcultures rather than being committed to a specific one. Rapidly evolving digital media seemed to allow the Korean *otaku* to easily access and navigate different media forms, without being firmly committed to one cultural from.

This process implies that the young Korean fans have evolved from the subcultural phase to the post-subcultural phase. That is, while some fans maintained subcultural strategies of consuming Japanese media by appropriating the forbidden cultural form in a relatively exclusive way; other fans—especially those who were interviewed in the later period—tended to show post-subcultural practices of media consumption, in which the fans eclectically navigated and enjoyed Japanese popular culture, along with other cultural forms. In a way, the *otaku* identity is no longer exclusive but rather similar with some mainstream audience members who navigate different media forms and explore participatory modes of consuming culture through interactive digital media.

Undoing the Transnational

The young Korean fans' subcultural practices are not only a challenge to national control over transnational cultural flows from Japan but also an attempt to appropriate transnational media content in a localized way. While questioning the national as a regulatory force in transnational cultural flows, the subcultural economy of Korean fans renationalizes the flows through its own cultural logic. In the respondents' subcultural translation of Japanese media, three modes of media consumption seemed to constitute a renationalizing force.

First, the fans' subcultural consumption of transnational popular cultures was accompanied by the implicit process of diluting the "Japaneseness" of Japanese popular cultural content. The Korean youth in the current study claimed that viewing J-dramas or listening to J-pop did not necessarily signify identification with Japan as a popular cultural origin. Rather, Japanese popular cultural texts were attractive because they could be consumed as a "cool" signifier without deep historical meanings. For some respondents, Japanese media content was appealing largely because of its unrealistic, decontextualized features; as Junha, a 27-year-old man, noted, J-dramas are "more or less unrealistically funny." By consuming Japanese popular cultural content without engaging with the context in which it was produced, some respondents seemed to minimize its cultural and historical implications. Throughout this process of undoing, by which Japan is consumed as a postmodern signifier dissociated from historical memories, Japanese media commodities were perceived as a form of pastiche, which is a set of signifiers without a signified (Cho, 2004). In this process of undoing, cultural consumption became devoid of the question of origin.

The fans' consumption of Japanese media as a set of signifiers through the subcultural strategy of undoing was not necessarily accompanied by neutral attitudes toward Japanese society. While attempting to dissociate Japanese media texts from their context (i.e., Japanese society), most respondents remained critical of Japan as the ex-colonizer. Despite their enthusiasm about and interest in Japanese popular culture, the interviewed fans tended not to describe Japan as a desired society. For example, Hana, a 22-year-old female fan, was critical of "some Korean kids" who yearned for Japan and who viewed it as an ideal society. According to Hana,

> Japanese popular culture may have diversity. It includes diverse tastes and diverse manias. That's an attraction. [. . .] However, although some Korean kids speak highly of Japan, Japanese society may be quite different from what they think. As far as I know, Japanese society does not always appreciate cultural diversity.

The young Korean fans' attempt to dissociate the desired texts (Japanese media content) from their context (Japanese society) implies that intensive exposure to Japanese media did not necessarily increase the Korean fans' favorable attitudes toward Japan.

Second, the young Korean fans' subcultural consumption of Japanese media content tended to remain national in terms of fan sociality. Regardless of their Japanese language ability, most respondents had not attempted to communicate with the Japanese or international fans of Japanese celebrities, J-dramas, and J-pop about which they were enthusiastic. The national boundary of fan sociality seemed to be maintained primarily by linguistic, cultural, and technological barriers.[4] Although the lack of Japanese language literacy was a common barrier discouraging some Korean fans from accessing Japanese or international online fan communities, this might not be the only reason for the limited transnational interactions. Moreover, despite their awareness of the well-known Korean-to-Japanese (or Japanese-to-Korean) translation functions offered by a few popular websites, most respondents had not attempted to communicate with the members of Japanese fan communities nor to access Japanese fan sites. Rather, the Korean fans sought to communicate with other Korean fans through fan sites, personal blogs, and online chatting. Even a few respondents who could speak Japanese primarily utilized their Japanese language ability to translate Japanese media content and share it with their Korean peers, rather than engaging with Japanese or international fan communities. It was difficult to find any consistent bonding or communication between Korean and Japanese fans who were enthusiastic about the same Japanese media items. In the subcultural economy as an imagined emotional locale, Korean fans tended not to consider their Japanese counterparts as peers. The sociality of the subcultural economy in the current study was largely limited to the national without being extended to the transnational. This implies that the Internet-mediated, transnational fan subcultures might not necessarily be as transnational and egalitarian as claimed in previous studies (e.g., Darling-Wolf, 2004). Rather, as shown in the present study, the subcultural economy might contribute to "peer-to-peer networks" (Benkler, 2006) primarily *within* the national as an affective space.

Third, the young Koreans in the study consistently translated and reappropriated Japanese media texts and, in so doing, exercised creative localization of the original materials, which are already, to some extent, a hybrid of Western cultural products (D. Y. Lee, 2007). The Korean fans in the study were aware of the cultural hybridity implicated in the transnational media, rather than seeking authentic Japaneseness in the cultural texts. This perspective questions the essentialized understanding of national popular culture, which reduces the meaning of popular cultural texts to a fixed, homogeneous attribute of the country in which they originate.[5] According to the Korean fans, Japanese popular cultural texts were appealing not because they exhibited an essentialized form of "Japaneseness" but because they effectively remixed various cultural references. They had a high regard for the hybrid nature of Japanese media content, which allowed for flexible methods of interpreting and appropriating it. The fans seemed to value "how to use it" rather than "where it was from." Some fans noted the importance of creatively reworking the transnational texts in the Korean context. For instance, Bora, a 20-year-old woman who had sometimes performed cosplay (costume play), commented on how "Koreanized" cosplay might differ from that of Japanese players and stated that it did not necessarily reproduce "Japanese color":

> Those who do cosplay and the general public have totally different opinions. The general public may consider cosplay as *waesaek* ("Japanese color" with a disapproving connotation) and speak ill of it. However, when we (i.e., Korean fans) do costume play, it is *totally* different from what Japanese players do. The (Korean) general public doesn't seem aware of such a difference though.

The Korean fans' emphasis on their ability to translate and "renationalize" Japanese content indicates their desire to minimize the negative public perception of Japanese popular culture, which has allegedly "contaminated" the purity of the Korean culture. The perceived hybridity of Japanese popular culture sometimes allowed the young fans to question the originality and purity of the Korean culture. Some fans claimed that more similarities might exist between the Japanese and Korean media formats than the Korean public assumed. They claimed that Japanese popular cultural content had been a significant reference and resource for the Korean popular cultural industries. This postcolonial irony of resisting yet internalizing the ex-colonizer has been especially observed in Korea's media system (H. M. Kim, 2003) and conceptualized as a process of "implicit Japanization" (*naejaejeok ilbohwa*) (D. Y. Lee, 2007). Some respondents seemed to be aware of this "implicit Japanization." As Jumi, a 19-year-old female, noted, "I would say that many things in Korea, from the education system to the TV dramas, may actually be copied from the Japanese. However, what [Korean] people do with the copied things is different from what Japanese people do." While acknowledging the influx of Japanese popular culture and its influence on its Korean counterpart, the young Korean fans tended to emphasize their ability to renationalize the influx.

In summary, Japanese popular culture appeared to become a resource that enabled the young Korean fans to denationalize and renationalize their cultural identity. The seemingly contradictory modes of the subcultural consumption of Japanese media are not necessarily mutually exclusive. Rather, they articulate with each other to some extent, resulting in critical engagement with and the reimagination of the dominant national subjectivity. The complexity of the denationalizing and renationalizing forces among the Korean fans in the current study calls into question the pervasive celebratory tone used in relation to the recent transnational cultural traffic.

Conclusion

This chapter has explored young Koreans' appropriation of Japanese popular cultural texts in the subcultural economy. Being a fan is not only an individual's personal choice but also implies a socially constructed process (Harrington & Bielby, 1995); therefore, it seems necessary to understand popular cultural fans in context—that is, in relation to the particular social forces influencing popular culture fans' cultural identities. For the young Koreans in this chapter, the nationalizing forces were significant, yet they were negotiated in several different ways. This chapter demonstrated how the postcolonial desires implied in transnational media consumption were articulated with the national. By negotiating the nation-state's regulation, distinguishing themselves from the mainstream national audience, and imagining Japanese media as a decontextualized, remixable resource devoid of historical memories, the young Korean fans in the study attempted to rework the national and its popular memories.

Thus, they contemplated the national boundaries and agency of popular culture without disregarding national identity in favor of transnational cultural power. Given the empirical findings of this chapter, the subcultural economy of transnational cultural flows in regard to Koreans' postcolonial memories seems to be constructed through a complicated process of undoing and doing. On the one hand, the subcultural economy involves consistently *undoing* the colonial memories associated with Japan as the historical other *and* popular cultural power. On the other hand, it engages with *doing* and appropriating Japanese popular cultural texts as a hybrid resource for remaking national identity.

The Korean *otaku*'s digitally mediated consumption of and participation in pop cultural content from Japan have facilitated the recent digital media-driven fan culture in Korea, which is often referred to as "*deokhu* culture." *Deokhu* is derived from the Japanese term *otaku*. *Deokhu* culture in Korea has gradually referred to a wide range of media fans (who are called *deok*, or "fans"); for example, female fans of female TV personalities or singers are called *yeodeok* (*yeo* means "women") (J. Ha, 2017). The neologism of *deok* does not simply mean a localized adoption of Japanese terminology; rather, it shows that the Korean *otaku*'s cultural practices have contributed to the exploration of various digital media fan practices, as exemplified by the recent media-driven transnational fandom of K-pop. *Deokhu* culture has emerged as a cultural phenomenon among Korean youth in the digital mediascape. It has become a way of expressing their cultural tastes and supporting their favorite stars and fan objects, such as particular brands and commodities.

Deokhu culture, which is inherently driven by digital media, might symptomatically reveal the accelerated tendency of post-subcultural consumption, through which subcultural resistance is diluted. Regarding post-subcultural consumption, the *deokhu* may not be subject to national gatekeeping, as their antecedents—the Korean *otaku* discussed in this chapter—were, and they engage with various fragmented cultural tastes. By navigating and clicking on social media, the *deokhu* may not necessarily challenge the dominant social order. In this regard, post-subcultural *deokhu* culture may be similar to the Japanese *otaku*, who are enthusiastic about surface narratives and minimalist interests, rather than about attempting to engage in subcultural struggles over the hegemony implicated in cultural forms (Azuma, 2009). Media fan culture has been more popularized via social media, through which users can conveniently endorse their favorite stars and materials. However, the popularization of social media-driven fan activities among young people may reveal the normalization of the subversive power of youth subculture through the consumption-driven youth culture. As Siriyuvasak (2004) argued in regard to current youth experiences, "Globalization is repressive because it confines youth to the sphere of consumption" (p. 197).

Given the research findings, the cosmopolitan hopes that are frequently represented in the recent discourse of transnational popular cultural flows need to be reexamined. This chapter suggests that the increasing technology-mediated, subcultural consumption of transnational cultural texts, which moves with relative ease beyond the regulatory regime of the nation-state, does not simply prove the declining cultural currency of the national. Rather, transnational cultural flows allow fans to rework their imagined relationships with the national. The most distinctive feature of young Koreans' consumption of Japanese popular culture may bear on their conflicting desire to reaffirm or renegotiate their national identity. While transnational and digital media flows increasingly challenge the role of the nation-state's gatekeeping, the national as an emotional and identifiable locale appears to still maintain its cultural currency among subcultural young people. Immediately following the Asian financial crisis of 1997, Korean anthropologist Cho Han (2000) lamented that "South Korean people have not been able to find a way to move beyond the dichotomy of a passionately defensive nationalism and passionless market principles" (p. 51). To some extent, this observation may still be valid, as the subsequent neoliberal regimes have recently boosted the nostalgic narratives of rapid modernization and the patriotic *kukmin*-based state. However, as this chapter's research findings indicate, the (post-)subcultural economy in transnational cultural flows may not simply be led by either defensive patriots or passionless consumerists.

The Korean *otaku*'s appropriation of transnational cultural texts as a way of negotiating the national in the 2000s is not a cultural practice in the past tense. It has implications for the ongoing cultural landscape of the Korean youth culture. The Korean *otaku*'s early adoption of and experimentation with digital media for transnational media access and participation have been incorporated extensively into the Korean digital mediascape. Since the 2000s, *deokhu* culture, which is partly rooted in the Korean *otaku*'s cultural practices, has become pervasive among young people. *Deokhu* culture has led and/or affected the evolution of Korea's cultural industries, as shown in K-pop idol groups' fan-based marketing and the social media-driven revenue structure, which is reliant on fans' participation and interaction. Indeed, fans have become an integral component in not only the consumption but also the production of K-pop idol groups; fans are "prosumers" who play a role in shaping how idols are designed and marketed (Kim & Yoon, 2012). The strong fan base, augmented through digital media, has been a major motivational factor behind K-pop's global penetration. For example, popular K-pop groups' global fans dedicate their time, attention, and digital literacy for their favorite idols' global recognition on YouTube and other social media. The Korean *otaku*'s strategies have evolved and influenced how transnational fans engage with Korean popular culture. The legacy of the Korean *otaku* culture that emerged in the intra-Asian cultural context may now be integrated into the global mediascape of the Korean Wave.

Notes

1 Of course, there are ongoing debates about the influence of Japanese popular culture across Asia. For example, Otmazgin (2013) argued that the official ban of Japanese popular culture in Korea and Taiwan did not necessarily decrease Japanese culture's intra-Asian influences, as pirated materials were widely circulated and attracted young people. Drawing on Japanese sources, he asserted that illegal Japanese music products constituted 10% of the Korean music market in the 1990s.

   As will be discussed later in this chapter, the Japanese popular culture industry has certain influences on its Korean counterpart. However, until recently, Japanese media content's ability to directly reach Korean mainstream audiences in official markets has been restricted.

2 In several best-selling nonfiction books on Japanese culture, written by Korean authors, for example, *There Is No Japan* (1993) and *I Want to Know about Japan: Samurai Shock* (1994), Japan was characterized by its exotic cultural aspects, such as its extreme individualism and sex industries, and was contrasted with Korea, which was portrayed as comparatively less individualized and commercialized and, thus, "healthier" (Kang, 2010).

3 The Japanese term *otaku* means "you" but typically refers to "youngsters driven by strong interest in contemporary culture and lifestyles" or "those who choose to facilitate social connections through specific, nonmainstream cultural practices such as cosplay" (Otmazgin, 2013, p. 61). The *otaku* are also known for their heavy uses of digital media technologies (Otmazgin, 2013). It is estimated that the term *otaku* was introduced to Korean fans of Japanese culture in the late 1990s and began to be used in the early 2000s (Im & Lee, 2013).

4 In addition to linguistic and cultural barriers, the technological environment seemed to be a factor that discouraged Korean fans from accessing Japanese materials. Several respondents complained about the inconvenient Japanese web interface and the lack of resources on Japanese websites. As Namho, a 19-year-old male fan, noted,

   > The Internet in Japan is not as well developed as it is in Korea. Korean websites are easy to access and well managed. However, it's not convenient to access Japanese sites and get information. Online information (about Japanese popular culture) is supposed to be easily accessible beyond national boundaries, but the reality is different.

5 The Korean fans' responses may be related to the way in which Japanese media products have been promoted and sold in their overseas markets. While Japanese cultural and media exports—from consumer technologies to animation—have had global impacts, Japanese cultural presence has not necessarily been incorporated into the sales of Japanese products. In the sales of Japan's major media exports such as consumer technologies, Japaneseness is not their appeal to overseas consumers in the way in which a Japanese way of life is promoted (Iwabuchi, 2002).

References

Allison, A. (2006). *Millennial monsters: Japanese toys and the global imagination*. Berkeley, CA: University of California Press.

Appadurai, A. (1996). *Modernity at large: Cultural dimensions of globalization*. Minneapolis, MN: University of Minnesota Press.

Appadurai, A. (2013). *The future as cultural fact: Essays on the global condition*. New York, NY: Verso.

Azuma, H. (2009). *Otaku: Japan's database animals*. Minneapolis, MN: University of Minnesota Press.

Benkler, Y. (2006). *The wealth of networks: How social production transforms markets and freedom*. New Haven, CT: Yale University Press.

Bennett, A., & Kahn-Harris, K. (Eds.). (2004). *After subculture: Critical studies in contemporary youth culture*. New York, NY: Palgrave Macmillan.

Berry, C., Liscutin, N., & Mackintosh, J. D. (2009). *Cultural studies and cultural industries in Northeast Asia: What a difference a region makes*. Hong Kong: Hong Kong University Press.

Bury, R. (2005). *Cyberspace of their own: Female fandoms online*. New York, NY: Peter Lang.

Calluori, R. A. (1985). The kids are alright: New wave subcultural theory. *Social Text, 12*, 43–53.

Cho, C. H. (2004). Discourses on "East Asia" and the influx of Japanese pop culture into South Korea. *The Korean Journal of Communication Studies, 12*(1), 105–120.

Cho Han, H. J. (2000). "You are entrapped in an imaginary well": The formation of subjectivity within compressed development—A feminist critique of modernity and Korean culture. *Inter-Asia Cultural Studies, 1*(1), 49–69.

Darling-Wolf, F. (2004). Virtually multicultural: Trans-Asian identity and gender in an international *fan* community of a Japanese star. *New Media & Society, 6*(4), 507–528.

Darling-Wolf, F. (2015). *Imagining the global: Transnational media and popular culture beyond East and West*. Ann Arbor, MI: University of Michigan Press.

Davis, D. W., & Yeh, E. Y. (2004). VCD as programmatic technology: Japanese television drama in Hong Kong. In K. Iwabuchi (Ed.), *Feeling Asian modernities: Transnational consumption of Japanese TV dramas* (pp. 227–247). Hong Kong: Hong Kong University Press.

Duffett, M. (2013). *Understanding fandom: An introduction to the study of media fan culture*. New York, NY: Bloomsbury.

Fiske, J. (1992). The cultural economy of fandom. In L. A. Lewis (Ed.), *The adoring audience: Fan culture and popular media* (pp. 30–49). London: Routledge.

Fiske, J. (2011). *Reading the popular* (2nd ed.). London: Routledge.

Fung, A. Y. H. (2009). Fandom, youth, and consumption in China. *European Journal of Cultural Studies, 12*(3), 285–303.

Fung, A. Y. H. (Ed.). (2013). *Asian popular culture: The global (dis)continuity*. New York, NY: Routledge.

Gray, J., Sandvoss, C., & Harrington, C. L. (Eds.). (2007). *Fandom: Identities and communities in a mediated world*. New York, NY: New York University Press.

Grossberg, L. (1992). Is there a fan in the house? The affective sensibility of fandom. In L. A. Lewis (Ed.), *The adoring audience: Fan culture and popular media* (pp. 50–65). London: Routledge.

Ha, J. (2017). The girl crush phenomenon: Why now? Retrieved from http://eng.kofice.or.kr/c00_hallyuInsights/c00_hallyuInsights_01_view. asp?seq=7864&page=4&find=&search=&genre=

Ha, S. J. (2010). Inflow of Japanese pop culture through its fandom in South Korea. *Korean Society for Entertainment Industry Studies Conference Proceeding, 7,* 77–89.

Hall, S., & Jefferson, T. (Eds). (1976). *Resistance through rituals: Youth subcultures in postwar Britain.* London: Hutchinson.

Han, S. M. (2001). Consuming the modern: Globalization, things Japanese and the politics of cultural identity in Korea. In H. Befu (Ed.), *Globalizing Japan: Ethnography of the Japanese presence in America, Asia and Europe* (pp. 194–208). London: Routledge.

Harrington, C., & Bielby, D. D. (1995). *Soap fans: Pursuing pleasure and making meaning in everyday life.* Philadelphia, PA: Temple University Press.

Hebdige, D. (1979). *Subculture: The meaning of style.* London: Routledge.

Hu, K. (2005). The power of circulation: Digital technologies and the online Chinese fans of Japanese TV drama. *Inter-Asia Cultural Studies, 6*(2), 171–186.

Hu, K. (2016). Chinese subtitle groups and flexible accumulation in the age of online viewing. In K. Iwabuchi, E. Tasi, & C. Berry (Eds.), *Routledge handbook of East Asian popular culture* (pp. 45–54). London: Routledge.

Im, C., & Lee, Y. (2013). Terms and meanings of Korean otaku. *Journal of Japanese Studies, 34,* 325–342.

Iwabuchi, K. (2002). *Recentering globalization: Popular culture and Japanese transnationalism.* Durham, NC: Duke University Press.

Iwabuchi, K. (Ed.). (2004). *Feeling Asian modernities: Transnational consumption of Japanese TV dramas.* Hong Kong: Hong Kong University Press.

Jenkins, H. (2006). *Convergence culture: Where old and new media collide.* New York, NY: New York University Press.

Jin, D. Y., & Su, W. (2019). *Asia-Pacific film co-productions: Theory, industry and aesthetics.* London: Routledge.

Jung, E. Y. (2007). Transnational cultural traffic in Northeast Asia: The "presence" of Japan in Korea's popular music culture (PhD thesis). University of Pittsburgh, Pittsburgh, PA

Jung, Y. (2007). Japan in the eye of the beholder: Its evolution and dilemma. *Japan Space, 2,* 70–91.

Kal, H. (2011). *Aesthetic construction of Korean nationalism: Spectacle, politics and history.* London: Routledge.

Kang, T. W. (2010). From refusal to acceptance: Characteristics of the popular books on Japanese Culture in the 1990s. *Korean Journal of Japanese Studies, 3,* 216–225.

Kim, H. (2011). A new wave in the Korean reception of Japanese popular culture after the emergence of Hallyu. *Orbis Sapientiae, 11,* 76–95.

Kim, H., & Yoon, T. (2012). How the idol system in Korean pop culture works: An explorative study on the dual structure of production/consumption of idol culture. *Broadcasting and Communication, 13*(4), 45–82.

Kim, H. M. (2003). J-pop consumption and the formation of fandom. *Korean Cultural Anthropology, 36*(1), 149–186.

Lee, D. H. (2004). Cultural contact with Japanese TV dramas: Modes of reception and narrative transparency. In K. Iwabuchi (Ed.), *Feeling Asian modernities: Transnational consumption of Japanese TV dramas* (pp. 251–274). Hong Kong: Hong Kong University Press.

Lee, D. H (2006). Transitional media consumption and cultural identity: Young Korean women's cultural appropriation of Japanese TV drama. *Asian Journal of Women's Studies, 12*(2), 64–87.

Lee, D. Y. (2005). *A society of cultural tribes: From hippie to pyein*. Seoul: Chaeksesang.

Lee, D. Y. (2007). *Imagining Asian cultural studies*. Seoul: Krinbi.

Lee, K. (2000). Detraditionalization of society and the rise of cultural studies. *Inter-Asia Cultural Studies, 1*(3), 477–490.

Lionnet, F., & Shih, S. (2005). Introduction: Thinking through the minor, transnationally. In F. Lionnet & S. Shih (Eds.), *Minor transnationalism* (pp. 1–23). Durham, NC: Duke University Press.

Maira, S., & Soep, E. (Eds.). (2004). *Youthscape: The popular, the national, the global*. Philadelphia, PA: University of Pennsylvania Press.

Moon, S. (2005). *Militarized modernity and gendered citizenship in South Korea*. Durham, NC: Duke University Press.

Nam, S. (2018). Japanese popular culture and Korea's governmentality. *Sanghur Hakbo: The Journal of Korean Modern Literature, 54*, 123–154.

Otmazgin, N., & Ben-Ari, E. (2012). Cultural industries and the state in East and Southeast Asia. In N. Otmazgin & E. Ben-Ari (Eds.), *Popular culture and the state in East and Southeast Asia* (pp. 3–26). London: Routledge.

Otmazgin, N. K. (2013). *Regionalizing culture: The political economy of Japanese popular culture in Asia*. Honolulu, HI: University of Hawaiʻi Press.

Park, J. W. (2006). An analysis of the impacts of import liberalization of Japanese pop culture. *The Korean Journal of Cultural Trade, 6*(1), 121–139.

Ryoo, W. (2009). Globalization, or the logic of cultural hybridization: The case of the Korean wave. *Asian Journal of Communication, 19*(2), 137–151.

Siriyuvasak, U. (2004). Popular culture and youth consumption: Modernity, identity and social transformation. In K. Iwabuchi (Ed.), *Feeling Asian modernities: Transnational consumption of Japanese TV dramas* (pp. 177–202). Hong Kong: Hong Kong University Press.

Smith, M. P., & Guarnizo, L. (Eds.). (1998). *Transnationalism from below*. New Brunswick, NJ: Transaction Books.

Straubhaar, J. D. (1991). Beyond media imperialism: Assymetrical interdependence and cultural proximity. *Critical Studies in Media Communication, 8*(1), 39–59.

Yoon, K. (2014). Looking east: Young Koreans consuming Japanese media in the intra-Asian youthscape. In D. Buckingham, S. Bragg, & M. J. Kehily (Eds.), *Youth cultures in the age of global media* (pp. 121–135). Basingstoke: Palgrave MacMillan.

Yoon, K., & Jin, D. Y. (2016). The Korean wave phenomenon in Asian diasporas in Canada. *Journal of Intercultural Studies, 37*(1): 69–83.

3 Digital Mediascape of the Korean Wave

Popular cultural content and styles from other countries—Japan and the United States (US) in particular—have until recently been influential in shaping young people's cultural practices in Korea. Some Korean critics and audiences have even considered Korean music, television (TV) shows, and films as more or less knockoffs of their Western or Japanese counterparts (Shin, 2013). The media producers have sometimes been accused of plagiarizing similar foreign—American or Japanese—texts.[1] In this regard, the recent flow of Korean popular culture has shown how a latecomer to the global cultural and media markets has not only caught up with global (e.g., the US) and regional (e.g., Japan) powerhouses but also explored enthusiastic fan bases around the world.

The global sensation of the K-pop group BTS since the mid-2010s demonstrates the emerging power of the Korean youth cultural form in the global mediascape. On April 12, 2019, the *Guinness World Records* recognized "Boy With Luv," a new BTS song, as the most viewed YouTube video in 24 hours; it garnered 74.6 million streaming views on the first day of its release. BTS had already broken the world record in the same category twice in the previous year—in August (the "Idol" music video) and May (the "Fake Love" music video). In June 2018, the seven-member K-pop group was recognized by *Time* magazine as one of "the 25 most influential people on the Internet." The group's fame was not limited to YouTube; rather, it was also observable in the mainstream media in several countries, as evidenced in the group's appearance on major network TV shows, including *Saturday Night Live*, *Jimmy Kimmel Live*, *The Ellen DeGeneres Show*, *Good Morning America*, and *Britain's Got Talent*. Furthermore, the group won in two major categories of the 2019 Billboard Music Awards and successfully continued stadium concerts in New York, London, and several other cities in 2019 (Frankenberg, 2019).

The global fandom of BTS is one of the latest examples of the transnational flow of Korean popular culture, known as the Korean Wave or *Hallyu* in Korean. The Korean Wave phenomenon forces us to ask how Korean popular culture, which has been deeply affected by, and has sought to catch up with, the West (and Japan), has emerged as a *global* cultural form that appeals to young people in numerous countries. As discussed in Chapter 2, Korea's media fan (*deokhu*) culture has evolved in young people's negotiation of overseas cultural forces, on the one hand, and the emerging environment of digital technologies, on the other. While Korean youth cultural styles inscribed in K-pop and other Korean Wave content are undeniably and to a large extent hybrid products of Western or Japanese cultural forms (Lie, 2012), Korean youth cultural forms have recently constituted a globally influential cultural trend. For example, BTS's global fan base, referred to as the ARMY, generates a vibrant and networked form of youth fandom that is equipped with digital literacy.

Global fans' engagement with K-pop illustrates an intriguing process of transnational cultural consumption in the social media era. As evidenced by the music video for Psy's global hit, "Gangnam Style," which was sung entirely in Korean without initially targeting an international audience, certain local cultural forms accidentally go viral through their integration into social media platforms beyond national and regional borders. In the emerging social media ecology, certain popular cultural forms are not only circulated through conventional channels, such as broadcast media, but also explore their own routes. K-pop has rapidly adapted to social media environments and has redefined itself as a visual/performative cultural form, thereby reducing probable linguistic barriers. K-pop's dispersed fan audiences are exposed to "free" content[2] on YouTube and share their feelings with fans who may be viewing the same music videos on the other side of the world. Intriguingly, K-pop's transnational flows reveal how cultural consumption involves media fans' networking and participation. Global K-pop fans not only consume cultural texts in a conventional way but also share, rework, reappropriate, and remediate the original texts through different forms of social media and user participation. For example, K-pop fans not only listen to K-pop and discuss their favorite K-pop idols but also practice these idols' choreographies and upload their own performances to YouTube. Some bilingual fans translate K-pop texts into different languages, sharing the translated subtitles on fan sites (i.e., "fansubbing"). These fan translations are often ongoing and collaborative processes in which some fans initially translate, while others revise to improve the early translations. Due to these fan practices, the boundaries between production and consumption are increasingly blurred. As a cultural form of *difference*, K-pop allows its overseas fans to "translate" it from their own perspectives and "re-localize" it (Yoon, 2017).

To examine how K-pop is transnationally circulated, translated, and re-localized by its overseas fans in social media environments, this chapter draws on a text analysis of K-pop fan videos and interviews with young Canadian K-pop fans. The field studies were conducted in

Canadian cities between 2015 and 2017, and 50 self-claimed K-pop fans were recruited via advertisements and snowballing, and interviewed individually. The interviewees, who had various ethno-cultural backgrounds (including Asian and White), were under the age of 30 years, and are presented under pseudonyms. In the semistructured interviews, these young Canadians discussed how they were introduced to K-pop, how they appropriated digital media for their fan activities, and how they enjoyed, felt, and thought about K-pop in their daily contexts. The field study period—from 2015 to 2017—overlapped with the rapid rise of K-pop among young people in Canada and numerous other countries. In particular, during this period, the Canadian news media depicted Vancouver and Toronto as emerging fan bases of global K-pop culture (Lee-Shanok, 2016; Nair, 2017; Shahzad, 2017). Drawing on the young Canadian fans' lived experiences, this chapter explores how K-pop as a youth cultural form originating and/or packaged in Korea is transnationally circulated, signified, and negotiated by overseas young people.

The chapter begins with reviewing the recent discussions of transnational flows of Korean popular culture, which is followed by an analysis of the emerging media environments enabling the global rise of K-pop. In particular, by looking at the interwoven processes of media convergence—corporate and grassroots convergence, the chapter proposes a framework for better understanding K-pop's participatory culture that is largely reliant on digital media-driven, global fan bases. The following sections have a close look at particular examples of digital media-driven fan practices—reaction videos and dance cover videos. While these examples reveal the participatory aspects of global K-pop fan culture as an audience-driven, grassroots phenomenon, K-pop fan practices are not free of structural forces, such as social media's technological structure and fans' racial and ethnic positions. Thus, it is suggested in the last section of the chapter that K-pop fans are not a homogenous group, but their sociocultural backgrounds may influence the way they participate in the digital mediascape of K-pop.

Global K-pop and Its Fans

There have been increasing discussions about how and why pop cultural forms of Korea—the country that was in the periphery of the global mediascape—have rapidly attracted global attention. The early Korean Wave in the 2000s, which was noticeable in Asian countries, was often explained by the probable cultural proximity between Asian consumers. The Confucianism-based cultural values, such as respect for elders and parents, and/or shared experiences of Asia's modernization were identified as appealing factors of Korean popular culture, especially Korean TV dramas for Asian audiences (Chua & Iwabuchi, 2008; Hogarth, 2013). In comparison, the recent Korean Wave, occurring since the early

2010s and represented by global K-pop fandom in not only Asia but also other regions, has often been attributed to the hybrid nature of the K-pop genre and its effective integration with social media environments beyond national and regional boundaries (Jin & Yoon, 2016; Lee & Nornes, 2015). Given the K-pop industry's efforts to remix and rework Western pop music, the hybridity of K-pop may not be surprising.

However, questions remain regarding the nature of K-pop's hybridity: Is it simply an inauthentic imitation of the hegemonic Western pop music (Jung, 2009; Unger, 2015)? Otherwise, does it imply "a potential node of cultural practice for new local identity formation" (Jin & Ryoo, 2014, p. 129)? For some, K-pop's hybridity might be a reproduction of Western musical styles (e.g., Unger, 2015), while others might see the possibility of "a third space" in the recent Korean Wave, moving beyond the dichotomy between center and periphery in the hybrid cultural genre (e.g., Jin, 2016).[3]

While K-pop refers to a popular music genre ("pop") by its name, this genre comprises more than musical components. Indeed, K-pop has been known for its "catchy tunes, good singing, attractive bodies, cool clothes, mesmerizing movements, and other attractive attributes, in a non-threatening, pleasant package" (Lie, 2012, p. 356). The fans who were interviewed for this chapter also described K-pop as "a package," primarily due to its variety of content,[4] systematic production process, and visual aspect. According to one fan, "K-pop is an overall performance package because there's so much that goes into it" (Jamie, 23 years old), while another stated, "K-pop is well packaged. It's an actual package because it has a training system going on, where pop music talents are trained for a long time" (Anne, 20 years old). K-pop was perceived as a package because of its visualized music: "You can distinguish K-pop [from other pop music] even without hearing the sound, because of the appearance [of K-pop idols], the fashion, the makeup, and the hairstyle . . . those are the whole package" (Carole, 20 years old). Additionally, it was stated that "if the package is pretty, why not look at it and wanna look at what's inside? So, yeah [laughs]. I'm pretty positive [about K-pop's emphasis on look]" (Nadia, 20 years old).

K-pop as a "package" has appealed to young audiences from different cultural backgrounds. For example, empirical studies in North America have identified ethnic minorities (diasporic youth of Asian heritage in particular) as the core fans of K-pop in the region (Park, 2013; Yoon, 2017; Yoon & Jin, 2016).[5] In the field studies conducted for this chapter, this demographic certainly constituted the core of K-pop fandom in Canada (Yoon & Jin, 2016); however, there were a noticeable number of non-Asian participants (including 11 White participants), which constituted over 20% of the total research participants. The Asian and non-Asian fans can be understood through Jenkins, Ford, and Green's (2013) framework of two key audience groups in transnational media circulation: (a) "diasporic audiences" (or "immigrants"), who transnationally consume the media of their origin (rather than that of the host society) and potentially act as "proselytizers" and (b) "pop cosmopolitans," who seek other cultural content beyond the boundaries of their own cultures.[6] According to this framework, diasporic media forms, such as Bollywood cinema, tend to be consumed primarily within diasporic communities, rather than by "pop cosmopolitans" (i.e., those who are not diasporic/immigrant audiences). In comparison, when certain transnational media forms, such as Japanese animation, are disseminated overseas, they attract dedicated "pop cosmopolitan" audiences, who have neither diasporic nor ethnic connections with the media forms they consume. Based on this cosmopolitan consumption pattern, transnational media forms are enjoyed without the cultural "odor" of the place of origin (Iwabuchi, 2002) or otherwise in a fetishized way through which the place of origin is stereotyped or fantasized (Jenkins et al., 2013).

The two categories can be applied to K-pop fandom in Canada, and interestingly, regarding K-pop fan bases in Canada, the two audience groups are not mutually exclusive and have both contributed to the global circulation of K-pop. It may be true that the earlier transnational flows of Korean popular culture were led by "diasporic" fans—that is, Asia-based fans or overseas fans of Asian descent. In the phase of diasporic consumption of K-pop, the cultural genre and its artists were often stereotyped or racialized by mainstream (non-diasporic) audiences. For example, when the K-pop superstar BoA showcased her US debut single in 2009, the *LA Times* described the native Korean star as "the heavily accented singer" (Amter, 2009). The American media's unfavorable responses to BoA's "accented" English may partly explain the Asian superstar's failure to penetrate the US market (Shin, 2013).[7]

However, the recent phase of the Korean Wave, often represented by enthusiastic young fans of Asian heritage and non-Asian heritage, appears to be moving beyond racial and cultural divides while exploring networked fans through social media. K-pop's language barriers and "accents" have been reduced through fans' networked consumption, which is facilitated by various digital and social media platforms. Canada-based fans in the study accessed information about K-pop idols through several English K-pop websites, such as allkpop.com and soompi.com, and social media, such as Twitter and Facebook. As Marianne, a 20-year-old fan in Toronto, pointed out, social media were frequently used for global *and* local fan networking:

> Twitter is the biggest way to find other international fans or people that are in Toronto. You guys can just go to events. If there's a Pop! Goes the World! [i.e., a Toronto-based K-pop event agency] event in Toronto and it is advertised on Facebook and Twitter. So, people just

go together. (…) I started getting into K-pop through my friends who already had Twitter [i.e., a Twitter account]. When I followed them, I realized that I got updates on different artists and groups. So, I got to know K-pop artists. If I tweeted about a K-pop group, someone would follow me [laughs]. And, after that, we would just talk [on Twitter] and would realize "Oh, look! We're both in Toronto!"

Locally *and* globally networked K-pop fans also were collaboratively immersed in the "universe" of their favorite K-pop idols.[8] As evidenced by BTS's "Love Yourself" campaign, K-pop idols encouraged their fans to participate in the K-pop universe, in which young people from different sociocultural backgrounds actualize themselves and share the feeling of growing up together. Moreover, digital media-driven, networked, and participatory consumption may significantly contribute to the inclusive universe of K-pop. The young fans in this study felt related to K-pop idols who were in their late teens or early twenties, as they share similar experiences regarding the struggle of transitioning to adulthood. Idols' extensive use of social media enables their fans to feel connected to them, as well as to other fans. For example, BTS's online channels on YouTube and V Live (Korean-based interactive application) connect the group's global fans by webcasting BTS members' everyday lives, thoughts, and music. BTS has also benefited from its dedicated fans who have contributed to different translations (primarily through fansubbing practices) on social media. The fans' participatory culture lowers the linguistic barriers and has, thus, attracted an increasing number of "pop cosmopolitans" to this new cultural genre. BTS has made continuous efforts to construct its performance and communication as a series of storytelling for the sake of their young fans. As Sugar, a BTS member, aptly summarized in an interview, BTS sings "what other people were feeling—like pain, anxieties and worries," and the group's goal is "to create this empathy that people can relate to" (Bruner, 2018, para. 6). Sharing the feeling of youthful struggles and showing efforts to cope with the struggles were highly appealing to the BTS fans in the study. Jane, a 20-year-old BTS fan, noted,

> BTS had the *Most Beautiful Moment in Life* trilogy [i.e., the compilation album by BTS released in 2016], and this whole story is about growing up and you would follow that. It's something that I find really interesting. And it has the continuation through one music video to another. One ends and the next music video is related to that last one. I like that there's a storyline to a music video.

In this manner, by participating in the imagined community of the K-pop universe, global fans might experience—at least temporarily—a sense of transcending their differences related to race, ethnicity, class, language, and age. As shown by BTS and its fan base ARMY, the K-pop universe expands through digital storytelling, which is facilitated by the process of digital media convergence.

Media Convergence from Above and Below

The global rise of K-pop vividly shows dimensions of media convergence as "an ongoing process occurring at various intersections between media technologies, industries, content, and audiences" (Jenkins, 2004, p. 154). In the global circulation of K-pop, media convergence occurs from above and below. On the one hand, the K-pop industry has exploited different media platforms to "package" its content by means of a process referred to as "corporate convergence" (Jenkins, 2006). On the other hand, the fans appropriate different media platforms for cultural consumption and participation by means of "grassroots convergence" (Jenkins, 2004).

K-pop is a cultural genre that has exploited social media extensively and has been customized for the emerging social media-driven cultural environment, which has been referred to as the "social mediascape" by Jin and Yoon (2016). K-pop may not yet be a globally dominant music genre in terms of conventional market measurements, such as song and album sales. However, the ability of major K-pop groups to penetrate the social mediascape has been remarkable. If measured by constant and intensive fan engagement (i.e., how often fans interact with an artist's social media account), rather than by simply following or clicking on social media, leading K-pop idol groups attract an exceptional number of social media mentions. For example, BTS had 61M Twitter mentions for 13M followers in a week of March, 2018, which "would look like every other artist in the world is failing to perform well on Twitter" (Benatar, Hughes, & Zee, 2018, para. 14).

The K-pop phenomenon has largely benefited from the industry's "corporate convergence"—that is, the vertical and horizontal concentrations of resources for production and distribution through its own packaging system (also known as the "in-house system"). The major K-pop corporations (known as the Big 3: SM, YG, and JYP Entertainment) have developed the "in-house" process of talent recruitment, training, marketing, music production, dissemination, and management. Media platforms play a key role in this vertical concentration, as evidenced by numerous reality audition shows, such as K-pop Star (2011–2017), Sixteen (2015), and Produce 101 (2016–2017), through which the entertainment companies form and promote their new idol groups. Meanwhile, K-pop promotion and dissemination have been strengthened by the industry's alliance with different media channels. In particular, YouTube has been essential to the circulation of K-pop on a global scale. Reportedly, over 90% of K-pop content on YouTube is consumed outside Korea (G. T. Lee, 2014). YouTube provides global audiences with convenient environments for accessing transnational media through its subtitles, automatic captions through speech recognition, and viewer comments and interactions (Jin, 2016, pp. 121–122). To overcome the initial lack of a solid offline infrastructure to enable the transnational dissemination of K-pop content, the K-pop industry quickly developed a new social media-based revenue model that bypasses traditional gatekeepers, such as broadcast media platforms. The industry has focused on viewers' attention on YouTube rather than on the sale of physical and digital materials, such as compact discs and files (Oh & Park, 2012). Major K-pop management companies marketize their idols through different platforms and versify their profit by extensively exploiting the appealing images of idols—for example, idols' endorsement deals with major companies, event performances, and merchandises including character goods (Y. Oh, 2018). Reliant on transmedia convergence, this revenue model has contributed to the effective global circulation of K-pop videos by allowing fans worldwide to conveniently access, share, and recreate them.[9] The visual consumption of K-pop not only entails activities on social media. The appealing visual aspect of K-pop but also facilitates a range of fan activities to "experience" K-pop, such as fan pilgrimages to Seoul, the "K-pop city" (Y. Oh, 2018).

The K-pop industry's deployment of digital platforms and early adoption of the business-to-business model, which is reliant on the profits generated by advertisements and the extensive release of free content on social media, have turned out to be successful strategies overall (Oh & Park, 2012). It is not only the K-pop industry but also the global platform provider YouTube that benefits from K-pop's revenue model through advertising on social media. Regarding the circulation of K-pop content on YouTube, the platform provider's profit share is much larger than that of the content provider—K-pop companies (Oh & Park, 2012). For this reason, seven major K-pop companies launched Music and Creative Partners Asia Ltd. (MCPA) in July 2018. According to its press release, MCPA aims to negotiate K-pop music videos' global distribution on YouTube and other global digital service platforms and to provide new platform services for K-pop video distribution. This project is known as the Korean counterpart to Vevo, which streams the music videos of three participating companies via its own site and YouTube, both of which share advertising and other profits (Milman, 2018).

As shown in MCPA's response to YouTube, the K-pop industry has not been exclusively reliant on global platforms for its worldwide reach. K-pop content producers have formed an alliance with Korean-based digital platforms. In particular, Korean-based platforms, such as Korean information technology (IT) giant Naver's V Live application (app), have helped facilitate transmedia digital storytelling practices, such as K-pop idols' personal broadcasts and their fans' video culture. Launched in 2015, the V Live app streams K-pop stars' personal live videos through an intimate and interactive format. The app, which offers foreign language support, has been especially popular among overseas fans who seek real-time communication with their Korean-based idols.[10] As exemplified by V Live's successful integration into K-pop fan bases, the K-pop industry has deployed different digital media platforms and technologies, including US-based global platforms—such as YouTube, Facebook, and Twitter—and Korean-based platforms—such as KakaoTalk, LINE, and V Live.

It is undeniable that global platforms, such as YouTube and Twitter, are far more influential than Korean-based platforms in the transnational social mediascape of K-pop. While K-pop's global social media platforms have contributed to spreading K-pop as a global youth cultural form, this process involves probable adverse effects on the ways in which cultural content is created and consumed. The global platforms not only enable "free" access but also restrict the expansion of local platforms and production companies; moreover, the global platforms might frame the ways in which fans interact with cultural texts. The dominant social media platforms are managed primarily by a few US-based global giant companies, which have become even bigger through continuous integration (e.g., mergers and acquisitions). Jin (2015) referred to major platform providers' tendency to dominate the platform media market as "platform imperialism." According to his argument, social and digital media do not necessarily provide opportunities for local industries and users, but they reinforce the existing economic and technological inequalities between Western and non-Western regions. Furthermore, platforms influence how users behave and appropriate content; for example, fans' methods of communicating with their stars and other fans are largely influenced by the technological affordances allowed by particular platforms. As boyd (2014) suggested, the dominant social media platforms have particular technological affordances, through which users' media consumption is framed. As discussed later in this chapter, K-pop fans' participation and user-generated content are not free of the design and structure of the media platforms they use. In particular, social media platforms engage with the commodification of user experiences and content by drawing on the interactive processes of users' participation as a source of revenue.

Although top-down media convergence ("corporate convergence"), which has been accelerated by media corporations (e.g., the K-pop music industry, IT industries, and global platform giants, such as Google), and particular technological affordances contribute to the rapid diffusion of K-pop on a global scale, the K-pop phenomenon would not have been possible without "grassroots convergence"—that is, global fans' active use of social media to translate, share, and recreate content. In particular, global fans' access to and engagement with K-pop across different media outlets, such as YouTube, Twitter, V Live, and fan sites, reveal how corporate convergence may be negotiated from below. K-pop fans do not simply consume ready-made content but, rather, actively *react* to and eventually *produce* content. For example, K-pop fans have utilized YouTube as their platform for sharing fan-generated content, such as fans' (a) editing of televised K-pop shows, (b) filming of K-pop stage performances (using their own video recorders or cell phones), (c) reactions to K-pop videos ("reaction videos"), and (d) "dance cover videos" (G. T. Lee, 2014).

Hugo, a 20-year-old fan, described how he accessed and enjoyed K-pop with others on social media:

> We share [information about] many different concerts and events that are happening here and especially if someone has a dance cover video or we love to share [the video]. I use Facebook Messenger a lot when something catches my ear or something new comes out. Especially with the YouTube group, I'm always like, "Yo, guys, check out this new video. We have to react to this."

K-pop fan activities are accompanied by networked consumption, which has also been referred to as "connected viewing" (Holt & Sanson, 2014), through which audience members are constantly connected with others via media platforms, and sharing content and information is not strictly controlled by institutionalized gatekeepers. Streaming sites have incorporated fan practices of connected viewing into their core interfaces. For example, the video streaming site Viki,[11] which specializes in Korean and East Asian content, shows the articulation of fans' participation and media corporations in the networked consumption of K-pop and the Korean Wave. Viki has effectively incorporated some of the fan-ish elements of file sharing, chatting, and interacting with other viewers on-line, as well as crowdsourced translations; thus, fans' participation is encouraged. Viki's interface design "solicits translation from the crowd yet offers multiple forums for community discussion and engagement, and encourages users to suggest new content, advocate for subtitles in their own language and self-organise subbing groups" (Dwyer, 2016, para. 2).

K-pop fan culture, which facilitates and is facilitated by grassroots convergence, blurs the boundaries between production and consumption. Equipped with mobile, ubiquitous, and mundane media technologies that allow for easy access and production, global fans enjoy K-pop through networked and producerly consumption. In particular, due to the digital media environments surrounding K-pop and the Korean Wave, overseas fans seem to easily interact with stars and other fans. Hilda, a 19-year-old fan in Vancouver, described how she took part in K-pop culture:

> There was a chance for international fans to write a message for their idol or trainee on *Produce 101* [i.e., on the web forum for the reality audition program *Produce 101*]. And then, someone would

put them together and translate them or keep them in English and then give them to the idols. There are obviously a lot of ways that fans can participate.

Not surprisingly, fansubbing is an important component of the global flows of K-pop. For K-pop music videos, equipped with production companies' official translations of the Korean lyrics, the official translations are limited to particularly popular songs and certain languages, such as English. Thus, bilingual fans contribute to fansubbing communities by offering their labor.

Moreover, user-generated videos have been popular forms of K-pop fan culture, in which fans not only consume but also actively interpret the content. Global K-pop fans are known for user-generated content, via which they express their feelings and share their thoughts with other K-pop fans. YouTubers' reactions to Psy's "Gangnam Style" video in 2012 were an early example of the vibrant K-pop fan video culture. When this Korean music video went viral, overseas YouTubers increasingly shot and uploaded their reactions to the original video primarily on YouTube while producing their own localized versions of OO (name of their own location) style—that is, dance covers and reactions. "Gangnam Style" fan videos show how global audiences express their emotional responses to and curiosity about the foreign content on YouTube. Among different forms of fan activities, making and sharing reaction videos and dance cover videos are particularly vivid examples of K-pop's fan culture. As Cho (2017) stated, K-pop fans' video culture is "a sign of a 'reactive' impetus in global K-pop reception, to assert that K-pop is less a pop-music genre than a performance culture" (p. 241). To examine the cultural meanings of fans' participation in K-pop culture through user-generated content, particular examples of reaction videos and dance cover videos will be discussed in the following two sections.

The Reaction Video Culture

Reaction videos have been rapidly integrated into K-pop's global fan communities for several reasons.[12] First, K-pop is an audiovisual genre that has been customized for YouTube and other social media platforms. Popular K-pop groups tend to promote their catchy songs in compact three- to five-minute music videos, which are often colorful and visually appealing. For K-pop musicians and producers who have no solid distribution channels in Western mainstream media industries, their global penetration has relied on YouTube's attention economy. As evidenced by BTS's global success, extensive and intensive integration into social media environments has been a particularly important component of K-pop's global distribution. The K-pop industry has developed its revenue model, which increasingly draws on YouTube viewing and related profits rather than content sales (Oh & Park, 2012). As a YouTube-customized music genre, K-pop has attracted enthusiastic audiences on YouTube and social media.

Second, as K-pop is a relatively new kind of music and is written in Korean, overseas fans want to talk and learn more about the context and content of its music videos. Regarding transnational and cross-cultural efforts to make sense of the foreign music form, YouTube and other social media platforms have been effective tools used by overseas fans to share their first impressions and interpretations of new K-pop music videos and know about others' thoughts on the new videos. By watching other fans' reaction videos, overseas fans know how others might think about and respond to particular K-pop music videos in which they are interested (Cho, 2017).

K-pop reaction videos reveal reactors' desires to watch (K-pop stars) and be watched (by other fans). Y. Kim (2015) pointed out succinctly the reactor's double role in regard to reaction videos—that is, the consumer, who assumes "the reactive position of appreciating the ready-made visual product," and the producer, who "makes and distributes self-reactive images" (p. 333).

While some reaction videos use advanced visual effects, most do not adopt particularly sophisticated production techniques; many comprise medium, close-up, or long-take shots of reactors' facial expressions and the narrations of their responses to K-pop music videos. Normally shot in front of the reactor's couch or desk, reaction videos prove that YouTube and other social media significantly lower the barrier of audiences' reworking of original cultural texts, as fans can easily upload and circulate their own video commentaries or reaction videos without having high level of digital media literacy.

Reaction videos largely comprise three parts: introduction (i.e., the part shot before the music video is played), reaction to the music video that is under examination (i.e., the part shot while the music video is being played), and the overall evaluation of the music video (i.e., the part shot after the music video is played) (Y. Kim, 2015). However, the simplicity of reaction videos in terms of their formats and narratives does not mean that they have no aesthetic value. As Y. Kim (2015) pointed out, reaction videos have their own aesthetics, such as ordinariness, naturalness, and self-immersion, and are produced and consumed in "ordinary people's everyday life and their habitual behaviors" (p. 337) while showing people's natural states and immersion in their own interiority in the process of watching K-pop videos.[13]

The practice of making and uploading reaction videos is often motivated by the fun derived from playful interactions with close peers and other fans. A few of the fans who were interviewed for this chapter had made and uploaded reaction videos. Initially, they were motivated by the pleasure of making funny videos, and then their continued production was encouraged by the increasing attention they received from other fans. For example, Adam, a 20-year-old student in Toronto, was a "micro-celebrity" YouTuber known for his K-pop reaction videos:

> [Interviewer: What made you start reaction videos?] Some people say I'm funny. I don't know why [laughs]. Uh, my friend was like, "Oh, I think you should do reaction videos." And I was like, "Okay. I'll try it." So, I sent her a few reaction videos that I didn't publish on YouTube. And she was like, "Oh my God! This is so funny!" which brought to my mind that maybe I could keep doing this. Maybe I could make other people laugh—not just this person. So, that's what happened. That's how I started.

Reaction videos are appealing to K-pop fans for several reasons. First of all, the videos are viewed because they are entertaining. For the viewers/fans (i.e., those who do not record their own reaction videos but enjoy watching others' reactions), reaction videos have additional functions—to make sense of the content and context of original K-pop video text, experience sameness by sharing similar reactions, and accumulate fan knowledge through "micro-celebrity" fans' reviews and recommendations.

By watching others watching K-pop music videos, overseas K-pop fans who do not understand the Korean language attempt to figure out the meanings and narratives of the videos. According to Alice (17 years old), K-pop videos tend to have complex narratives and many idol members in one short video; thus, she sometimes refers to K-pop fan vloggers' reaction videos for a better understanding of particular new videos:

> I watch reaction videos. [. . .] Because there are too many people in an idol group, I feel like, *Okay, but is there too much going on?* It's mostly like, *I like the beat, I like how catchy it is, and I like how they dance; it's so cool.* But then, there's just too much visually within the music video. [. . .] Because I have only one friend to share my feelings [about K-pop] with [in real life], watching other people react [helps me see] if they react the same. Then, I'll be like, *Oh! Someone else likes this too.* And there are really funny people on reaction channels, so . . . it's just entertainment basically.

Moreover, by watching others' reactions, fans affirm that their reactions differ only minimally from others'. According to Nora, a 19-year-old fan, "How they [reactors] are reacting, their facial expressions and stuff like that, is what I actually do when I watch [K-pop videos]." This feeling of sameness regarding reactions to K-pop music videos was also provided as a reason for watching reaction videos. For example, Hilda (19 years old) stated the following:

> Reaction videos are fun to watch because if I'm really into this one music video, and I want to hear other people's opinions about it, I might watch one person's reaction. I kind of want other people to feel the same way I do about this K-pop idol; so, that's why I watch them.

By watching other fans watching and reacting to K-pop videos, K-pop fans may allow themselves "to experience, at a time of increasing cultural difference, the comforting universality of human nature" through "a comforting restoration of order and unity" (Anderson, 2011, para. 14).

Furthermore, reaction videos produced by "micro-celebrity" fans can help fan viewers better understand various K-pop videos. As Carole, a 20-year-old fan in Vancouver, noted, famous YouTuber fans play the role of reviewers, which differs little from that of professional film or music reviewers:

> Lately, too many groups are appearing, and the majority of reaction videos are made by people who dedicate themselves to doing reaction videos. They tend to choose different kinds of . . . well, actually all the new groups, and they suggest groups [to pay attention to]. They introduce new songs coming out.

The reaction video facilitates the networked consumption of the transnational cultural text (K-pop) and potentially contributes to intercultural communication. As Swan (2018) pointed out, the reaction video is an "integration of reactive dialogue, emotional gasps, and conversation that encourages the participation of other fans" (p. 13).

While the reaction video is often considered an example of K-pop's participatory culture, it has been viewed skeptically by some critics and fans. Cho (2017) pointed out that the reaction video culture may reinforce a standardized and homogenized mode of human reactions. Reaction videos' format and aesthetics, which can be summarized as "ordinary" viewers' "natural" responses, are often conventional and manufactured. To some extent, viewers learn *how to* react by watching reaction videos. These videos may reproduce "the form of voluntary activeness to be reactive" (Y. Kim, 2015, p. 339) and may commodify being reactive. By watching others watching, fans are encouraged to feel, react, and translate a text in the way that other fans (reactors) do. The reaction video may narrowly frame the way in which a transnational cultural form is translated in different cultural contexts. Moreover, some

Western "micro-celebrity" YouTubers exude Oriental exoticism. As D. C. Oh's (2017) analysis illustrated with regard to K-pop, White YouTubers' reaction videos reveal to some extent the liberatory potential of cultural hybridity but also unveil White fans' power to fetishize non-Western cultural texts and to rework the dominant racial order.

Skeptical views regarding the reaction video culture were also evident among several fans who were interviewed for this chapter. Whereas some fans enjoyed uploading or watching reaction videos, others did not necessarily appreciate the reaction videos as a core fan activity. According to the skeptics, reaction videos reproduce stereotypes of K-pop and its fans. As Florence, a 21-year-old fan who is of Chinese heritage, noted, some Westerners' reaction videos reveal cultural misunderstandings: "It's very interesting to me to see the reaction of Westernized people, and most of them are like, 'Wow, this is really really strange.'" In this regard, several fans viewed some reaction videos as childish and even offensive rather than as representing cultural diversity regarding the reception of K-pop. These critical views reveal that the practice of making reaction videos may not always contribute to the participatory fan culture; rather, depending on *who reacts* and *how to react*, the reaction video culture may imply different meanings.

Dance Covers and the Video Culture

K-pop is circulated globally in the form of compact three- to five-minute videos, which are often freely available on social media platforms. The idols' collective choreographies, presented in colorful music videos, have contributed to K-pop's transnational appeal. By performing ("covering") the dance moves, global fans identify with, and embody their dedication to, the idols while attracting their own audiences. Fans' dance covers refer to dances that imitate the original artists' choreography. Fans' efforts to copy their idols' dance moves have been an important component of the K-pop fan culture (Billboard, 2011). The fans who were interviewed for this chapter indicated that they tended to enjoy the dance cover culture as dancers and/or viewers. Dance cover videos show a facet of the participatory K-pop fan culture, in which collaborative performance is digitally archived and shared. Young fans imitate, adjust, and appropriate original K-pop music videos and, thus, localize K-pop as an embodied cultural form. However, the cover dancers may not be free of the ongoing commodification of K-pop, through which audiences' performance and participation are incorporated into the circuit of K-pop as a commodity form.

K-pop is often recognized by its signature dance moves. According to the fans who were interviewed for this chapter, it was K-pop's choreography that initially attracted them to the genre. Olivia, a 19-year-old fan, described how her friends danced to K-pop: "There were a lot of people in high school who were really strong K-pop fans, and there were all kinds of people would just dance to it [a K-pop song], like 'Fantastic Baby,' just because it's really catchy." As 28-year-old Vancouver-based fan Cora noted, K-pop seemed to be integrated into the urban club culture:

> In Vancouver, there's a "Soju [i.e., a popular Korean liquor] Sunday," where they book a club on Sundays on a long weekend to play K-pop, and there are dance covers. Dance groups come and perform, too. And that's a lot of fun. [. . .] I love watching dance covers that people do, and I follow a couple of different dance crews that are here. They make videos and stuff like that. Sometimes, they react to the music videos, too, before they cover them.

Some fans learned to perform original K-pop dances by watching and analyzing K-pop music videos. By making and uploading dance cover videos, amateur fan dancers make an effort to improve their performances and present them to other fans and the public via social media platforms. Thus, once a new K-pop music video is released, K-pop cover dancers begin to exercise while aiming to perform the original choreography as accurately as possible. Once they are confident about their performances, they may record their dance moves in locations such as studios, public places, and even their bedrooms. Dance covering is a process involving fans' embodied participation in their K-pop idols' choreographic worlds. Cover dancing fans are highly committed and emotionally attached to the idols (groups) they replicate, and "the potency of the performance comes from the perfection of the dance and the precision in personifying the star" (Kang, 2014, p. 566). Some cover dancers attract their own fans and perform at events, becoming "microcelebrities" or "demi-idols" in their own right (Kang, 2014). Popular cover groups even created "a cottage industry selling prints, T-shirts, hats, and other fan paraphernalia" (Kang, 2014, p. 566).

The aesthetics of dance cover videos focuses on their similarity to original K-pop videos, primarily in regard to gestures, choreography, and costumes (Kang, 2014). Some dance cover videos are filmed in a way that imitates the original K-pop music video texts in terms of camera movements and mise-en-scènes. The cover dancers' efforts to imitate the original dances and texts can be considered a form of mimicry, in which certain hybrid effects and meanings are generated intentionally or unintentionally. As postcolonial theory suggests, the term *mimicry* implies the political effects of colonial subjects. According to Bhabha (1994), colonial mimicry is "the desire for a reformed, recognizable Other, *as a subject of a difference that is almost the same, but not quite*" (italics in original, p. 122). Dance cover videos reveal not only fans' desires to imitate the originals but also their (in)ability to do so identically.

Although dance cover videos imitate original K-pop music videos, amateur videos are inevitably different from the originals. Fans' dance cover videos often reveal their localities, which are contrasted with those of their original counterparts. With some exceptions, such as Psy's "Gangnam Style" and TWICE's "Likey," K-pop music videos are often shot in highly staged studio environments, and locations, therefore, remain unrecognizable (Liew, 2013). Common K-pop dance cover videos are simply shot in studios, where fans practice their dance moves, or in public places; however, even when filmed in a studio, a fan dance video does not completely remove the local atmosphere of the particular studio. Fans' dance cover videos tend to reveal "undecorated actual space instead of the staged elaborate settings of mainstream music videos" (Liew, 2013, p. 171). Additionally, some fan videos are set in public spaces in front of anonymous, pedestrian audiences. In such cases, the K-pop fans show not only their local contexts but also their creative engagement in public spaces, which function as the stage of their corporeal movements and collaboration. The fans resignify public locations, which would otherwise remain distant to them.

Many K-pop dance cover videos also present corporeal movements that may not coincide with the K-pop idols' narrowly defined standards of beauty. Liew (2013) claimed the following:

> From the intimate space of the bedrooms and living rooms to the dance studios and public arenas, the most striking deviation of the mirror dances from the artistes that they are following lies in the fan-performers' deeper sense of place and body.
>
> (p. 173)

In addition to showing fans' dedication and efforts to imitate K-pop idols, dance cover videos reveal moments of hybridity or mimicry. For example, shortly after the release of K-pop girl group TWICE's "Likey" music video (2017), which was shot entirely in Vancouver, several fan groups uploaded their dance cover videos that were shot in several locations that appeared in the original video. They clearly imitated the choreography of the original music video and presented nine members—the number of members in TWICE.

However, the fans had some changes of the original video by including behind-the-scenes segments, flash mobs in public spaces, and/or male performers. For example, Vancouver-based Flying Dancing Studio's fan dance cover video imitates the original "Likey" video, as nine East Asian-looking young women perform in several Vancouver locations that were featured in the original video. In this video, which was uploaded only seven days after the release of the original, the fan dancers imitate the choreography and atmosphere of the original as closely as possible. On the same day, K-City, a Vancouver-based dance cover group, also uploaded a "Likey" cover video. While Flying Dance Studio's video presented young Asian women, the dancers in the K-City video were relatively mixed in terms of gender (including two male members) and ethnicity (including several non-East Asian-looking members). Moreover, as K-pop idol groups are typically composed of many members (four or more), dance cover groups tend to have the same number of members as the original K-pop groups they cover. Thus, dance cover groups sometimes need to collaborate with other cover dancers or groups to make up for any shortages in this regard. For example, K-City's "Likey" video is based on the group's collaborative performance with other K-pop dance teams. In this manner, K-pop cover dancers often work collaboratively, sharing their feelings and corporeal movements.

K-pop cover dancers also perform in public places or clubs, thereby exposing the public to K-pop. Jamie, a K-pop fan and cover dancer in Vancouver, recalled being introduced to K-pop in a flash mob and later learning the dance moves through YouTube:

> In the summer of 2011, a big K-pop flash mob happened in Granville [i.e., the entertainment district of downtown Vancouver]. My friends wanted to participate in it, and this was when I had no idea what K-pop was. They said, "You know, we really want to do this, but we can't learn to dance off of YouTube. So, you should learn it, then you should teach us." Then I was like, "OK. I like you guys. I like dancing. I'll give this a shot." And that's when the whole thing just snowballed. And I started. That was my first experience learning dances off a computer.

Cover dancers perform as groups and/or do flash mobs in public places. In so doing, K-pop transforms public spaces into young people's symbolic territories, which would otherwise have remained distant to them. The fans' corporeal movements are also recorded for other fans and anonymous others. For example, "random dance cover games" are playful flash mob-style dance events that are popular among K-pop fans. This dance cover format allows participants to dance to random mixes of different K-pop songs in public places while replicating particular songs' signature choreography. Anyone can join and dance to each segment, as there is a short break (three to five seconds) between each segment. Random dance cover games tend to be performed in public places, such as shopping malls, public squares, and KCON. The way in which fans use technology and public spaces can be analyzed based on Molnár's (2014) study: "Flash mobs illuminate how everyday technological tools can be used ingeniously to create urban interventions, to break the routine of the everyday, by reframing public space around unexpected outbursts of sociability" (p. 55).

Popular cover dancers often shoot different versions of cover dance in different locations, such as public places and studios. They also upload tutorial videos to help other fans learn how to dance. This culture of sharing and mutual learning invites more and more young people to *do* (i.e., embody and perform) K-pop. Sasha, a 21-year-old fan who enjoys dance covers, noted,

> It's just easy to follow, and because there are so many YouTube tutorials online showing how to do Korean girl group dances, it's very easy for anybody to follow along. So, I sang, and my friends did the girl group dances.

Similar to K-pop reaction videos, dance cover videos show how global K-pop fan activities are heavily mediated and rely on digital media. Fans learn how to dance by watching music videos and other fans' dance tutorials (Kang, 2014). Dance cover videos reveal how fans accelerate translational cultural flows through the creative appropriation of different digital and social media platforms. Fans make use of corporate social media platforms, such as YouTube, to re-localize overseas cultural texts and globally share fan-generated content. Cover dancers' playful performances and videos, circulated on social media and beyond linguistic and cultural barriers, vividly illustrate the transnationalization of a Korean youth cultural form. The young people's bodily engagement with K-pop reveals how global youth localize and appropriate this cultural form rather than repetitively and passively consume it.

However, the culture of K-pop dance cover videos may not be free of the commodification of user-generated content and fans' labor (De Kosnik, 2013); by "covering" and referring to the original text/commodity, fans might contribute to attracting attention to it. The fan-generated content of dance cover videos serves the attention economy of K-pop on social media. In particular, media platform providers, such as YouTube, and the K-pop industry (the production companies of original K-pop music videos) benefit from a wide range of online fan activities, from uploading user-generated content to clicking on likes. Arguably, K-pop fans' "free labor" is not necessarily rewarded but eventually contributes to the reproduction and growth of digital capitalism (Y. Kim, 2015). For example, a Korean network TV channel, JTBC, recently launched the reality TV show *Stage K* (2019), in which global K-pop cover dancers compete, and a final winner is given the opportunity to perform with K-pop idols. This example reveals how fans' participatory culture is at least partly subject to, and in negotiation with, commodification forced by cultural industries.

Conclusion

The Korean Wave has been deeply integrated into the digital mediascape, through which its transnational circulation is accelerated substantially. As illustrated in this chapter, young people who are surrounded by ubiquitous digital media forms access and engage in the global fandom of K-pop and, in so doing, generate a participatory culture in which consumers become "produsers" (productive consumers) and explore their identities. K-pop fans' media-making practices illustrate how transnational fans make sense of and use of the text originating in a distant cultural context. As shown in the case of reaction videos and cover dance videos, K-pop fans produce, share, watch, and comment on idols' performance and other fans' performances through social media. The fans are seamlessly and constantly networked with other fans, while re-localizing the original texts.

By engaging with K-pop idols and other fans via different media forms, fans take part in transmedia storytelling and explore transnational imagination. As Jenkins (2006) suggested, media convergence facilitates not only the synergy of different media platforms and technologies but also the collaborative and networked methods of media creation and participatory culture, especially among young media users. In other words, in the era of digital and social media, media convergence is accelerated at the level of institution ("corporate convergence"), such as IT and media corporations, and simultaneously at the level of grassroots media users, artists, and activists ("grassroots convergence").

In the process of media convergence, K-pop fandom has emerged as a new mode of transnational youth cultural form. According to the young fans' accounts in the study, K-pop was considered as a cultural package that includes different cultural components. By engaging with this versatile cultural resource, the fans were globally *and* locally connected to the K-pop universe. Whereas the fans imagined an egalitarian K-pop community, the fans might not always go beyond their subject positions such as gender, race, ethnicity, and social class. The K-pop universe may be interpreted from many different perspectives. For example, "pop cosmopolitans" and "diasporic audiences" (Jenkins et al., 2013) might have different understandings or perspectives of K-pop. The diasporic audiences of Asian heritage have, to some extent, engaged with K-pop partly as a way to positively affirm their Asian identity (Yoon & Jin, 2016). In comparison, pop cosmopolitans, who were neither ethnically nor racially connected to the "K" in K-pop, seemed to be interested in K-pop owing to its difference from mainstream Western pop music. These differing perspectives of the pop cosmopolitans and diasporic audiences in this study resonate with D. C. Oh's (2017) analysis of racial orders in the Western K-pop fan community: White fans might be in a racially privileged position consuming K-pop as a non-Western (often racialized) cultural form, whereas Asian Canadian fans relate to K-pop as a resource for their identity politics.

Digital and social media may not be free of the existing (offline) power relations between different audience groups (including fans and nonfans) of K-pop. For example, trolling on social media and online forums has increased the number of negative stereotypes about K-pop idols and fans. When the K-pop group Girls' Generation won the Video of the Year award at the YouTube Awards in November 2013, a racist viral campaign built around the tag "Ching Chong Girls" was run against the group. The campaign was reportedly led by fans of White pop singers who were in competition with Girls' Generation (Jakubowicz et al., 2017). The K-pop fans in the study were sometimes offended by anonymous others who stigmatize K-pop and its fans as "immature" and "Asian" or describe the phenomenon as an "Asian-fetishizing" cultural taste. The fans' common responses to racist trolling or other forms of stigmatization of K-pop included "not coming out" (i.e., not publicly admitting their interest in and enthusiasm for K-pop), "ignoring the trolls," and "seeking allied fans." A few fans in the study fought back against trolls, rather than ignoring them or remaining silent. For example, Julia, a 19-year-old fan, consistently confronted those who teased K-pop fans online: "I've already fought so many people on Facebook about separate things [to do] with racism. I've already fought a ton of people. I've got into fights with lots of really White girls over [their] racism." For Julia, the social and digital mediascape involves ongoing tensions between fans and nonfans, on the one hand, and the racialization of non-Western music and its fans, on the other. Interestingly, Julia, who is a young White woman, assumed that "really White girls," who are not fans, virtually attacked K-pop fans and that this trolling was racist in nature. Julia's experience reveals that, despite digital media's potential for inclusive cosmopolitanism, the digital mediascape of transnational cultural flows is affected by the existing power relations.

This chapter explored the digital media-driven mobility of a local form of youth culture on a global scale. As a transnational media practice, K-pop fandom shows how digital and social media shape a participatory youth culture that moves beyond the temporal, spatial, and financial limitations with which young people cope. By accessing and re-localizing K-pop at a low cost and without geographic restrictions, the fans experience a sense of belonging and growing up together. In so doing, they may potentially feel empowered (Grossberg, 1992). K-pop's narrative of growing up together may serve to reproduce a particular mode of subjectivity, which idealizes self-regulated, self-developing, competitive, and young individuals (G. Kim, 2019; Y. Kim, 2011; Yoon, 2017). As Y. Oh (2018) aptly described, what K-pop's youthful narratives imply may be "the neoliberal enforcement of the refined body and the commodification of youth" (p. 134). Moreover, S. Y. Kim (2018) argued that K-pop fans' sense of togetherness might be an ideological and technological effect of liveness, which is digitally enhanced and involves dualistic meanings—the illusion of intimacy and a sense of community.

While the K-pop industry may produce and reproduce competitive idols oriented toward neoliberal subjectivity, this does not necessarily mean that the fans conform to the dominant neoliberal ideology. Popular cultural forms are always decoded and resignified by its audiences of different socio-cultural positions. K-pop can be reappropriated by young people to question the dominant social order. For example, "Into the New World," a song by the popular K-pop girl group Girls' Generation, was sung by a group of Ewha Womans University students in Seoul in 2017 during their protest against undemocratic school administration. Earlier, the prestigious private university announced the establishment of a new degree-granting college without consultation with the student body; this protest incidentally publicized the involved university executives' corruption, which later turned out to be a part of a larger political corruption, and then ignited nation-wide "candlelight" protests to impeach the president (Y. Lee, 2017). The students' appropriation of a song by the K-pop group that is considered a highly commercial, girlish group reveals how K-pop as a commodity form can be resignified by its audiences and thus, meaningfully incorporated into young people's social engagement.[14]

As Sandvoss (2005) argued, the "particular affection of the object of fandom" bridges "the fan's self and the object world" and operates as "a meaningful device in integrating internal and external reality" (p. 161). As vividly shown in this chapter, the global K-pop phenomenon has engaged with corporate and grassroots processes of digital media convergence, in which fans negotiate structural forces, such as corporations' commodification of fan culture. Global fans' reflexive engagement with K-pop may show how young people are growing up along with popular culture and digital media across geocultural boundaries.

Notes

1 The plagiarism of foreign media content and its format has been reported not only in Korea but also in other Asian countries. According to a recent report, many Korean TV shows have increasingly been copied without proper license agreements by numerous Asian media productions and repackaged as if they were original programs (The Chosun Ilbo, 2017).

2 While K-pop music videos on social media and YouTube are typically free in the sense that users do not have to pay for content, audiences have to provide their attention, data, and information in return. For a comprehensive discussion of audiences' consumption as labor, see McGuigan and Manzerolle (2014).

3 Either way, K-pop has been considered a new breed of cultural commodity developed in relation to the influence of Western popular culture, as evidenced by the Korean music industry's increasing contracts with American composers and producers, as well as the trend of including English lyrics in numerous K-pop songs (Jin & Ryoo, 2014). In addition to Western influences on K-pop, Japanese pop music (J-pop)'s influences were also noted by a few K-pop fans in the study. Several K-pop fans who were interviewed for this chapter were familiar with J-pop and compared K-pop and J-pop. According to their evaluations, J-pop did not sound "universal" or was "way too cute" (Maya, 18 years old). In addition, J-pop songs and music videos

were deemed less available than K-pop ones, which were widely available on social media platforms. Consequently, J-pop seemed to appeal to particular demographics of domestic and international fans, while K-pop was considered to have the potential to be spread globally.

4 In particular, K-pop idols are more than singers; they often appear in different cultural genres, such as variety shows, TV dramas, films, and TV commercial. Due to the nature of K-pop idols as "one source multi-use content," as promoted by the Korean cultural industries, they play a role as transmedia storytellers across different media platforms and forms (Shin, 2016).

5 By comparison, Latin American case studies have found that the young members of lower-income families constitute the main fan base (Carranza Ko, Kim, & Simoes, 2014; Min, 2017).

6 Despite the convenience and simplicity of their comparison, these two categories may need to be applied carefully. Otherwise, various people of color can be simply reduced to the category of "immigrants," while White people or those who are not minorities are contrastingly referred to as "cosmopolitans." In this binary opposition, diasporic populations might be essentialized to those who are excluded from the mainstream culture but inherently attracted to their ancestral and ethnic cultures.

7 Psy's success in Western markets has been explained in part by his easily consumable image as the funny, racialized, and demasculinized other in the eyes of Western audiences (Glynn & Kim, 2013). Some mainstream American media racialized Psy's "Gangnam Style" rather than engaging with the cultural context of the music (e.g., a parody of the nouveau riche of the Gangnam district in Seoul). Fox News presenter Bill O'Reilly depicted Psy as "a little fat guy from Yong Yang, or some place, and he's jumping up and down," after stating that "the most popular music apparently is that without intelligible words," which obviously referred to the apparent unintelligibility of "Gangnam Style" that was written in Korean (Davis, 2013).

8 Both fans and journalists sometimes call the virtual world of K-pop idols a "universe." One idol group constitutes a universe, while it can cross another idol group's universe and be incorporated into another universe. The term "universe" may correspond to the term "storyworld" used in narrative studies. Storyworlds

> encompass not only the story per se, but also the backstory, and sometimes the afterstory (such as the later life of the protagonists, as represented in epilogues), and not only the scene of the story, but all the places that characters think or talk about.
>
> (Ryan, 2016, p. 14)

By this definition, K-pop idols' universe can be defined as a form of storyworld in which not only music texts but also background stories and after stories about idols are generated and circulated through fans' enunciative participation in social media. The Internet and social media appear to be integral components of the K-pop universe. Several platforms allow K-pops to do chatting with other fans, while some K-pop idols frequently upload their everyday video segments. Moreover, many fan-based websites, such as Netizenbuzz, provide translations of Korean-based K-pop fans' online comments about K-pop stories, gossip, and news. The abundant information appears to provide the overseas fans with important resources for developing the K-pop universe.

9 It is estimated that K-pop fans' pilgrimage has also contributed to the boost of tourism. Indeed, many K-pop fans interviewed for this chapter have been to Korea for sightseeing, motivated by their interest in K-pop. According

to them, the SM Entertainment, the leading K-pop management company's theme park (SM Town Coexatrium) in the Gangnam district, Seoul, was a popular tourist attraction, where they can purchase SM-affiliated K-pop idols' merchandise. In the study, two fans recalled that while they were staying in Korea, they made train trip to a small café in Gwangju (located approximately 260 km away from Seoul), owned by the mother of Suzy, a popular K-pop idol to "feel" the atmosphere and meet with the mother.

10 In December 2018, V Live had over 973 channels, many of which stream segments of the everyday lives of young Korean pop stars. The live streaming service also includes the stars' live chat sessions with their fans. While watching the stars' live streaming, which is archived and re-playable, viewers can volunteer to provide fansubbing and chat with other viewers. V Live's content includes a wide range of celebrity shows, such as the webcam-style monologues of stars, reality shows, and visual radio shows. While most materials are streamed in Korean, this service has targeted and attracted global audiences. As of November 2018, most visitors (approximately 76%) of this service have been from outside Korea (see vlive.tv Traffic Statistics on November 17, 2018, retrieved from www.alexa.com/siteinfo/vlive.tv). To reach global audiences, V Live relies heavily on fansubbing, rather than providing official translations. Due to the fan viewers' "free labor," some video clips have over ten versions of subtitles. Fansubbers are rewarded in nonmonetary ways (e.g., given opportunities to call their favorite stars).

11 In 2007, Viki was established by three American students as a class project to provide video streaming and language services for primarily Asian (Korean in particular) TV content. The streaming site was purchased by the Japanese electronics company Rakuten in 2013 and was relaunched as a for-profit service targeting a global audience. Today, the site provides video content in numerous languages and is syndicated to major streaming service companies, such as Netflix.

12 The reaction video is a relatively new cultural form that was reportedly started online in the mid-2000s. A famous early example is the circulation of numerous short videos capturing people's reactions to the one-minute trailer for the 2007 Brazilian pornographic film *Hungry Bitches*. The trailer video clip, nicknamed *2 Girls 1 Cup*, was widely reacted to by numerous people on video and contributed to popularizing the term "reaction videos" (Skelton, 2018). The reaction video has emerged as a popular YouTube genre, and some YouTubers who regularly release reaction videos have been recognized as "micro celebrities" who have their own fan bases (Marwick, 2015). Some celebrity YouTubers have even become professional media producers and/or entrepreneurs. For example, FBE (originally known as Fine Brothers Entertainment)—the two-man video team best known for its REACT channel on YouTube and its attempt to trademark the term *react*—has established itself as a for-profit media company.

13 Among numerous K-pop reaction channels on YouTube, ReacttotheK is one of the most widely known. This channel, established in 2016 by a classical music student at the Eastman School of Music in New York, has attracted a large number of subscribers (approximately 550,000 as of June 1, 2019) and has gained exceptional popularity among K-pop fans. Thus, the channel's regular reactors were even invited to KCON (the annual Korean Wave convention) in Los Angeles in 2018 as special guests. This channel regularly releases reaction videos, its "Classical Musicians React" series, focusing on classical music students' takes on K-pop. By reviewing music components of K-pop videos from classical music students' perspectives, ReacttotheK's videos are distinguished from typical reaction videos, which primarily present reactors'

(exaggerated) emotional responses to K-pop videos. While this channel was started "for fun" by the main creator, Umu, who was about to graduate from high school in 2016, the creator and reactors have attracted their own fans and have, thus, become keenly aware of their audiences' responses. That is, reaction video makers are not only audience members but also performers who have their own audiences. It is uncertain whether the channel will become for-profit. The channel has recently begun fundraising by introducing patron memberships (https://www.patreon.com/reacttothek) so that it can improve video quality by using better equipment and paying for the labor.

14 While this incident was examined by some critics as an intriguing example of new social movement that may move beyond the exclusive nature of earlier Korean student movements (e.g., Y. Lee, 2017), others are relatively skeptical about this appropriation of K-pop (e.g., G. Kim, 2019). For example, G. Kim (2019, p. 24) claims that, although this example of appropriation of K-pop for a protest shows how young people "utilize the neoliberal cultural device for their critical cause", the protest is no other than "a consumer movement" that requests the university to maintain its degrees' value and to better serve its students as consumers.

References

Amter, C. (2009). Utada, Boa set sights on America with dueling English-language discs. Retrieved from http://latimesblogs.latimes.com/music_blog/2009/03/utada-boaset-si.html

Anderson, S. (2011, November 27). Watching people watching people watching. *New York Times Magazine*. Retrieved from https://www.nytimes.com/2011/11/27/magazine/reaction-videos.html

Benatar, J., Hughes, S., & Zee, A. (2018). Next big sound introduces: Weekly performance insights. Retrieved from https://blog.nextbigsound.com/weekly-performance-insights-e2a9e149d91

Bhabha, H. (1994). *The location of culture*. New York, NY: Routledge.

Billboard. (2011). A look inside the "K-pop cover dance" trend. Retrieved from. https://www.billboard.com/articles/news/465675/a-look-inside-the-k-pop-cover-dance-trend

boyd, d. (2014). *It's complicated: The social lives of networked teens*. New Haven, CT: Yale University Press.

Bruner, R. (2018, October 10). How BTS is taking over the world. *Time*. Retrieved from https://time.com/collection-post/5414052/bts-next-generation-leaders/

Carranza Ko, N., Kim, J. N., No, S., & Simoes, R. G. (2014). Landing of the wave: Hallyu in Peru and Brazil. *Development and Society, 43*(2), 297–350.

Cho, M. (2017). Pop cosmopolitics and K-pop video culture. In J. Neves & B. Sarkar (Eds.), *Asian video cultures: In the penumbra of the global* (pp. 240–265). Durham, NC: Duke University Press.

Chua, B. H., & Iwabuchi, K. (Eds.). (2008). *East Asian pop culture: Analysing the Korean Wave*. Hong Kong: Hong Kong University Press.

Davis, L. (2013, May 22). Is the hilarious Fox News analysis of Gangnam Style racist?" *The Independent*. Retrieved from http://www.independent.co.uk/voices/iv-drip/must-watch-is-the-hilarious-fox-news-analysis-of-gangnam-styleracist-8371793.html

De Kosnik, A. (2013). Fandom as free labor. In T. Scholz (Ed.), *Digital labor: The Internet as playground and factory* (pp. 98–111). London: Routledge.

Dwyer, T. (2016). Welcome to Viki! Fansubbing and media change. Retrieved from http://mediacommons.org/fieldguide/question/what-ways-do-internet-tools-and-culture-recursively-affect-both-international-and-localiz-4

Frankenberg, E. (2019, June 27). BTS surpasses $50 million in May with the month's top-grossing tour. *Billboard*. Retrieved from https://www.billboard.com/articles/columns/chart-beat/8517718/bts-surpasses-50-million-top-grossing-tour-may-2019

Glynn, B., & Kim, J. (2013). "Oppa"-tunity knocks: Psy, Gangnam Style and the critical reception of K-pop in Britain. *Situations: Cultural Studies in the East Asian Context, 7*(1), 1–20.

Grossberg, L. (1992). Is there a fan in the house? The affective sensibility of fandom. In L. A. Lewis (Ed.), *The adoring audience: Fan culture and popular media* (pp. 50–65). London: Routledge.

Hogarth, H. K. K. (2013). The Korean Wave: An Asian reaction to western-dominated globalization. *Perspectives on Global Development and Technology, 12*(1–2), 135–151.

Holt, J., & Sanson, K. (Eds.). (2014). *Connected viewing: Selling, streaming, and sharing media in the digital age*. New York, NY: Routledge.

Iwabuchi, K. (2002). *Recentering globalization: Popular culture and Japanese transnationalism*. Durham, NC: Duke University Press.

Jakubowicz, A., Dunn, K., Mason, G., Paradies, Y., Bliuc, A. M., Bahfen, N., ... Connelly, K. (2017). *Cyber racism and community resilience*. London: Palgrave.

Jenkins, H. (2004). The cultural logic of media convergence. *International Journal of Cultural Studies, 7*(1), 33–43.

Jenkins, H. (2006). *Convergence culture: Where old and new media collide*. New York, NY: New York University Press.

Jenkins, H., Ford. S., & Green, J. (2013). *Spreadable media: Creating value and meaning in a networked culture*. New York, NY: New York University Press.

Jin, D. Y. (2015). *Digital platforms, imperialism and political culture*. London: Routledge.

Jin, D. Y. (2016). *New Korean Wave: Transnational cultural power in the age of social media*. Champaign, IL: University of Illinois Press.

Jin, D. Y., & Ryoo, W. (2014). Critical interpretation of hybrid K-pop: The global-local paradigm of English mixing in lyrics. *Popular Music & Society, 37*(2), 113–131.

Jin, D. Y., & Yoon, K. (2016). The social mediascape of transnational Korean pop culture: Hallyu 2.0 as spreadable media practice. *New Media & Society, 18*(7), 1277–1292.

Jung, E. Y. (2009). Transnational Korea: A critical assessment of the Korean Wave in Asia and the United States. *Southeast Review of Asian Studies, 31*, 69–80.

Kang, D. B. C. (2014). Idols of development: Transnational transgender performance in Thai K-pop cover dance. *Transgender Studies Quarterly, 1*(4), 559–571.

Kim, G. (2019). *From factory girls to K-pop idols girls: Cultural politics of developmentalism, patriarchy, and neoliberalism in South Korea's popular music industry*. Lanham, MD: Lexington Books.

Kim, S. Y. (2018). *K-pop live: Fans, idols, and multimedia performance.* Stanford, CA: Stanford University Press.

Kim, Y. (2011). Idol republic: The global emergence of girl industries and the commercialization of girl bodies. *Journal of Gender Studies, 20*(4), 333–345.

Kim, Y. (2015). Globalization of the privatized self-image: The reaction video and its attention economy on YouTube. In L. Hjorth & O. Khoo (Eds.), *Routledge handbook of new media in Asia* (pp. 333–342). London: Routledge.

Lee, G. T. (2014). Digitalization and globalization of K-pop-YouTube reaction video and cover dance festivals. *The Journal of Hallyu Business, 1*(1), 73–107.

Lee, S. J., & Nornes, A. M. (Eds.). (2015). *Hallyu 2.0: Korean Wave in the age of social media.* Ann Arbor: University of Michigan Press.

Lee, Y. (2017, March 14). How sparks at S. Korean women's school led to anti-Park fire. *The Associate Press.* Retrieved from https://www.apnews.com/f26782acb46246a0835ecfc412ed7db1

Lee-Shanok, P. (2016, May 6). Hallyu North festival brings K-pop music to Toronto Friday night. Retrieved from http://www.cbc.ca/news/canada/toronto/hallyu-north-festival-brings-k-pop-music-to-toronto-friday-night-1.3569328

Lie, J. (2012). What is the K in K-pop? South Korean popular music, the culture industry, and national identity. *Korea Observer, 43*(3), 339–363.

Liew, K. K. (2013). K-pop dance trackers and cover dancers. In Y. Kim (Ed.), *The Korean Wave: Korean media go global* (pp. 165–182). London: Routledge.

Marwick, A. (2015). You may know me from YouTube: (Micro-)celebrity in social media. In P. D. Marshall & S. Redmond (Eds.), *A companion to celebrity* (pp. 333–350). Oxford: Wiley-Blackwell.

McGuigan, L., & Manzerolle, V. (2014). *The audience commodity in a digital age: Revisiting a critical theory of commercial media.* New York, NY: Peter Lang.

Milman, L. (2018). BTS' label & other major K-pop companies launch service referred to as a "Korean Vevo." Retrieved from https://www.billboard.com/articles/business/8466156/mcpa-korean-vevo-launch-kpop-music-video-distribution

Min, W. J. (2017). Korean Wave reception and the participatory fan culture in Latin America: What lies beyond the media reports. In T. J. Yoon & D.Y. Jin (Eds.), *The Korean Wave: evolution, fandom, and transnationality* (pp. 145–161). Lanham, MD: Lexington.

Molnár, V. (2014). Reframing public space through digital mobilization: Flash mobs and contemporary urban youth culture. *Space and Culture, 17*(1), 43–58.

Nair, R. (2017). Is Vancouver the new Gangnam? Korean pop video filmed in Vancouver gets millions of views upon debut. Retrieved from http://www.cbc.ca/news/canada/british-columbia/is-vancouver-the-new-gangnam-korean-pop-video-filmed-in-vancouver-gets-millions-of-views-upon-debut-1.4380373

Oh, D. C. (2017). K-Pop fans react: Hybridity and the White celebrity-fan on YouTube. *International Journal of Communication, 11*, 2270–2287.

Oh, I., & Park, G. S. (2012). From B2C to B2B: Selling Korean pop music in the age of new social media. *Korea Observer, 43*(3), 365–397.

Oh, Y. (2018). *Pop city: Korean popular culture and the selling of place.* Ithaca, NY: Cornell University Press.

Park, J. S. (2013). Negotiating identity and power in transnational cultural consumption: Korean American youths and the Korean Wave. In Y. Kim

(Ed.), *The Korean Wave: Korean media go global* (pp. 120–134). London: Routledge.

Ryan, M. L. (2016). Texts, worlds, stories. In M. Hatavara, M. Hyvärinen, M. Mäkelä, & F. Mäyrä (Eds.), *Narrative theory, literature, and new media: Narrative minds and virtual worlds* (pp. 11–28). New York, NY: Routledge.

Sandvoss, C. (2005). *Fans: The mirror of consumption*. Oxford: Polity.

Shahzad, R. (2017, May 13). Here's the unexpected reason why Korean language courses are so popular at U of T. Retrieved from http://www.cbc.ca/news/canada/toronto/programs/metromorning/korean-interst-1.4022395

Shin, H. (2013). *Gayo, K-pop, and beyond*. Paju: Dolbaege.

Shin, H. (2016). K-pop, the sound of subaltern cosmopolitanism? In K. Iwabuchi, E. Tsai & C. Berry (Eds.), *Routledge handbook of East Asian popular culture* (pp. 116–123). London: Routledge.

Skelton, E. (2018). The fascinating rise of YouTube music reaction videos. Retrieved from https://www.complex.com/pigeons-and-planes/2018/01/youtube-music-reaction-videos-rise-science-understanding

Swan, L. A. (2018). Transnational identities and feeling in fandom: Place and embodiment in K-pop fan reaction videos. *Communication, Culture and Critique, 11*(4), 548–565.

The Chosun Ilbo. (2017). Why Chinese broadcasters' copy of Korean entertainment programs continue. Retrieved from http://news.chosun.com/site/data/html_dir/2017/08/20/2017082000358.html

Unger, M. A. (2015). The aporia of presentation: Deconstructing the genre of K-pop girl group music videos in South Korea. *Journal of Popular Music Studies, 27*(1), 25–47.

Yoon, K. (2017). Cultural translation of K-pop among Asian Canadian fans. *International Journal of Communication, 11*, 2350–2366.

Yoon, K., & Jin, D. Y. (2016). The Korean Wave phenomenon in Asian diasporas in Canada. *Journal of Intercultural Studies, 37*(1), 69–83.

4 Digital Mediascape of Global Experiences

As discussed in Chapters 2 and 3, the digital media-driven flows of popular culture have facilitated the transnationalization of Korean youth culture, especially since the early 2000s. The two chapters illustrated the flows of popular culture both within and outside Korea in relation to young fans engaging with overseas media. In comparison, the current and the following two chapters focus more on the flows of people—young media users on the transnational move. In particular, this chapter discusses young Korean sojourners' digital media practices in Canada.

Each year, many young Koreans go abroad for travel, education, work, and immigration purposes. An increasing number of temporary young sojourners from Korea are reportedly being observed in the urban areas of English-speaking countries (Chun & Han, 2015; Yoon, 2014). For example, as of 2017, over 54,000 and 50,000 Koreans who hold working holiday visas, temporary working visas, or student visas resided in Canada and Australia, respectively (Korean Ministry of Foreign Affairs, 2017).

While sojourners do not typically become permanent residents of the host country, the constant flow of young sojourners has indeed changed the urban landscape of Canadian cities (Chun & Han, 2015). For example, flourishing tourism industries targeting transnational sojourners provide services, such as short-term English language programs, volunteer opportunities, tourism agencies, short-term housing, and homestay services in the host country. Various agencies promote programs that provide young people with overseas experiences (Yoon, 2014). Young Korean sojourners overseas often connect with diasporic communities and are involved in the ethnic economy, which consists of immigrants' small businesses and diasporic labor power (Yoon, 2014). Moreover, they may transnationally disseminate particular popular cultural forms, such as K-pop, especially when they encounter other sojourners of different national origins (Shin, 2012). Furthermore, young sojourners' transient use of digital media facilitates the evolution of low-cost communication technologies with different groups of people in the transnational context. For example, owing to their transient status, young sojourners often explore certain media strategies, such as exploring free Internet access spots and sporadic/mobile viewing of television (TV) through steaming services.

Transnational young sojourners are not only consumers but can also be workers who are temporarily involved in the host country's labor market. Some countries, such as Canada and Australia, have used "working holiday" programs to attract young temporary, inexpensive labor power (Helleiner, 2017; Yoon, 2015). Working holidaymakers constitute a particularly interesting demographic among many types of young sojourners, from short-term backpackers to relatively long-term international students. Working holidaymakers include a wide range of sojourners, as the working holiday is a visa program that allows young people (typically aged 18–30 years) to stay, study, and/or work in another country usually for one year. Thus, while working holidaymakers might literally refer to those who are working *and* enjoying holidays overseas, they often hold this particular type of visa.[1] This program offers young Koreans opportunities to go abroad for a relatively long period. As of 2016, Korea has working holiday visa agreements with 21 countries, including Australia, Japan, Canada, and New Zealand, which constitute the most popular destination countries among young Korean working holidaymakers. According to recent statistics, 37,637 young Koreans went abroad through this program in 2016 (Working Holiday Info Center, 2019). Each year for the past decade, 30,000–50,000 young people have left for one of the working holiday destinations (Working Holiday Info Center, 2019).

Some young people with working holiday visas work, study, and holiday, whereas others either travel long term or work full-time. The Korean working holidaymakers who were interviewed for this chapter tended to refer to themselves and others like them as *woholleo* (Korean for "working holidaymaker"). *Woholleo*s constitute a specific group of sojourners, whose transnational mobility is driven primarily by their desire for "global experiences" (Chun & Han, 2015; Yoon, 2014). Thus, they can be compared with other types of sojourners, such as international students seeking academic credentials and migrants who are permanently relocated. The working holiday scheme is popular among young Koreans due to its flexibility, which enables participants to decide how they spend one year overseas; the scheme seems to offer an ideal combination of activities that cannot be experienced by individuals with other visa types (such as international student or short-term tourist visas, which do not typically grant eligibility for full-time employment). For young people, this flexibility can be an opportunity to explore aptitudes and interests, especially during a gap year before the transition to adulthood or full-time employment. However, this flexible year can also be a highly precarious time of uncertainty and anxiety (Chun & Han, 2015).

Given this context, this chapter explores how young Korean sojourners in Canada negotiate the opportunities and precariousness of transnational mobility, especially in relation to their digital media practices. To examine sojourners' transnational experiences and media practices, 57 individual interviews were conducted in three Canadian cities–Toronto, Vancouver, and Kelowna–between 2010 and 2014, after which three follow-up interviews were conducted in Seoul. The participants, presented under pseudonyms, were Koreans who had entered Canada with working holiday visas and had been in the country for at least three months. In addition to in-depth interviews, policy documents, news media, online forums, and blogs were analyzed to examine how global experiences through overseas sojourning were discursively constructed in Korea.

This chapter begins with a review of key themes arising in recent studies of sojourners' media use. This is followed by an analysis of the global experience discourse in Korean media and government documents. The chapter explores how the discourse of global experience has been constructed and has had the ideological effects of reorienting young people's frustrations and struggles with the country regarding the neoliberal ethos of self-development and transnational mobility (Dardot & Laval, 2014). This constructed discourse of global experience is brought into question based on the young sojourners' accounts of their actual working holiday experiences in Canada. Moreover, the young people's transnational lives are examined in relation to their media use. The empirical analysis explores how young Koreans engage with digital media to cope with their transnational and transient lives.

Studying Sojourners' Media Practices

Recent media studies have examined young sojourners whose transient lives are deeply immersed in digital media environments (Gomes, 2017, 2018; S. Jung, 2013; Y. Kim, 2011; Lee & Ahn, 2018; Pham & Lim, 2016; Wong, 2017). These studies explore how young people on the transnational move negotiate the transient nature of sojourning through their media practices. One of the most frequent themes in these recent studies is the role of digital media in sojourners' transnational communication. In particular, existing studies have addressed how digital communication technologies facilitate sojourners' connections with their home countries and their overseas locations of residence and, thus, shape their sense of place. In the existing studies, three recurring themes that are especially relevant to this chapter can be identified.

First, according to the literature, young sojourners use media to facilitate their cultural adjustment to the host country. S. Jung (2013) found that newly arrived Korean sojourners in Australia sought information to help them understand the host country's social system. New sojourners who feel socially unstable in the new environment participate in the online ethnic community to find an avenue through which to understand and connect to the host country and, in so doing, negotiate their ambiguous social status as transient migrants (Gomes, 2017, 2018; S. Jung, 2013).

Second, studies have shown that young sojourners use media to connect with the home country and, in so doing, maintain emotional continuity and stability before and after their transnational migration (Lee & Ahn, 2018; Wong, 2017). Furthermore, sojourners reportedly consume home country media as a way of coping with their homesickness and challenges in the host country (Gomes, 2017, 2018; Lee & Ahn, 2018; Wong & Hjorth, 2016). This media consumption enables them to feel temporally and spatially closer to their homeland. However, maintaining a connection with the homeland may not always empower the sojourners, as it can disrupt transnational life (Gomes, 2017, 2018). As Y. Kim (2011) claimed, the sojourners' "imaginary connection with home is ambiguous and paradoxical in its effects on their everyday transnational lives, both constraining and facilitating the subsequent development of a felt, functioning sense of belonging and of their subsequent actions 'here' or 'there'" (p. 97).

Third, sojourners' media practices involve the processes of self-expression and self-actualization (Gomes, 2017, 2018; Hjorth, 2007; Wong, 2017). As sojourning involves a process of self-realization in an unfamiliar location, sojourners' media practices engage with space-making. Social media storytelling is an exemplary practice through which young sojourners maintain and explore their cultural identities (Wong, 2017). By sharing narratives of life overseas, sojourners are "effectively giving power to the multiple instantaneous and intimate publics to reshape their migrant identities" (Wong, p. 126). For example, online community forums function as platforms on which young sojourners share their feelings and overseas experiences with other sojourners (S. Jung, 2013).

Overall, the existing studies have closely examined the transient and ambivalent nature of sojourners' transnational mediascape, focusing on two dimensions: (a) connection/disconnection and (b) online/offline. On the one hand, digital connection occurs in relation to disconnection. Connecting with the homeland can disrupt the connection with the host society's mainstream media, thus resulting in a certain level of disconnection, and vice versa. As Gomes (2018) argued, "transient migrants use the digital platforms they bring with them from the sender nation and may not cross over to the digital platforms of their receiver nations" (p. 59). In digital media-saturated environments, even relatively short-term sojourners, such as backpackers, are increasingly forced to manage their online persona and social identities due to their use of social media (Berger & Paris, 2013). On the other hand, intensive immersion in digital media environments can disrupt sojourners' integration into the offline context of the host society (Gomes, 2018; Rosenberg, 2019). These two dimensions, however, are not necessarily mutually exclusive. Due to the increasing incorporation of digital communication technologies into everyday lives, online and offline contexts are seamlessly interwoven. Moreover, connection with the homeland may not always entail disconnection and disengagement from the host land. The dichotomy between online connection with the homeland and offline integration with the host society seems to draw on an ideal type, as sojourners' media practices may be more complicated than the dichotomous user pattern. For example, digital communication technologies— the smartphone in particular—might not necessarily disrupt but might also facilitate sojourners' opportunities to connect with the host society and explore different human networks. Communication technologies may serve as tools and resources that enable young sojourners to participate in transnational living and explore new sociocultural contexts.

Despite offering some insights into how media are utilized to negotiate the transient processes of transnational mobility, the existing studies tend to focus more on particular types of transient sojourners, such as international students, and, thus, fail to capture diverse sojourning subjects, such as working holidaymakers, whose migrant status is highly transient and precarious (e.g., a one- or two-year stay in a foreign country). Compared with international students, whose main aim is to complete their program and obtain a degree, working holidaymakers illustrate the uncertainty and transience of sojourning overseas. This chapter focuses on working holidaymakers as a group of sojourners who have not been sufficiently addressed in the existing studies. It explores how working holidaymakers, whose stay overseas is relatively short term, transient, and flexible, may experience transnational mobility and how digital media technologies are incorporated into experiences of transnational mobility.

Construction of Transnational Youth Mobility

Young people's transnational mobility has been represented as a positive attribute that constitutes a new subjectivity in a rapidly globalizing world (Heath, 2007; Yoon, 2014). Scholarly literature has increasingly addressed how transnational mobility and overseas experiences become an integral component of young people's transition to adulthood (Heath, 2007; Simpson, 2005; Snee, 2016). While there are ongoing debates about the effects of overseas experiences (e.g., whether they enhance intercultural understanding or reproduce a dominant way of understanding difference) (Snee, 2016), going abroad has become a popular option for young people who are in school and transitioning to employment. Young people's transnational sojourns have emerged as a popular coming-of-age ritual, as evidenced by various forms of youth mobility experiences and programs, such as gap year programs among young Europeans (Heath, 2007; Snee, 2016) and overseas experiences among young Australians and New Zealanders (Haverig & Roberts, 2011).

Korea has witnessed a significant increase in young people's outbound sojourning. For young Koreans, working holidays, overseas language learning, and overseas backpacking experiences have been popular forms of transnational youth mobility. With the exception of China and Japan, due to their close economic relations with Korea, the young Koreans' destinations are often limited to Western countries, primarily owing to the pursuit of narrowly defined global experiences comprising English language skills and lived experiences in economically advanced countries. Global experiences have become important components for young people's career development and self-actualization (Yoon, 2014). A large number of Korean youth go abroad for a form of study break or career break.

The increasing transnational mobility of young Koreans has been affected by pull and push factors. A particular mode of youth subjectivity has emerged and been popularized among the public. In particular, the "global generation" discourse has reinforced the ideal image of young people as being equipped with globally competitive and transferrable skills, experience, and knowledge (Yoon, 2014). The pull factors include the importance of global experiences, such as English language skills and overseas internships. The push factors include the stagnant domestic youth labor market and a lack of social mobility (Cho Han et al, 2016; Fifield, 2016). Of course, pull and push factors are neither clearly demarcated nor mutually exclusive. For many of the young people who were interviewed for this chapter, the decision to go overseas for several months to one year was not motivated by a single factor. They often had a sense of being pushed by their homeland's socioeconomic conditions and/or pulled by the benefits of overseas experiences. Moreover, structural and personal factors affect young people's transnational mobility: structurally, overseas experiences have become a necessary attribute on one's résumé (Yoon, 2014), while young people pursue personal growth by being independent from their family homes and disconnecting themselves temporarily from their families and peers (Kato, 2013; Tsai & Collins, 2017).

Among the structural forces that have shaped the dominant "global generation" discourse of 21st-century Korea, the media, the government, and the tourism and education industries have played significant roles. Especially since the early 2000s, government documents and different forms of media have emphasized the important role of overseas experience in becoming the "global generation" (Hong & Ryu, 2013; C. J. Lee, 2013). Since 2008, successive governments have promoted transnational youth mobility programs. In his inaugural speech, President Lee emphasized the overseas training of young Koreans to meet the "global standard", and soon thereafter, his administration launched the Global Youth Leaders Training program, which aims to dispatch 100,000 young Koreans overseas to undergo job training and acquire work-related experience over a five-year period.[2] The Global Youth Leaders Training program is one of the major national policies implemented during Lee's tenure. Despite mounting questions about the program's effectiveness, it was continued and even expanded under the Park government (2013–2017) and rebranded as a forward-looking youth initiative, referred to as K-Move.[3]

The global generation discourse was not limited to government programs for overseas job training. The discourse has been constructed synergistically through diverse outlets: government policies, the news media, personal blogs, and travelogues. Flourishing narratives about transnational youth mobility have enhanced the celebratory representation of global experiences in a narrowly defined mode. In the dominant media representation, youth on the transnational move were defined as forward-looking, adventurous subjects (Yoon, 2015). In the late 2000s, the mainstream news media covered the aforementioned Global Youth Leaders Training initiative while frequently reporting on the adventurous aspects of different types of transnational sojourning. In particular, throughout the 2000s, several newspapers introduced the transnational working holiday program as a new type of youth travel. In 2009, the Korean broadsheet *Hankyoreh* selected *working holiday* and *gap year* as two of "the tourism-related trendy keywords you should know in 2009" (Kim et al., 2008). The news media has covered different types of overseas youth travel while reporting the stories of high-profile sojourners—that is, those whose overseas experience has earned them successful careers (Kim & Lee, 2014). Overseas experience was described as a key to enhancing one's résumé for employment and/or a channel that eventually opens up opportunities to obtain overseas jobs. Throughout the 2000s, the newspapers introduced stories of young Korean professionals whose overseas experiences contributed to their employment and, in so-doing, these articles reinforced the narratives of overseas sojourning and internship as a method of self-development (e.g., C. J. Lee, 2013; Yoon, 2014).

The government has also diligently reproduced celebratory images of overseas experiences. The Ministry of Labor has widely encouraged and distributed young people's essays on their overseas experiences since the mid 2010s. The ministry has also hosted an annual open competition for young people to write about their overseas experiences regarding employment, internship, and volunteering. The award-winning essays are published online and introduce narratives of overcoming challenges and self-development. For example, an essay written by a young Korean working as a professional in the Netherlands tells her story of backpacking in India for six months and working holidaymaking in New Zealand for six months, both of which facilitated her pursuit of overseas jobs. She wrote, "Every moment we challenge gives our lives a significant meaning" (Ryu, 2018, p. 99). Working holidaymakers' experiences have also been narrated in online blogs, web forums, and publications. Some have been organized and promoted through the government-sponsored

Working Holiday Information Center, which has played an important role in attracting young Koreans. By regularly updating the information, stories, and statistics of young Korean sojourners overseas, this center seems to reinforce the dominant discourse of the global generation.

The dominant discourse of global experiences in the 2010s has promoted youth mobility, drawing on its pull factors. The discourse has emphasized the pragmatic benefits of going overseas, such as obtaining particular skill sets, which is often presented alongside romanticized images of particular (often Western) destinations as places for personal growth. The dominant discourse of global experiences engages with the celebration of pull factor-driven mobility. However, paradoxically, young Koreans' increasing transnational sojourning has also been triggered by push factors, such as social inequality and severe competition in the labor market. That is, while some young people conform to the dominant discourse of global experiences, those who consider their future to be precarious seem to seek opportunities to escape the country.

Young Koreans' sense of being pushed from their country has been evident, especially since the 2010s. As observed in numerous online forums, owing to the increasing precariousness of the transition to adulthood and employment, young Koreans have referred to the country metaphorically as "Hell" since the early 2010s (Fifield, 2016; M. Y. Lee, 2019). Young people in numerous online communities often referred to the country as *Hell Joseon*, which is a coinage to compare contemporary Korea with the feudal *Joseon* dynasty, during which Confucian hierarchies and order determined individuals' social positions and suppressed their freedom (Fifield, 2016). The *Hell Joseon* discourse has been circulated among young people in online communities, who sometimes refer to themselves as *ingyeo* (i.e., useless, surplus human beings) and attempt to undertake an imaginary escape to the illusionary world of cynicism and self-depreciation in response to the dominant discourse of self-development and globally competitive youth (S. M. Kim, 2015). Moreover, escape is not only imaginary but is also exercised in the form of overseas sojourning or immigration; this increasing desire to escape Korea was called *tal* (i.e., leaving) *Joseon*. *Hell Joseon* escapers constitute a group of Korean overseas sojourners to places such as India (M. Y. Lee, 2019).

Young Koreans who are frustrated with their country and are, thus, pushed to go abroad have been vividly captured in Kang-Myoung Chang's (2015) novel *Because I Hate South Korea*, in which he tells the story of a young woman who is tired of the hopelessness of Korea and, thus, embarks on working holidays in Australia. This best-selling fiction presents the first-person narrative of this young Korean woman as she challenges the dominant discourse of global experiences regarding self-development and successful employment. The protagonist, Gye-na, leaves Korea not because of the promise of global experiences but due to her frustration with the country. While in Australia, she contrasts

Korea, which is characterized by competition and high social pressure to achieve success, with Australia, the location of her sojourn, which is depicted as a society in which individuals' different ways of life are relatively respected.

In addition to these critical responses to the dominant discourse of global experiences, counter-hegemonic narratives have questioned the myth of global sojourning. For example, several media outlets have published critical views on the aforementioned Global Youth Leaders Training program and other government initiatives that are geared toward facilitating young people's global experiences, noting that the government had inadequate infrastructure and resources to secure the opportunities for a large number of young Koreans to undertake internships and acquire experience in overseas workplaces (Choi, 2014). Several news articles have criticized the government's lack of systematic support by quoting young sojourners (e.g., C. J. Lee, 2013), whose voices have also emerged through mainstream news media and alternative media, such as personal blogs. In particular, a few alternative travelogues written by former sojourners have gradually been published since the 2010s (Jeon, 2018; J. Jung, 2015; Tak, 2010). They present an alternative and critical view, compared with the earlier popular travelogues that romanticize successful sojourning experiences that can be transferred into cultural capital. For example, J. Jung (2015), who was a working holidaymaker in Australia, stated,

> My life in Australia was tough. As everything was tough, it was difficult to pick one particularly tough aspect. Whenever I felt that my life in Australia was tough, I reread the travelogues I had read in Korea to remind myself of the courage I had before leaving for Australia, but I felt even tougher after reading those books again. Those books made me feel that I was struggling because I wasn't making enough effort or wasn't thinking positively. Thus, I blamed myself, and I was ashamed to say that my life was tough. My life in Australia was tough. So were the lives of all of my working holiday colleagues. Nevertheless, no one—no books, news articles, statistics, nor people at the Korean consulates—talked about this toughness. Even my fellow working holidaymakers did not talk about it. The material that I read in Korea about overseas working holidays was so focused on what dreams can be achieved during the period. They did not include information about whether the participants achieved their dreams, if it was even possible to do so, and if any problems arose during the process.
>
> (p. 13)

Such alternative critical perspectives have revealed that the dominant discourse of global experience may have particular ideological effects that conceal the fact that the existing structural contradictions, such as the stagnant youth labor market and ineffective youth policy, might be responsible for the precariousness of Korean society, about which young people are worried. The dominant discourse emphasizes individual young people's responsibility for obtaining overseas experiences and, thus, preparing them for global competition. By reinforcing and reproducing a particular mode of youth subjectivity equipped with narrowly defined global experiences, the dominant discourse might obfuscate structural factors that may be responsible for *Hell Joseon*. The discourse might attribute the *hellish* state of the country to young individuals who should make a maximum effort to become the global generation. Owing to the global experience discourse, young Koreans have been encouraged to go abroad (often at their own expense) and compete with their counterparts on a global scale. However, the proposed overseas opportunities may conceal the realities of the precarious domestic labor market for young Koreans, spreading the promises of gaining certain skill sets and personal growth through transnational sojourning (Yoon, 2015).

Overall, the dominant discourse of global experiences, which appears to be constructed through the alliance of the neoliberal state, corporations, and mass media, reinforces the myth that emphasizes the benefits of transnational youth mobility. In contrast, the alternative narratives of critical journalism, academia, and young people themselves reveal the push factors affecting the popular phenomenon of global experiences among young Koreans.

Realities of the Global Experience

According to the young sojourners who were interviewed for this chapter, Canada seemed to be an ideal destination that projected the dominant discourse of global experience. The young working holidaymakers considered Canada to be a place in which global experiences and skill sets, such as English proficiency, can be obtained and as a romanticized location in the exotic West.

Pragmatically, Canada was a desired destination for the young sojourners in the study because it was a developed, English-speaking country. Canada was preferred to other English-speaking working holiday destinations, such as Australia, because it was considered to be geographically and culturally "close to America," the country that has socioeconomically influenced Korea to a large extent since the latter's liberation from Japanese colonial power (1945), but does not participate in working holiday visa programs. Several respondents in the study described a short-term trip to the United States (US) as one of the goals of their working holidays in Canada.

Moreover, in the young sojourners' narratives, the romanticization of Canada as a destination was represented by components such as its relaxing lifestyle, individual freedom, clean nature, advanced welfare system, and safe atmosphere. For several interviewees, the romanticized image of Canada they had before their working holidays involved a racialized imagination of the country. For example, Sangjoon, a 24-year-old man who moved to Toronto after first several months in Halifax, recalled how an exotic location in which White people far outnumbered people of color was recommended by Korea's tourism industry:

> After I got a working holiday visa, I consulted a *yuhakwon* (a private study-abroad agency) in Korea. The consultant recommended locations where there are many White people but few Koreans. I also wanted somewhere exotic. So, I landed in Halifax first.

Interestingly, whereas Canada is an attractive destination option for global experiences, Korean sojourners did not consider it the sole option. For most working holidaymakers in the study, Canada was primarily a location for overseas sojourning through which young people could pursue personal growth and/or retreat in a foreign country. Thus, their chosen locations could have been Canada or elsewhere. For the research participants, it was common to think about going or living outside Korea, which most respondents described as "a small country." For example, Hyena, a 21-year-old woman, who was on a leave of absence from her university in Korea, recalled her old dream of going abroad to live a unique life:

> Since childhood, I have been thinking about living a special life. The world is large, and so staying in Korea felt unfair. I wanted to go abroad and learn many languages. So, I didn't finish university all at once; I took this time off. I wanted to live uniquely rather than following the ordinary pattern of life.

According to the sojourners, personal growth involved independence from their parents and distance from familiar local contexts. Consequently, working and studying, rather than short-term backpacking or travel, were important components of their sojourns. In addition to the desire for personal growth, most working holidaymakers in the study commonly identified several goals of their overseas sojourns. As Hyena summarized, "First, learning and improving one's English; second, traveling; and, third, experiences [that are not available in Korea]. These may be the three goals that all *woholleos* pursue." Indeed, most interviewees commonly emphasized the aims to improve their English and have unique experiences. However, ironically, their desire for unique overseas experiences led them to a similarly structured process of working holidaymaking, comprising studying, working, volunteering, and traveling. Their 12 months in Canada began with studying part-time in an English language program while looking for a part-time job. During the first three to four months of studying English, they engaged in volunteer work as a way of getting to know their Canadian and international peers. Typically, at a later phase of the 12-month sojourn, and depending on their financial circumstances, the respondents traveled within Canada and to the US.[4]

While sharing the common goals of working holidaymakers in Canada, some sojourners who were on leaves of absence from their Korean universities sought the pragmatic benefits of overseas stay—that is, experience to strengthen their résumés. They aimed to develop specific skill sets, such as English proficiency, and to acquire work experience in Canada, which can be assets for job hunting upon their return to Korea. In particular, those who were entering the labor market in the next couple of years were eager to improve their English and have internship experiences. When interviewed in Seoul in 2013 after her one-year working holiday in Toronto, 23-year-old Nuri recalled that one of the first things she did upon returning to Korea was taking the Test of English for International Communication (better known as its acronym TOEIC among young Koreans), which is required for job applications to Korean corporations, to determine how much her English had improved. In a previous interview conducted in Toronto in 2012, she had a clear plan for how her one-year overseas would facilitate her career preparation. By identifying herself as an undergraduate at a mediocre university, Nuri was under pressure to engage in self-development during her time in Toronto:

> I have to compete with graduates from prestigious universities and those who have great English skills. I thought that the overseas stay could make my résumé stronger, and so, I decided to invest one year to [enable me to] move beyond my weakness [i.e., my mediocre academic credentials].

Nuri's parents and peers in Korea also expected her to engage in self-development while overseas. When interviewed in Seoul after her overseas sojourn, she noted,

> People ask me a lot, "How much has your English improved?" People around me expect too much. So, I have been stressed out since I've been back. You know, working holidaymakers tend to take an English test upon their return. It's a bit odd. The working holiday has unique characteristics, but *woholleo*s are asked to prove their English skill improvement as if they were *eohagyeonsusaeng* [i.e., English language program students]. I have to prove how much my skills, such as English, improved during my time in Canada.

Most working holidaymakers admitted that the pragmatic goals of overseas sojourns, such as improvement in English skills and the acquisition of global experiences, were far more difficult to achieve than they had anticipated. Due to their full-time employment in precarious, small-business sectors, the sojourners have neither the time nor the resources to improve their English skills, to acquire relevant work experience, and to socialize with Canadian peers.

To make ends meet during their stay overseas, most interviewees, except for a few who were financially supported by their parents, worked full-time as service or manual workers. Sangmi, a 26-year-old woman who had left her big corporate job to "recharge" herself for a better future, was working at a Korean immigrant-owned small restaurant after applying for numerous jobs at offices and franchise coffee shops, such as Starbucks. She lamented,

> No one here [i.e., Kelowna, a White-dominant medium-sized city where the interview was conducted] hired me for any office position. Even franchise coffee shops here wouldn't hire Asians. It is tough to learn English and enjoy life while working full-time. I wish I could work in a Canadian environment [i.e., work with Canadians]. I am so envious of those who are fully supported by their parents.

The sojourners were employed in the service industry (small restaurants, franchises, and convenience stores); approximately half of the interviewees had worked or were working for small businesses owned by Korean immigrants. The majority were working at Asian-owned (including Korean-owned) businesses. The interviewees frequently viewed the work experience negatively, as they were not necessarily relevant to their future jobs. The sojourners did not believe that their work experience in small businesses might enhance their résumés. Among service industry experiences, working at Starbucks was relatively preferred by the sojourners, partly because of the company's global brand value and partly because of the job's positive stereotypes repeated in travelogues and blogs written by Korean sojourners. Some assumed working at Starbucks would be a good way to immerse in Canadian environments and to socialize with Canadian coworkers. However, even though Starbucks and other global franchise coffee shops were relatively preferred workplaces, Dorim, a 24-year-old woman who had been working at Starbucks in Toronto for over six months, described her work as monotonous and, thus, planned to leave to undertake volunteer work in the US after completing her working holiday in Canada.

Due to their workplace and full-time work arrangements, which often involved irregular shifts, many sojourners who were interviewed for this chapter had few opportunities to meet up with their local friends. Jiman, a 26-year-old man in Toronto, lamented,

> It is every Korean working holidaymaker's dream to have Canadian friends, but in reality, it rarely happens. I now understand that there would be no reason for Canadians to make friends with those

learning English like me. [. . .] My goal (during working holidays) was to experience the Western culture and lifestyle, but I didn't have many opportunities to socialize with Canadians or experience their culture.

Realizing the limitations of pursuing the global experience that they had imagined, most young sojourners in the study seemed to adjust their initial plans and their romanticized image of Canada. In comparison, a few interviewees, who worked even in the low-paid, small-business sector, preferred working and living in Canada because returning to the homeland held no promise of a better future.

Whether or not their pragmatic goals were achievable, the sojourners considered their stay overseas as time for them to experience personal growth away from their parents and friends. Some sojourners, especially those who were in the final phases of their sojourns and were about to return to their home country, shared the lessons that they learned from their sojourns overseas, including those resulting from unpleasant experiences, such as discrimination, loneliness, and even abuses in the workplace. They wanted to remember their experiences of working and living in Canada as a time of meaningful personal growth. "My struggles here can make a good life story when I look back in the future. I can also tell others about my experiences," noted Moohan, a 25-year-old man.

Overall, most sojourners in the study had difficulty pursuing their pragmatic goals. Due to financial pressure and the inability to find relevant work, the realities of sojourning were harsher than most sojourners had anticipated. For many working holidaymakers, there is a gap between "imagined freedoms and lived constraints" (Tsai & Collins, 2017). Moreover, due to their limited interactions with members of the local community, they did not gain the global experiences that they had anticipated. In retrospect, the interviewees were critical of the romanticized images of overseas sojourning to which they had been exposed prior to arriving in Canada. To negotiate the often harsh realities of working holidays, in which they appeared to be treated as ethnic minority temporary workers rather than as members of the promising "global generation," the young Koreans in the study seemed to redefine the journey as one of personal growth through their various struggles overseas.

Negotiating Transient Lives through Digital Media

Digital media are important facilitators of transnational mobility. Simultaneously, people's transnational movements and lifestyles influence how digital media evolve and are used. For the young sojourners in the study, digital media affected how they imagined Canada as the ideal location in which to acquire global experience. Moreover, digital media played an important role in regard to how they negotiated their over-seas realities and the extent to which they became mobile during their daily routines. Furthermore, their transient lifestyles seemed to influence how they accessed and used different forms of digital media in the host country. Among the sojourners' various media practices, this section discusses (a) how material and physical contexts interplay with digital media and (b) how sojourning is transformed into stories through the particular digital technology of blogging.

Due to their transient lifestyles, exemplified by short-term renting and room sharing with other sojourners, as well as limited financial resources, the sojourners utilized digital media strategically. Most of the working holidaymakers in this chapter aimed to be financially independent—that is, to function without receiving remittances from their parents in Korea. Thus, they had to negotiate their limited financial and material resources in the host country. The transient nature of their stay in Canada limited their mobility and access to media to some extent.

Due to their dwelling types, most interviewees had no TV sets nor subscription-based TV packages. In fact, a few interviewees had no Internet at home for a certain period because they lived their lives on the move. Even if their rented accommodation was equipped with the Internet, they subscribed to a mediocre package that provided limited speed and data. Given the context, it is not surprising that most interviewees were not fully satisfied with their access to the Internet and other communication technologies in Canada. Among the sojourners, a common first impression of Canada was the lack of connectivity and the general unavailability of Wi-Fi in public places, as evidenced by the following interview excerpts: "Cell phones often don't work on the subway. There is no WiFi on the subway either" (Jongsu, 26-year-old male) and "The Internet is so slow here, but no one seems to complain about it. So, I thought, *Canadians are so patient!*" (Minji, 27-year-old female). The sojourners' dissatisfaction with Canada's media environment may be comparable to their overall satisfaction with the country's other available public resources, such as its public libraries and free English classes.

Several interviewees in the study had extremely limited media access. For example, 21-year-old Somi did not subscribe to Internet services in her rented accommodation; thus, public Internet and Wi-Fi were important sources of contact with Korea. Moreover, as she worked for seven days per week to make ends meet, she had little free time for regular TV watching. In comparison with most sojourners in the study, who were not regularly exposed to various local and global English language media, a few who had at least partial financial support from their parents or had already developed a consistent interest in Western (e.g., American) TV shows during the premigration period in Korea regularly accessed local media primarily to improve their English proficiency. For them, CBC (Canadian Broadcasting Corporation) news or American dramas were helpful tools for learning English. Interestingly, even the Korean sojourners keen to immerse in the Canadian environment and improve English through media tended not to distinguish clearly Canadian media from its American counterparts. For them, both Canadian and American mass media content was often indistinguishable and, thus, used to learn about Western ways of life.

The sojourners gradually developed certain strategies to negotiate the media environment—most commonly, their controlled use of digital media. Given that one of the main aims of the overseas sojourn was the pursuit of independence from their parents and friends in Korea and having time off in an unfamiliar environment, the intentional reduction of media-use time and activities may be unsurprising. Due to the relatively short period of residence—a maximum of one year but often shorter—that sometimes involves relocation within the same city or to another one after the first few months, the working holidaymakers in the study tended not to own sedentary devices, such as TVs and radios. At the time of the interviews (the early 2010s), several sojourners did not yet own smartphones equipped with mobile apps and the Internet, although all interviewees owned at least one second-generation (also known as 2-G) mobile phone. While smartphones were increasingly adopted in the latter period of the field study (2013), laptops were also a common tool for transnational communication and archiving. Given the rapid popularization of smartphones in the early to mid-2010s, it is probable that smartphones equipped with various communicative functions, such as Internet access, picture-taking capabilities, and cloud storage, are replacing laptops among sojourners who have transient status. Several interviewees did not bring their laptops to Canada, anticipating that their immersion in the new environment would be facilitated by the lack of communication technologies. For example, 25-year-old Homin noted that he avoided using KakaoTalk, the Korean-based application (app) for messaging and group chatting so that he would be better integrated into Canadian life:

> KakaoTalk is very convenient, so I sometimes want to send messages and chat with Korean kids. But I am trying hard not to do so, because I abstain from hanging out with Korean kids here. So, I feel a bit lonely here. But I don't think I should compromise.

These interviewees resonate with Rosenberg's (2019) analysis of Israeli backpackers in India who attempted to disconnect from communication technologies and, thus, prove their ability to be independent of familiar contexts—that is, family and friends—in their homeland. According to the study, backpackers' effort to temporarily avoid the use of digital media technologies is associated with a sense of maturity and "authentic" sojourner identity—the sojourners distinguish themselves from other tourists who "have one foot at home" (p. 154).

Whether or not they owned personal communication technologies that allowed Internet access, the sojourners often relied on the Internet in reality, as it was a common tool for job hunting, information seeking, and social networking. Due to the transient status of their residence and accommodation (e.g., sublease, short-term rental, or sharing with other renters), Internet access was not constant. The type of accommodation tended to affect the types of media that the young sojourners used. As most interviewees shared a house or room with more than one person, they had insufficient time, space, and resources to access diverse local media, such as TV programs. Thus, some sojourners in the study used public libraries or organizations on a regular basis to access the Internet. For example, the public libraries located in downtown Toronto were popular locations in which young Korean sojourners gathered, shared information, and accessed the Internet. It was important for a few sojourners to seek and identify free Wi-Fi locations daily.

While for several interviewees, the use of digital media had to be controlled during their stay overseas to enhance their immersion in local contexts and authentic sojourning, most tried to use digital media extensively to further their integration into the Canadian environment. Indeed, most considered digital media, such as the Internet, TV, and smartphone, as tools for learning about English and Canadian lifestyles. For them, exposure to Canadian or American media and communicating with local people seemed to be important components of the overseas experience. In particular, as they realized that it was difficult to befriend Canadians in practice, they gradually began to think that mediated experiences through TV shows and news might be alternative methods of learning about Canada. However, Canadian TV shows were often described as "not so interesting"; thus, few interviewees consistently attempted to watch Canadian TV shows regularly. Bora, a 26-year-old woman, noted,

> I listened to local radio when I walked to work and home. When I home-stayed, I had a TV set in my room, so I had it turned on all the time. I did so intentionally to improve my English. However, since I moved out (from the homestay) and live alone, I don't watch much TV. Well, I would say that TV programs here are not so interesting.

In comparison with some sojourners who intended to distance themselves from Korean-based media content to enable better immersion in the Canadian environment, others enjoyed accessing Korean TV and portal sites for comfort and relaxation. Woojin, a 29-year-old man in Kelowna, which is a relatively White-dominant, medium-sized city, recalled his first few months there: "It was wintertime, and there didn't seem to be many people outside. I watched Korean TV on the Internet. Well, I didn't know any local people, and so I stayed alone. I felt lonely." Jiyou, a 23-year-old woman in Kelowna, also accessed the Internet to watch popular Korean TV shows. She worked as a cashier in a Korean-owned small business, which was not in keeping with her initial plan to work at Starbucks, and experienced racial discrimination in White-dominant Kelowna on a number of occasions. For her, watching Korean TV was an escape from the local environment that she encountered. For Kiho, a 23-year-old man in Toronto, chatting and texting with his Korean friends were important daily routines after a day of full-time work. "Whenever I've had a tough day, I seek out Korean friends. I use my smartphone to contact my friends here or in Korea."

Overall, most sojourners in the study faced the dilemma of disconnection or connection. That is, they tried to control their media use for independent and "authentic" sojourning, on the one hand, while needing access to media to enable immersion in the local context, on the other. In practice, the young people gradually relied on the Internet for local information gathering and networking. Depending on several factors, such as the season and work hours, some sojourners used the Internet to learn more about Canadian culture, while others used it to stay connected with their family members and friends in Korea or to access Korean media. Most sojourners in the study worked full-time or close to full-time especially to afford the high cost of living in Canada–Vancouver and Toronto in particular; thus, their free time was limited. Owing to the limited material resources and accessibility of the Internet and media, the young sojourners in the study had to negotiate when and how to use digital media.

Overseas sojourns are increasingly archived and transformed into stories through various forms of digital media, such as social media, digital cameras, smartphones, blogs, apps, and online forums. As young Koreans holding working holiday visas typically remain in Canada for one year, they aim to seek memorable experiences while there. The sojourners in the study, especially those in the first half of their stay overseas, considered various activities they would do before completing their sojourns—for example, visiting several Canadian landmarks, such as the Canadian Rockies, and volunteering at a recognized international event, such as the Toronto International Film Festival. They frequently used mobile media to capture moments of their transient gap years, and it was common for them to diligently take pictures and share them with their family members and peers in Korea through social media or personal blogs. Numerous pictures taken during their stay in and travels across Canada, especially during the early period of their sojourns, constitute their storytelling and narratives of transition to a new phase of their lives.

While smartphones and desktops were popular digital media devices among the sojourners, some apps—for example, Facebook and the Korean-based messaging app KakaoTalk—were especially popular.

Facebook was widely used to expand locally based networks and befriend non-Koreans, while KakaoTalk was a primary tool for communicating with family members in Korea and other Korean working holidaymakers. In particular, blog apps and services were used effectively by some interviewees who kept their overseas stories open to the public and as a proof of their self-development and transformation. For example, the aforementioned Nuri, who would graduate from university within a year of her return, managed a popular personal blog that addressed her experiences in Canada. She archived her journey and experiences in Toronto and, thus, received many inquiries from young Koreans seeking opportunities to go to Canada. For her, the media-based archiving of her overseas experiences was an integral component of her transnational mobility and self-development. She was aware that diligent blogging is an effective method of networking and promoting herself. Her status as a micro-celebrity appeared to provide a sense of connection and community during her stay in Canada as she lived apart from her parents for the first time.

This use of blogs for the self-archiving of transnational mobility may be related to how Korea's neoliberal labor market has sought human resources equipped with soft skills, such as communication and presentation abilities (Han, 2013; Kim & Yoon, 2013). Overseas life experience has recently been considered a key asset for employment. J. T. Kim (2010) outlined in his bestselling self-help book, *A Story Defeats Specs*, which claims that each individual's well-narrated experience is highly valued in the emerging knowledge-based labor market. Ironically, despite Kim's suggestion to move beyond a "spec"[5]-obsessed trend, the book's emphasis on the economy of experience over the standardized elements of a spec seems to define well-narrated experience as a new spec element. This idea was reflected in the description provided by Nabi (25-year-old female) regarding her plans to prepare her job applications after completing her working holiday: "I keep my personal blog updated while I am in Canada. Who knows? My postings and journals on this blog might be an asset for my portfolio when I'm job hunting someday."

Of course, blog-based storytelling was not always strategically intended for bloggers' spec building. While several sojourners thought that their online stories and archives could potentially contribute to their portfolios, various forms of storytelling through digital media were often improvident and were motivated by their desire to express themselves and communicate with others while coping with the new environment. Blogging has been a popular media practice, especially among young Koreans, since the 2000s, during which several Korean platforms offer free aesthetic and interactive blog services. For Korean users, according to E. M. Kim (2016), the major appeal of blogging is its function as "space for expressing individualism" in family-oriented and highly networked Korean society (p. 235). For Korean sojourners-bloggers in the study, expression of individualism was also a motivation for blogging practices—not to be solitary from highly networked everyday life in Korea, but rather to be alive and connected, in foreign, solitary contexts in Canada. Sojourners' blog-based storytelling has gradually evolved into the video platform such as YouTube in recent years. Since the field studies conducted for this chapter in the first half of the 2010s, travel-vlogs have become popular for young Koreans. This audio–visual format of travelogues seems to increasingly replace its blog format counterpart.

For several interviewees, blogging was primarily a practice of self-archiving during the transient period and a method of communicating with other Korean sojourners and their family members and peers in Korea. Several sojourners in the study posted their experiences on their personal blogs or online communities to share their stories about their trials and errors. Sinjoo, a 28-year-old sojourner in Toronto, noted,

> I have noticed that *woholleos* have the same questions. It was difficult finding a room for me, and it was the same for others [i.e., other Korean working holidaymakers]. I searched to see if there was any information I was curious about. So, I keep posting on my blogs to share information with those you are looking for the information I looked for.

By sharing information, as well as feelings, via blogging, sojourners appeared to feel connected to other Korean sojourners. However, some blogs and postings on online communities may partly reproduce the romanticized images of global experiences. For example, one online community, the Country of a Red Sesame Leaf (http://cafe.daum.net/roy815), has been particularly popular since 2000 and has over 100,000 members as of June 2019.[6] All the young people who were interviewed for this study were either occasional or frequent users of this community. The community's online site, which comprises numerous web forums for working holiday information (e.g., about visas, taxes, and other guidelines), questions and answers, and stories, primarily targets Korean working holidaymakers but also attracts other newly arrived sojourners and landed immigrants. Hongjin, a 25-year-old sojourner, noted that the stories and images posted on these community forums motivated her decision to choose Kelowna, which is not popularly known among Korean working holidaymakers, instead of larger cities:

> Someone's postings on the Read Sesame Leaf community influenced me. She wrote about her day-to-day experiences in Kelowna, from getting on the flight to job hunting, all of which was told along with pictures . . . mostly very nice pictures. So, I must have been attracted by those pictures and decided to come here.

Several interviewees accused travel blogs and postings, such as those in the Country of a Red Sesame Leaf community, of reproducing "fantasy about Canadian experiences, which is often unfounded" (Seokjoon, 24-year-old male).

As discussed in this section, young sojourners cope with their overseas lives by engaging with digital media in different ways. Owing to several factors, such as limited material resources and the desire to immerse in the local community, the young people sometimes controlled their media-use time and methods. Moreover, they strategically utilized digital media to expand networks and/or for storytelling. The young sojourners communicated, sought and shared information, expressed their feelings, and archived their transnational journeys. For a few interviewees who tried to keep their blogs updated for their readers as well as themselves, the aesthetic aspect of their blogs was important to express their emotions and feelings. This aesthetic practice is enabled by the Korean portal sites, such as Naver, the platforms that the sojourners' blogs utilize. The service users are offered with free emoticons, fonts, and templates from time to time. As Nyboe and Drotner (2008) stated, aesthetic practice of digital storytelling involves "disclosure and articulation of inner states and lived experiences" and a "strong sense of ownership" (p. 172). Moreover, the young sojourners' storytelling in the digital environments shows how they engage with others and reflect on themselves. Overall, the sojourners' digital media practices involved transient control, negotiation, and storytelling. By appropriating different media forms, they coped with transient process of transnational living and narrative on the self and others.

Conclusion

Drawing on the accounts of young Korean working holidaymakers in Canada, this chapter has examined how the dominant discourse of the global experience has been constructed and how young people negotiate the constructed discourse through their lived experiences. The global experience discourse has emerged in alliance with a particular mode of neoliberal subjectivity that pursues self-development to become the "global citizen." The neoliberal subjectivity has been deeply incorporated into social worlds surrounding young Koreans—sectors of popular culture, education, and the labor market. For example, as discussed in Chapter 3, K-pop stars and their fans seemed to admire and romanticize versatile, self-developing young talents. In comparison, young sojourners desired to be globally minded, entrepreneurial individuals through their overseas experiences (Yoon, 2014). However, as shown in this chapter, young sojourners did not necessarily always internalize the dominant discourse of "global experiences"; rather, some sought overseas working holidays as a way to escape their country, which is considered as *Hell*.

This chapter has addressed two aspects of transnational sojourning and media practices: first, the interaction between material contexts and digital media use and, second, digital storytelling and the sense of self-development and community through digital media practices. Some sojourners' attempts to practice self-control in regard to their digital media use imply the ambivalent potential of digital media as both a disruptor and a facilitator of transnational communication. Moreover, the sojourners' practices of digital storytelling show how digital media can be utilized as tools of self-promotion and/or self-reflection. Sojourners' stories on blogs and online communities may also partly contribute to the reproduction of the romanticized images of global experiences.

The recent discourse of global experiences, which has been disseminated by the media, government, and industries, and partly by the young people themselves, may reproduce a particular youth subjectivity—that is, youth who are continuously self-developing and relentlessly seeking to outdo their competitors on a global scale. However, by experiencing the precarious condition and prospect of overseas sojourns, young Koreans critically engage with the dominant discourse of global experiences to some extent. While they may not achieve the pragmatic goals of global experiences, they rather paradoxically engage with the contradictions of the global economy, in which young people are "pushed" by the precarious domestic labor market yet deceivingly "pulled" by the celebratory rhetoric of global generation. By appropriating digital media during their sojourns, transnational young Koreans may capture the moments of structural contradictions and their own negotiation.

Notes

1 Any two countries can have their own bilateral agreements on the conditions, numbers, and annual quotas for their intake of working holiday-makers. These agreements do not necessarily mean that the participating countries have identical terms and conditions for inbound working holiday-makers. For example, Canada issues 24-month visas for Australian and Irish working holiday makers, while granting their Korean counterparts unrenewable 12-month visas. Canada sets different quotas for different nationals but has no set quota for Australian working holiday applicants. Moreover, in Canadian government policies and media, Irish working holidaymakers are represented as "culturally compatible," while their non-White counterparts tend to be marginalized and racialized (Helleiner, 2017).

2 The government's youth mobility initiatives do not only involve regular internship and training schemes. They also included working holidaymaking and short-term skills training. In particular, as the Lee government's target to train 100,000 youth overseas was beyond the actual capacity of overseas internship positions, other outbound youth mobility programs that do not necessarily include overseas internships, such as the working holiday scheme, were also promoted (Yoon, 2015).

3 In a public meeting to promote trade and investment in 2015, the Korean Minister of Labor outlined the government's plans to further inform young

people of overseas employment opportunities. Acknowledging the minister's efforts, the then Korean president, Park Geun-hye, noted humorously, "Please pursue the plan so hard that there are no young people left in Korea. Then, people would ask 'Where are Korea's young people?' We would say that they have all gone to the Middle East to work." President Park also noted, "There are many overseas jobs waiting for Korean youth. The mismatch [between education and employment] can be resolved by sending our young people overseas to find work, because there are many jobs out there." President Park's comments reminded many Koreans of the country's earlier history, in which construction and manual workers were dispatched to the Middle East, and their remittances contributed to the growth of the Korean national economy in the 1970s. The president's comments were received skeptically by many young Koreans, as they revealed the government's outdated understanding of youth labor markets (Jung & Seok, 2015).

4 The ironic standardization of transnational sojourns is not unique to Korean working holidaymakers. The seemingly independent transnational youth travel has been increasingly structured, commercialized, and standardized by the overlapping interests and practices of the tourism industry, governments, and media (Haverig & Roberts, 2011; Simpson, 2005). The tourism industry has encouraged young populations to engage in customized longterm travel, while it sells the promise of differentiated global experiences via overseas travel, which is allegedly distinguished from that of one's peers or job market competitors (Simpson, 2005). Some critics argue that the packaged difference in travel experience seldom differs from the standardized version (Heath, 2007; Simpson, 2005). Additionally, the governments of advanced capitalist countries, often in collaboration with corporations and the media, have a high regard for young people's global experiences and disseminate the discourse of the "knowledge-driven society" or "new economy." Furthermore, higher education sectors have facilitated students' global experiences under rhetoric such as "global citizenship" (Abelmann, Park, & Kim, 2009).

5 The term "spec," derived from the English term "specification," has been used widely in Korea since the mid-2000s. The term refers to individuals' résumé -building activities, such as university grades, qualifications, internships, and high English language exam scores (Cho, 2015).

6 Red sesame (perilla) leaves are widely used in Korean cuisine, such as barbeque. The "Red Sesame Leaf" in the community's name is a humorous replacement for the maple leaf, which is a Canadian national symbol.

References

Abelmann, N., Park, S. J., & Kim, H. (2009). College rank and neo-liberal subjectivity in South Korea: The burden of self-development. *Inter-Asia Cultural Studies, 10*(2), 229–247.

Berger, E. A., & Paris, C. M. (2013). Exploring the role of Facebook in re-shaping backpacker's social interactions. In Z. Xiang & I. Tussyadiah (Eds.), *Information and communication technologies in tourism 2014* (pp. 299–312). New York, NY: Springer.

Chang, K. M. (2015). *Because I hate Korea.* Seoul: Minumsa.

Cho, H. (2015). The spec generation who can't say "No": Overeducated and underemployed youth in contemporary South Korea. *positions: east asia cultures critique, 23*(3), 437–462.

Cho Han, H., Eum, G., Kang, J., Na, I., Lee, C., Lee, Y., ...Yang, G. (2016). *The betrayal of efforts: The state denying youth, the youth denying society.* Paju: Changbi.

Choi, Y. (2014, August 4). The illusion of overseas employment. *Weekly Donga.* Retrieved from https://weekly.donga.com/3/all/11/97931/1

Chun, J. J., & Han, J. H. J. (2015). Language travels and global aspirations of Korean youth. *positions: east asia cultures critique, 23*(3), 565–593.

Dardot, P., & Laval, C. (2014). *The new way of the world: On neoliberal society.* New York, NY: Verso.

Fifield, A. (2016, January 31). Young South Koreans call their country "hell" and look for ways out. *The Washington Post.* Retrieved from https://www.washingtonpost.com/world/asia_pacific/young-south-koreans-call-their-country-hell-and-look-for-ways-out/2016/01/30/34737c06-b967-11e5-85cd-5ad59bc19432_story.html?noredirect=on&utm_term=.7618665b999e

Gomes, C. (2017). *Transient mobility and middle class identity: Media and migration in Australia and Singapore.* New York, NY: Springer.

Gomes, C. (2018). *Siloed diversity.* New York, NY: Palgrave.

Han S. (2013). The governmentality of becoming the economic subject in the network era: A qualitative study of university students participating in competitions (*gongmojeon*). *Korean Journal of Journalism & Communication Studies, 57*(3), 431–454.

Haverig, A., & Roberts, S. (2011). The New Zealand OE as governance through freedom: rethinking "the apex of freedom." *Journal of Youth Studies, 14*(5), 587–603.

Heath, S. (2007). Widening the gap: Pre-university gap years and the "economy of experience." *British Journal of Sociology of Education, 28*(1), 89–103.

Helleiner, J. (2017). Recruiting the "culturally compatible" migrant: Irish working holiday migration and white settler Canadianness. *Ethnicities, 17*(3), 299–319.

Hjorth, L. (2007). Home and away: A case study of the use of Cyworld mini-hompy by Korean students studying in Australia. *Asian Studies Review, 31*(4), 397–407.

Hong, S. H., & Ryu, W. (2013). Becoming a global talent in the era of unlimited global competition: A critical discourse analysis of the global talent. *Communication Theory, 9*(4), 4–57.

Jeon, N. (2018). *I work in Germany.* Paju: Idambooks.

Jung, J. (2015). *A 25-year-old young person's story of struggling with working holidays.* Seoul: Humanitas.

Jung, S. (2013). Ambivalent cosmopolitan desires: Newly arrived Koreans in Australia and community websites. *Continuum: Journal of Media and Cultural Studies, 27*(2), 193–213.

Jung, Y., & Seok, J. (2015, March 21). Young people scoff at Pres. Park's plan for another "Middle East boom." *Hankyoreh.* Retrieved from http://www.hani.co.kr/arti/english_edition/e_national/683318.html

Kato, E. (2013). Self-searching migrants: Youth and adulthood, work and holiday in the lives of Japanese temporary residents in Canada and Australia. *Asian Anthropology, 12*(1), 20–34.

Kim, E. H., Lee, B. H., Park, M. H., Nam, J. Y., Go, N. M., & Hyun, S. W. (2008, December 31). Tourism-related trendy keywords you should know in 2009. *The Hankyoreh*. Retrieved from http://www.hani.co.kr/arti/specialsection/esc_section/330763.html

Kim, E. M. (2016). Digital media and connected individuals. In Y. Kim (Ed.), *Routledge handbook of Korean culture and society* (pp. 231–242). London: Routledge.

Kim, J. T. (2010). *A story defeats spec*. Seoul: Gallion.

Kim, M. S., & Lee, M. Y. (2014, January 25). Working holidays: Stories of success and failure. *Seoul Sinmun*, p. 1. Retrieved from http://www.seoul.co.kr/news/newsView.php?id=20140125012011

Kim, S. M. (2015). *Being surplus in the age of new media: Ing-yeo subjectivity and youth culture in South Korea* (PhD thesis). George Mason University, Fairfax, VA.

Kim, Y. (2011). *Transnational migration, media and identity of Asian women: Diasporic daughters*. London: Routledge.

Kim, Y., & Yoon, T. (2013). Cultural meaning of "presentation": An investigation of the new communication culture in Korea. *Speech & Communication*, 20, 150–187.

Korean Ministry of Foreign Affairs. (2017). *Statistics of overseas Koreans*. Seoul: Korean Ministry of Foreign Affairs.

Lee, C. J. (2013, November 19). Five times increase of Korean working holiday-makers going to Germany. "Global generation" seeking new challenges. *The Hankyoreh*. Retrieved from http://www.hani.co.kr/arti/international/international_general/611895.html#csidxb870ab9583f54059ef657844b2b95a0

Lee, C. S., & Ahn, J. H. (2019). Imagining homeland: New media use among Korean international graduate students in the U.S. In A. Atay & M. U. D'Silva (Eds.), *Mediated intercultural communication in digital age* (pp. 185–203). London: Routledge.

Lee, M. (2008, February 26). Inaugural address. *The Hankuk Ilbo*, p. 28.

Lee, M. Y. (2019). "Escape from Hell-Joseon": A study of Korean long-term travelers in India. *Korean Anthropology Review*, 3(19), 45–78.

Nyboe, L., & Drotner, K. (2008). Identity, aesthetics, and digital narration. In K. Lundby (Ed.), *Digital storytelling, mediatized stories: Self-representations in new media* (pp. 161–176). New York, NY: Peter Lang.

Pham, B., & Lim, S. S. (2016). Empowering interactions, sustaining ties: Vietnamese migrant students' communication with left-behind family and friends. In S. S. Lim (Ed.), *Mobile communication and the family: Asian experiences in technology domestication* (pp. 109–126). New York, NY: Springer.

Rosenberg, H. (2019). The "flashpacker" and the "unplugger": Cell phone (dis)connection and the backpacking experience. *Mobile Media & Communication*, 7(1), 111–130.

Ryu, J. (2018). What I learned through backpacking and my overseas employment. In Worldjobs (Ed.), *Youth making their dreams of overseas employment true* (pp. 94–99). Ulsan: Human Resources Development Service of Korea.

Simpson, K. (2005). Dropping out or signing up? The professionalisation of youth travel. *Antipode*, 37(3), 447–469.

Shin, H. (2012). From FOB to cool: Transnational migrant students in Toronto and the styling of global linguistic capital. *Journal of Sociolinguistics*, 16(2), 184–200.

Snee, H. (2016). *A cosmopolitan journey? Difference, distinction and identity work in gap year travel.* London: Routledge.

Tak, S. (2010). *Own your own New York: A biased report on the chic neoliberal city New York.* Seoul: Inmulgwasasang.

Tsai, L. L., & Collins, F. L. (2017). Youth and mobility in working holidays: Imagined freedoms and lived constraints in lives of Taiwanese working holidaymakers in New Zealand. *New Zealand Geographer, 73*(2), 129–140.

Wong, J., & Hjorth, L. (2016). Media and mobilities in Australia: A case study of Southeast Asian international students' media use for well-being. In C. Gomes (Ed.), *The Asia Pacific in the age of transnational mobility* (pp. 41–62). London: Anthem Press.

Wong, J. W. (2017). "So that she feels a part of my life": How international students connect to home through digital media technologies. In L. Tran & C. Gomes (Eds.), *International student connectedness and identity* (pp. 115–135). New York, NY: Springer.

Working Holiday Info Center. (2019). The number of outbound working holiday program participants. Retrieved from http://whic.mofa.go.kr/contents.do?contentsNo=4&menuNo=6

Yoon, K. (2014). Transnational youth mobility in the neoliberal economy of experience. *Journal of Youth Studies, 17*(8), 1014–1028.

Yoon, K. (2015). A national construction of transnational mobility in the "overseas working holiday phenomenon" in Korea. *Journal of Intercultural Studies, 36*(1), 71–87.

5 Digital Mediascape of Transnational Families

As discussed in previous chapters, Korean youth culture has increasingly been transnationalized especially since the 1990s. The introduction of the neoliberal system after the financial crisis of 1997 had economic impacts and facilitated a particular ethos and subjectivity among Koreans (Seo, 2011). In the past two decades, the neoliberal version of globalization has enhanced the zeal for English education among Koreans. English has become a significant source of cultural capital for social mobility in Korea (Park, 2011; Park & Abelmann, 2004); thus, studying in English-speaking countries at an early age (i.e., usually prior to the teenage years or during the early teens) has emerged as an option for the children of Korean middle-class families. Among this class, studying abroad at an early age (*jogiyuhak*) has created new forms of transnational families—for example, (a) the child lives overseas with his or her guardian, where he or she attends school, and his or her parents are left behind in the home country, and (b) the child's mother accompanies him or her abroad, while the father remains in the home country and financially supports the family members who are overseas. This latter family type is often referred to metaphorically as the "geese family."[1]

Transnationally split families driven by the pursuit of an overseas education and lifestyle have increasingly been observed among the Asian middle class (Abelmann, Newendorp, & Lee-Chung, 2014; Finch & Kim, 2012), and can be compared with other forms of transnational families that are often forced to become transnational by economic factors, such as overseas employment opportunities or poverty in the home country. Among the Korean middle class, the transnational family phenomenon, motivated by the children's precollege overseas education, has become visible since the 1990s. Korea was one of the Asian countries in which the precollege study-abroad phenomenon mushroomed throughout the 2000s. The annual number of precollege Korean students attending school overseas, such as in the United States (US), Canada, and New Zealand, increased nearly fourfold between 2001 (7,944) and 2006 (29,511) (Korean Educational Development Institute, 2013). What may be even more significant is the fact that an increasing number of middle-class Korean families are considering their children's precollege study abroad as a probable option (Finch & Kim, 2012).

The Korean phenomenon of education-driven transnational families can be explained by a combination of two kinds of "social fever": the traditional "education fever," which defines education as the central duty of the family and educational credentials as a crucial component of the family's social status (Seth, 2002), and the recent "globalization fever," evident since the 1990s, which pressures Koreans to reap the benefits of acquiring English skills and an overseas education (Park, 2011).

The emergence of these overseas education-driven transnational families shows the reworking and redefinition of traditional family values in the transnational context. Sending children (sometimes accompanied by their mothers) to the West for precollege study is thus seen as one of the emerging "family-based strategies responding to globalization and educational ambition" (Finch & Kim, 2012, p. 489). These new types of family, whose members are voluntarily separated across national borders, reveal that young people's transitions to adulthood are no longer local but, rather, are shaped by global forces. For the Korean transnational families motivated by the children's education opportunities, growing up overseas separating from one or both parents is considered the preparation for and the cost of becoming "global citizens" who possess cultural capital (Abelmann et al., 2014). The recent phenomenon of the Korean transnational family involves the flow of not only Korean international students and their parents but also the communication technologies that families use when on the move. Compared to forced low-income migrant workers, the middle-class Korean families in the study seemed more willing to be separated in pursuit of the children's "global" cultural capital, which consists of English proficiency and academic credentials. Whereas the mediated communication of "forced" migrants and their families tended to be constrained significantly by relatively poorer material and technological resources (Law & Peng, 2008), the transnational middle-class children in this study were not similarly encumbered, instead manifesting cultural negotiation between mediated and face-to-face communication.

The need for constant, mobile, and mediated communication between transnational family members facilitates the extensive appropriation of emerging forms of communication technologies. These new technologies have influenced transnational migration, whereas migrants' experiences have contributed to technological innovation (Fortunati, Pertierra, & Vincent, 2013). This chapter explores how the smartphone, among other communication technologies, is incorporated into the communication practices of young people of Korean transnational families. As the interviewees' stay overseas overlaps with the period during which the smartphone was introduced and began to be popularized (i.e., the late 2000s and onward), this chapter reveals how a new form of communication technology is integrated into transnational family interactions and young people's transitions to adulthood.

Drawing on in-depth interviews with the young adult children of Korean transnational families in Canada, this study examines how the family is reimagined in the mediated, mobile, and transnational communication among its members and how transitioning to adulthood is becoming a transnational practice among middle-class Korean families. Individual interviews with 38 young members of transnationally split Korean families were conducted in Canadian cities in the provinces of British Columbia and Ontario between February and July of 2014. The interviews were conducted in Korean, as this was the participants' first language. The participants, presented under pseudonyms, were aged between 19 and 30 years, and the average age at which they moved to Canada was 15 years. About two-thirds of the participants (n=25) were separated from both parents, who remained in Korea, while the remainder (n=13) resided with their mothers in Canada. Twenty-four participants initially entered Canada as international student visa holders and remained the same, while 14 acquired permanent residency at the time of entry or later.[2]

The interview questions focused on how the young adult children of Korean transnational families narrated the process of adopting and appropriating smartphones, especially in their relationships with their family members. To enable a better understanding of the technology appropriation process, the respondents were asked to address their present and past media practices, especially for the purposes of family communication, throughout their lives in Canada. Thus, they were given opportunities to narrate and contemplate both their past and current experiences. Although this process relies on participants' personal memories, the reconstructed stories seemed to meaningfully reveal how their transnational media experiences were retold from their current perspectives.

Contextualizing the Smartphone in Transnational Families

The emergence of new communication technologies, such as smartphones, has led to attempts to explore the process and meaning of technology consumption in everyday life. Cultural studies-inspired media ethnographies have provided a vivid picture of the cultural appropriation of emerging technologies (e.g., Hjorth, 2009; Horst & Miller, 2005; Lim, 2005; Madianou & Miller, 2012; Wallis, 2013). The role and meaning of communication technologies in transnational families can be examined from different perspectives.

One group of studies focuses on the social and cultural contexts of transnational family's use of communication technologies (e.g., Clark & Sywyj, 2012; Elias & Lemish, 2008; Hoang & Yeoh, 2012; Madianou, 2014; Parreñas, 2005; Pearce, Slaker, & Ahmad, 2013; Wilding, 2006). From this perspective, the transnational family's pattern of engagement and ability to engage in transnational communication via technology are influenced by factors such as members' working conditions and available media resources (Hoang & Yeoh, 2012), cultural norms (Clark & Sywyj, 2012), premigration histories of media use (Wilding, 2006), and generational differences (Elias & Lemish, 2008).

The other perspective focuses more on technological features that significantly affect transnational families' communication practices (e.g., Francisco, 2015; Vancea & Olivera, 2013). This perspective suggests that transnational family relationships tend to be deeply affected by the technological features of digital media that enable or constrain certain aspects of communication. In particular, the technological infrastructure that is available to the users at the macro level (Vancea & Olivera, 2013) or the particular technological affordances of the new communication technologies, such as their visual components (Francisco, 2015), can enhance the intensity and frequency of transnational family communication. Furthermore, the ability of communication technologies to compress time and space empowers migrants or at least enables them to cope with the isolation resulting from their marginal social position and their separation from their family members who have been left behind (Uy-Tioco, 2007).

The aforementioned two ways of understanding transnational families' use of communication technologies (i.e., sociocultural and technological foci) are not necessarily mutually exclusive. They have been articulated together in a few recent studies that have applied the technology domestication approach in a contextualized way (e.g., Madianou, 2014; Madianou & Miller, 2012). For instance, Madianou and Miller (2012) addressed the social context of media users and technological affordances in equal measure. While focusing on technological affordances with a view to exploring how particular media forms facilitate certain communication patterns, Madianou and Miller (2012) did not ignore the sociocultural context in which technology is adopted, utilized, and negotiated. Similarly, this chapter articulates the sociocultural and technological aspects of communication technologies in transnational youth's family interactions. In so doing, it aims to move beyond a one-dimensional explanation of technology consumption. The study, therefore, focuses on young, education-driven migrants from middle-class backgrounds, who constitute a relatively under-researched demographic in transnational media studies.

Among the various forms of communication technologies that are utilized for transnational interactions among Korean families, the smartphone is particularly intriguing. Like numerous other countries, Korea has witnessed the rapid diffusion of communication technologies over the past two decades. In particular, the smartphone, one of the most recent forms of communication technology, has been so popular among Koreans that the country's smartphone penetration rate has been consistently ranked among the top five worldwide since 2010 (Yonhap News,

2013). The extensive use of the smartphone, which is not only a form of mobile telephony but also a platform for various Internet-based communication and computing tools (Madianou, 2014), may reconfigure the ways in which the family is connected, organized, and imagined. Moreover, this reconfiguration may be further enhanced when new communication technologies are appropriated by transnationally separated family members (Madianou & Miller, 2012).

Due to its mobility and convenience, the smartphone is deeply integrated into the rhythm of the user's everyday lives and bodily movements. It also reveals the ongoing process of media convergence, in which different media content and platforms are merged and reinvented. The smartphone as a multifaceted form of information and communication technology is an assemblage that involves earlier media forms and experiences and is, thus, contextualized in relation to media communication technologies. Especially through its various apps, the smartphone enables users to reengage with various media practices, such as interpersonal communication, listening, video watching, information search, and content generation (Gardner & Davis, 2013). In this regard, it reifies remediation processes in which the memories of earlier media are embedded (Bolter & Grusin, 1998). The smartphone as a tool of remediation illustrates how technology use becomes a complicated process involving various places, users, expectations, and practices.

This study examines how the smartphone is used by transnational families in relation to other communication technologies. In addition, it addresses the popular use of the Korean-developed communication app KakaoTalk among the transnational family members. In so doing, this chapter examines how technology and culture mutually affect the redefinition of the family and young people's transitions to adulthood. On the one hand, this chapter explores the cultural forces influencing the appropriation of new communication technologies—that is, how smartphones are integrated into the continuous practice of "doing family" by enacting familial roles (such as gender roles) and reproducing the existing family norms (Kaur & Shruti, 2016). On the other hand, this chapter examines how the smartphone's apps and technological features may, to some extent, shape transnational family interactions. For example, the young people's accounts reveal how particular local communication apps—that is, Kakao and Facebook—affect the ways in which they engage in different modes of family interaction.

As communication technologies enhance the family's connectivity across transnational contexts, forms of family interaction, which were conventionally based on geographic proximity, are seemingly becoming diversified. Especially for the increasing number of transnationally split families, mediated connection with family members residing in other countries or locales is an essential component of what constitutes family. For these families, the digital media environment and offline space are not mutually exclusive but are almost interchangeable. For the young people in transnational families, growing up involves being in the family not only physically but also from a distance.

Connected Presence in Transnational Families

Transnational families, whose members have to maintain long-distance relationships, tend to adopt and test various forms of communication technologies and are, thus, relatively heavy users and early adopters of new technologies (Madianou & Miller, 2012; Parreñas, 2005). For the younger members of these families, who had to cope with prolonged separation from their parents, it seemed that being online continually was the default position for family communication (Madianou, 2014). For this reason, a few respondents felt more comfortable engaging in mediated rather than face-to-face interaction with their parents. For the past five years, Ara, a 19-year-old undergraduate, had been separated from her father, who had remained in Korea, and she described how she felt about talking to him via telephone versus in person: "It's more comfortable to talk with my dad over the phone than face to face. This might be because my dad and I have been separated for quite some time." Ara, who lived with her stay-at-home mother in Vancouver, communicated frequently with her father in Seoul via her smartphone. Although her face-to-face contact with her father was limited to an average of once a year or less, it was supplemented by various forms of communication technology. Her father regularly used programs such as KakaoTalk, Facebook, and Skype to communicate via his laptop, smartphone, or office computer, while her mother did not even have her own mobile phone and used only the home telephone.[3]

The significance of smartphones was emphasized by a few respondents who did not acquire their own until a relatively late stage of their transnational lives. For example, Minju, a 22-year-old female student in Toronto, who had been living apart from her family in Korea since the age of 17, was one of the few respondents who were relatively ill-equipped with regard to personal communication technologies. As her parents did not allow her to have a personal technology device, she did not own a mobile phone or personal computer until her final year of high school; thus, she had to rely on her homestay family's home computer or telephone for transnational communication during this period. In addition to having no access to personal communication technologies, Minju had insufficient time in which to connect with her parents, as both were employed full-time:

> At first, living overseas was tough . . . because I didn't have my family here, and I was young. Things [i.e., communication technologies] were so inconvenient back then [i.e. in the late 2000s]. I called my family using the homestay's house phone. I didn't have a laptop nor

a mobile phone at that time. In those early days, my mom and dad called me once a month, and we talked over the phone for 30 minutes. That was it. I was so lonely.

The families in the study adapted to the development of communication technologies since their transnational separation. The respondents recalled that, especially before adopting smartphones, they had initially used landline telephones with prepaid international telephone cards, after which they had begun to use Internet-based voice communications (Voice over Internet Protocol [VoIP], also known among the respondents as "Internet phones") via home computers or Internet-customized telephone handsets. Transnational families' use of different communication technologies prior to the emergence of the smartphone was described in detail by the older respondents. For example, Chan, a 27-year-old Vancouver-based man, recalled the early 2000s, when he first came to Canada alone as a precollege student:

> There was no Skype in those days [laughs]. To contact my family in Korea, I would buy and use international telephone cards. I would also email. I used Buddy Buddy [i.e., an early Korean web-based messenger] with my friends in Korea, but my parents used email only [among Internet-based tools]. Because of the time difference, I couldn't get responses immediately when using email. Moreover, international phone cards [. . .] ran out of funds too quickly. Even if I bought a 10-hour card, the 10 hours would go by too fast. Those things were very, very inconvenient. [. . .] These days, I use KakaoTalk [to communicate with my parents] because my parents seem to feel comfortable using it.

As evidenced by Chan's recollection, the smartphone seems to have contributed to considerable changes in the ways in which transnational families communicate. The respondents had their own smartphones, which they had primarily purchased in Canada during their mid- to late teens, and the devices had been incorporated into the rhythm of their everyday lives. As Han, a 24-year-old male university student in Toronto, noted, "As soon as I get up, I check messages on my KakaoTalk. Then, I start playing music on my [smart]phone and get ready to go to school while responding to the overnight KakaoTalk messages." Similarly, Suna, a 24-year-old female university student in Vancouver, stated, "I use my iPhone anytime and anywhere [laughs]. Whenever I'm waiting in line or in traffic, or even when I'm eating, it's easy to use and small to carry. I can carry it wherever I go."

The smartphone offered the young people a mediated copresence with the rest of their family members and friends in Korea. This sense of "connected presence" (Licoppe, 2004) was enhanced by various smartphone apps, such as KakaoTalk, Facebook, and Skype.[4] As Licoppe (2004) indicated, telephony, whether landline or mobile, facilitates two modes of mediated interactions between individuals: *the conversational mode*, which comprises long and even ritualized interactions via technology, and *the connected mode*, which consists of short, frequent, mediated interactions. Due to mobile phones and, more recently, smartphones, the connected mode of mediated interactions has increased and is probably a default mode. That is, along with flourishing free wireless networks and infrastructure, especially in urban settings, the smartphone's various apps allow users to always be online and connected with someone.

For the young people in the study, who were separated from their parent(s), the sense of connected presence was an essential component of their daily lives. By exchanging frequent yet brief "link-up" messages or calls (Horst & Miller, 2005), they maintained their family ties and sense of belonging. Several respondents shared their everyday stories, which were frequently accompanied by selfies and emoticons indicating their feelings, with their overseas family members and friends. Several smartphone apps and other technological tools were widely used by the young people and their families. In particular, the Korean-developed Kakao app platform was especially popular among the interviewees and their families. The platform comprises several apps, such as KakaoTalk (messenger app), KakaoStory (social media app), and additive gaming apps. Launched by a Korean venture company in 2010, the platform has been the most popular communication tool among Korean smartphone users. The number of active monthly KakaoTalk users was estimated to be 43,526,000 in Korea and 50,348,000 globally as of the first quarter of 2018 (Kakao, 2018). As of 2017, nearly all Korean Internet messenger service users (99.2%) use KakaoTalk, while the Kakao platform's social networking app, KakaoStory, is more widely used than Facebook in Korea (Ramirez, 2017). KakaoTalk is widely used across generations, distinguishing it from other social network apps, such as Facebook (Kim & Shin, 2013). KakaoTalk's particular technological features have been considered an important factor in its popularity (Clayton, 2013). Among other merits, the coexistence of both older and newer media forms in its simplistic interface design might appeal to parents, which might be an important factor driving the wide use of KakaoTalk among Korean transnational families. The enormous popularity of Kakao apps among Koreans is evidenced by several interviewees, who identified access to these apps as their most important motivation for owning their first smartphones. For example, Suna, a 24-year-old female university student, noted, "These days, I can use KakaoTalk on my computer. However, previously, I had to use the smartphone a lot because of Kakao Talk."[5]

Overall, KakaoTalk was used extensively in family contexts, in comparison with other communication apps, such as Facebook, which were widely used with networked contacts. KakaoTalk's circle of "Friends" tended to represent contacts who were bound by their physical and emotional localities. Since KakaoTalk allows only users who share their smartphone numbers to be included in each other's contact lists, an individual's KakaoTalk contacts tend to comprise the people whom he or she has met in person and calls via telephone at least occasionally. This small, circular, phone number-based network system seems to distinguish KakaoTalk from other communication apps that tend to accelerate the economy of size. KakaoTalk contacts are neither exclusively online nor networked to the public.

As the Kakao platform offers various communication services, such as text messages, voice calls, group chats, photo sharing, attractive stickers, and other social media services, it facilitates diverse modes of storytelling and communication. Via the platform, conversational and connected modes of communication coexist and are merged. For example, users can switch from text messages and stickers to longer conversations (e.g., voice or video calls) and then archive these as stories or photo diaries (e.g., social media timelines and stories).

Media Convergence

In addition to the pervasive use of KakaoTalk, video calls via Skype on smartphones or laptops seemed to enhance the sense of copresence. In particular, built-in cameras on smartphones and webcams on laptops were widely used among the young people in the study. As observed in recent studies (Francisco, 2015; Hoang & Yeoh, 2012), visual technologies are being increasingly embraced by transnational families who desire to "actually *see* their family when they are away" (Francisco, 2015, p. 181).

For some respondents, it was evident, at least during the initial period overseas following family separation, that any single method of mediated communication—voice call, text message, or video message—could not fulfill their desire for copresence: "Although I would call my mom and dad every day, I still felt somewhat limited. So, I tried Skype as well. Then, the Internet phone," noted Somi, a 22-year-old woman who relocated to Canada alone at the age of 15. She recalled using different forms of communication technology to attempt to maintain as much contact as possible with her overseas family members while coping with separation anxiety during her adolescence alone in Vancouver:

> The most difficult thing was . . . well, I was young and alone. I had been the kind of child who had an extremely close bond with my mom but was suddenly left alone. It was so . . . so very challenging.

The extensive use of smartphones among the respondents seemed to correlate in particular with the ever-increasing availability of and need for mobile Internet. At the time of the interviews, the respondents, with a few exceptions, accessed the Internet more via smartphones than via computers. Yuri, a 19-year-old female student in Vancouver, explained while pointing to her smartphone, "*This* is often more convenient than *that* [pointing to the interviewer's laptop]. With the laptop, I have to use a mouse, but I can touch the whole screen once with this [i.e., her smartphone]."

Nonetheless, the smartphone did not completely replace nor displace earlier communication technologies, such as landline and pre-smartphone era phones (referred to as second generation mobile phones, or 2G phones), but rather coexisted with them (Madianou, 2014). At the time of the interviews, some respondents still used VoIP for family communication—at least while at home—because their parents, who were not completely comfortable using smartphones (at least in the early phase of their smartphone adoption), preferred VoIP, which was highly similar to that of traditional landline phones. Various smartphone apps and instant messaging services were often used along with voice calls via smartphones or VoIP services.

Instant messaging was incorporated extensively into the respondents' family interactions, for which the importance and necessity of voice were not necessarily replaced by the practice of text messaging (Horst & Miller, 2006). Rather than relying on a single form of communication technology, most respondents used voice calling, text messaging, and video calling supplementally. For instance, text messaging was sometimes used to arrange voice or video calls (Bonini, 2011). In particular, the smartphone appeared to provide a platform for switching easily between different forms of mediated communication, such as conversational and connected modes.

The smartphone reifies the process of media convergence, through which different content and technologies are merged and activated. The smartphone offers written, audiovisual, and haptic modes of communication by enabling engagement with previously separated technologies (such as landline phones and television). This convergence often involves a level of remediation of another, often older form of media technology (Bolter & Grusin, 1998). The smartphone's remediation of landline telephones might necessarily be favored by some parents. However, while a few parents were not completely comfortable using smartphones, most were using them or at least adapting to the technology; they did not seem to simply resist or reject emerging technologies. For example, Mona, a 23-year-old woman who recently began living with her mother in Toronto after several years of being separated from her parents and living alone, described how her mother was adapting to smartphone use:

My mom recently switched to a smartphone [from a 2G phone]. These days, I'm teaching her how to use it. My mom is very pleased to have a smartphone because she can now send Dad [in Korea] photos. Although he lives abroad, they [Mom and Dad] can see each other by sharing photos. My mom used to use text messaging frequently in Korea [via a 2G phone]. However, when she came to Canada, she rarely used text messaging. That's probably because text messaging is more expensive here [than in Korea], and she had to type in English [on her 2G phone in Canada]. But now she can type in Korean with her smartphone; so, she began text messaging, although she calls more. Thus, I usually use voice call [on my smartphone] when I contact my mom.

Despite transnational families' enhanced connectivity via mobile communication technologies, it is uncertain how effectively mediated interaction compensates for the lack of face-to-face interaction. In the present study, the sense of virtual togetherness was questioned by several respondents. Mediated interaction did not necessarily fulfill the young people's need for proximity-based emotional ties with the family. As some respondents described, mediated family interaction occasionally caused miscommunication and created distance between family members. For example, when asked to compare communication with her parents via smartphone and face-to-face, Yuri, the aforementioned 19-year-old student, noted,

> I prefer to talk face to face. It's difficult to fully express what I really want to say via phone calls and texts. However, if I see Mom, I can look her in the face and see how she's responding.

Moreover, some respondents considered face-to-face conversation to be more meaningful than technology-mediated connection. For example, Songhee, a 25-year-old woman in Toronto, noted that, despite her being always online with her family in Seoul, she felt "a little empty":

> I went back [to Korea] and stayed for about six months last year after graduation. I realized why I had been feeling a little empty. It was the family. It was so good being there [in Korea] with the family. However, I also realized that I had changed since leaving Korea; I thought I might have a greater sense of belonging to Canada now.

Songhee, a recent graduate who hoped to acquire Canadian permanent residency in the near future, had been communicating frequently with her family members in Korea since her entry into Canada at the age of 14. She had been using various smartphone functions extensively, such as KakaoTalk, iPhone's FaceTime, and Skype, to maintain contact with her family on a daily basis. However, she noted the absence of her physical proximity to her family as a missing part of her adolescence. Songhee's account suggests that the virtual togetherness of transnational families that is maintained by mediated interaction is felt to be noticeably incomplete when compared with physical togetherness. This finding echoes the previous observation that mediated communication between transnational families involves certain costs, such as emotional distance (Lan, 2003).

The connected mode of communication via smartphones might decrease the intensity of familial communications. Han, the aforementioned 24-year-old man in Toronto, stated that communication apps can be a "supplement to actual communication" and explained that "if I can click on *like* (on Facebook), I don't have to talk in person. It lets others know I am doing OK." For several interviewees, smartphone-mediated communication was also considered to be playful. In particular, the various stickers and emoticons available on the KakaoTalk platform allowed the young people to reduce the distance caused by transnational and mediated modes of communication. For example, the young people sent their Korean friends and family members KakaoTalk's various cute emoticons and stickers. In response, their parents sometimes, if not often, sent them emoticons as well. For the transnational KakaoTalk users, the KakaoTalk-specific emoticon was not simply a supplement to texts but, rather, an essential communication tool. The expression of users' emotions via KakaoTalk's humorous and cute emoticons seemed to mediate any tensions that might arise in distant, mediated communication.

Growing Up Transnational and Uncertain

The smartphone was a resource for not only young people but also their parents. The respondents recalled the occasions on which their parents had kept track of the minor details of their everyday routines. The mobile Internet and various communication apps enabled on smartphones appeared to intensify the micromanagement or even surveillance of the users by others in networked contact (Madianou, 2014). In the connected presence allowed by smartphones, it seemed difficult to opt out of being online continually. Such "mobile parenting" or "mediated parenting" has been reported in existing studies (Chib, Malik, Aricat, & Kadir, 2014; Lim, 2008; Ling & Yttri, 2006; Madianou & Miller, 2012; Uy-Tioco, 2007), although the specifics of parenting may depend on cultural contexts.

Transnational mobile parenting was often the extension of preexisting parental control over communication technologies prior to the respondents' migration, in which they had been allowed to use the Internet and/or mobile phones for a restricted period. However, since their migration to Canada, the respondents had been released, to some extent, from social and parental pressures due to their physical distance from their parental homes. Even for those who lived with their mothers in Canada, parental control over technology use tended to be more relaxed than it had been prior to their migration. While this does not mean that parental supervision of their children's technology use disappeared in the transnational context, the focus of parental monitoring with regard to children's technology use seemed to be transformed from direct control of technology use to indirect yet mobile control through smartphones (Chib et al., 2014). In this process of mobile parenting, preexisting cultural norms seemed to reemerge.

First, the role of preexisting family norms was observed in the obligatory family ties between parents and children via mobile communication, which is a topic that has been addressed in media studies of Asian families (Lim, 2008; Madianou & Miller, 2012; Yoon, 2003). In particular, the use of KakaoTalk by the respondents and their parents appeared to reaffirm the reciprocal yet obligatory process of family interaction. Similar to other communication apps, KakaoTalk notifies message senders as soon as their messages are seen by the receivers; thus, children seemed to feel obliged to respond promptly to their parents. In this regard, KakaoTalk might work as a "parent app" (Clark, 2012) with which parents can keep track of their children and, thus, be assured of their safety via mobile communication.

As observed in previous studies (Chib et al., 2014) and based on the respondents' accounts, many parents—especially mothers—wanted to frequently confirm their children's daily routines from a distance. Jihee, a 19-year-old woman who had been living alone in Toronto as an international student for over five years while her parents had remained in Korea, described the way in which the smartphone kept her connected to her mother, which, at times, made her feel obliged to respond. She explained how her mother kept track of her via the popular smartphone app KakaoTalk to ensure that she was all right:

> As usual, one day, my mom sent KaTalk [i.e., KakaoTalk] messages to me and then made KaTalk voice calls, but I didn't answer. When I got back to her two hours later, she was wailing. I felt bad, so I try to reply to her quickly these days. [That time,] my mom [in Korea] contacted me before she went to bed, but I didn't know that I got those messages because it was daytime here [in Canada], and I was in quite a noisy place. My mom said she was worried because I didn't reply quickly.

Second, mobile parenting tended to be gendered in its pattern, as the traditional gender roles of breadwinning fathers and nurturing mothers were by and large maintained. With the exception of a few cases in which both parents were employed full-time, most respondents relied on the financial remittances of their left-behind fathers. The preexisting mode of gendered parenting appeared in the respondents' accounts of the relatively caring, intimate mother, compared to the strict, distant father. In particular, the respondents who lived with their mothers in Canada described their fathers as both physically and emotionally distant figures. For instance, Yuri, the aforementioned woman who had moved to Vancouver with her mother six years ago, described how she communicated with her parents:

> It's not quite necessary to contact Mom on the mobile phone, because she is with me [living together in Vancouver]. Well, in regard to Dad [in Korea] . . . he has been away for over six years now, so I am no longer likely to talk to him about every single detail of my life, which I still talk to my mom about.

This emotional distance from fathers and intimacy with mothers was especially evident in several female respondents' mediated communication with their parents. Even for respondents with both parents in Korea, mediated communication with their mothers tended to be more frequent than with their fathers. In addition, some respondents preferred to contact their fathers via written communication using the KakaoTalk app or emails, whereas they contacted their mothers in Korea via voice calls and KakaoTalk messaging. Based on a few young people's accounts, mothers, rather than fathers, preferred voice calls via home telephones, smartphones, or Internet phones over text messaging. In such cases, the mothers were relatively less comfortable with new technology than the fathers, who seemed to have high accessibility to various communication technologies at both work and home. Most respondents described the fathers as being "busy with work" or relatively "traditional." Songhee, the aforementioned 25-year-old woman in Toronto, stated the following:

> Dad is really busy all the time [. . .] My dad is somewhat traditional, so he doesn't do much Skype or KakaoTalk [. . .] I often talk with my family [i.e., each of my family members via media], but it is rare for all of my family members to be together on the phone or Skype. [It happens] just a couple of times per year, I suppose.

Owing to the relative emotional distance between fathers in Korea and their children in Canada, mothers, whether in Canada or Korea, played the role of moderators with regard to the communication between their children overseas and other family members.

The mother's role echoes the findings of previous research on Korean families' use of technology. For example, Lim and Soon's (2010) ethnographic study found that Korean mothers used communication technology to not only monitor their children but also enhance mother–child bonding, while some appropriated communication technology to improve the relatively distant father–child relationship that is commonly observed in patriarchal family cultures. As shown in the examples of mediated and mobile parenting in the present study, the smartphone and other communication technologies serve to maintain the bonds between separated family members. This does not necessarily mean that smartphone-mediated communication substantially transforms the preexisting cultural norms in which parenting roles remained largely gendered (Cabanes & Acedera, 2012; Madianou, 2014). For the transnational families in the study, with the exception of those in which both parents were employed, parenting roles were rather similar to the conventional mode of the father as the breadwinner in the public domain and the mother as the stay-at-home, intimate figure.[6]

As is evident in smartphone-driven mobile parenting, new communication technologies play a supplemental role rather than operating as a replacement for conventional, face-to-face family interactions. Thus, the connected, mediated copresence with the parent(s), other family members (such as siblings), and/or old friends was sometimes described as a missing piece of the lives of these transnational young people as they grew up. For example, although Jongsu, a 26-year-old man who moved to Canada alone at the age of 16, was a successful young professional in Toronto's financial sector, he recalled his adolescence in Canada with mixed feelings: "Sometimes, it didn't feel like home, because I didn't have family here. When I am at work, it's OK, but at other times, I still feel strange living here." In this way, being raised in a transnational and mobile way with the aim of becoming the "global citizen" involves feelings of uncertainty and un-rootedness.

Smartphone Storytelling

The smartphone is not simply a tool for communication, as it remediates different media forms and stores particular personalized content. Similar to personal computers, smartphones can store users' personal histories. For the interviewees, personal technology devices, such as laptops and smartphones, seemed to be secret and intimate locations in which personal stories and histories are stored. There might be an increasingly popular tendency among young people to use communication technologies as journal-keeping tools that replace print-copy journaling (Lincoln & Robards, 2017). However, this tendency might be significant for young people with a highly transnational upbringing and whose sense of a permanent, physical home is relatively ambiguous. For example, Mira, a 20-year-old female undergraduate whose parents reside in Korea, lives with her older sister in a relatively small rented condo in downtown Toronto. For Mira, the transition from handwritten to digital journaling was partly motivated by her pursuit of personal space:

> I used to keep journals (by hand). I had hard times (in Canada), and so my struggles were handwritten in my diaries. Later, I was concerned that my older sister might read my diaries. So, I tore them up, and I use my smartphone now.

Several young people in the study used their laptops and early social media sites, such as Cyworld (a Korean-developed social networking site: 1999–2015), prior to owning a smartphone. For example, Jongsu, the aforementioned 26-year-old man, recalled how he kept his personal notes in the pre-smartphone era: "I used to keep journals on Cyworld. I also emailed myself quite often [. . .] if there was anything I wanted to write or anything to remember."

Cyworld was described as a popular early form of digital journal keeping and social networking. In particular, the young people who had already used home computers (or laptops) back in Korea prior to their relocation to Canada in their early or mid-teens commonly recalled accessing Cyworld frequently. Given Cyworld's national popularity in the 2000s, this recollection is not surprising. Following its launch as an early form of social networking site in 1999, Cyworld enjoyed exceptional popularity. While it offered computer-based social networking, it also provided each user with a virtual room (called a *minihompy*), in which the user was encouraged to decorate, play his or her own soundtrack, and keep photo/text diaries. However, at the time of the interviews (2014), in the era of the smartphone, Cyworld was rapidly losing its user base and, thus, terminated its services in 2015. As of 2014, some respondents sometimes logged into Cyworld to revisit their old diaries (postings), photos, peers' comments, and even soundtracks in their minihompies whenever they felt nostalgic about their earlier days in Korea. As several young people agreed, Cyworld played a unique role by providing digital diaries that were written not only personally but also collaboratively with close friends who regularly posted in their minihompies.

In regard to journal-keeping functions, the young people in the study compared Cyworld with newer, smartphone-based apps while admitting that the former might not be replaced by other apps, in particular Facebook or Instagram.[7] This lamentation might imply that the young people have an emotional attachment to the early communication technology; it also reveals that newer technology may not necessarily and entirely replace older technology in regard to the roles they play. Nevertheless, the smartphone and social media apps appeared to gradually supplement for laptops as their primary journal-keeping technology. Domi, a 19-year-old student who had homestayed in Toronto, having been separated from her parents since the age of 16, frequently used the smartphone and its apps (Facebook in particular) for not only networking but also archiving her daily life:

> I write what I think and feel on my phone. If there is anything special, I write. Personal thoughts and stuff are stored in my phone. Whenever I am on the Internet, I am on Facebook. I check linked recipes, funny videos, and stuff. I tend to comment on others' postings.

For Domi, Facebook was a useful tool for keeping journals, partly because it is not accessed by her parents, who do not have accounts.

In comparison, several interviewees used social networking apps to share their stories and thereby keep their families and left-behind friends updated about their lives in Canada. For example, Namjun, a 27-year-old man who had resided with his mother in Vancouver since the age of 14, used KakaoStory to keep his father in Seoul updated about his daily life: "KakaoTalk is easy to use. KakaoTalk has KakaoStory, and so people can easily post their selfies, well . . . with some notes on them. It's like a good combination of texting and Facebook." While KakaoTalk and KakaoStory were widely used, Facebook appeared to be increasingly popular, especially among university students, at the time of the interviews (2014). Changwoo, a 24-year-old student in Toronto, used Facebook for visual and shared storytelling to communicate with his peers in Canada and Korea, as well as his parents in Korea:

> Whenever there were interesting things happening, I took pictures and uploaded them to Facebook—for example, when the first snow fell and when the snow melted . . . stuff like that. Especially in my early days in Toronto, I took quite a few pictures. These days, I don't do anything special, as I go back and forth between home and school. I still picture and upload foods that I have tried for the first time, exceptionally expensive cars parked on the street, and so on.

In this manner, the smartphone and its apps enable transnational youth to record moments and feelings related to their lives in Canada and to share them in their mother tongue with their peers and family members in the home country. While for some respondents, smartphone-assisted journal keeping meant more personal and private storytelling, others tended to share their stories via smartphone apps to enable them to enhance the connected presence. The KakaoStory app was especially popular for online storytelling.

The transnational young Koreans' practice of engaging in smartphone-assisted storytelling illustrates that journal keeping has been transformed into a more mobile, fragmented, and/or shared process in the era of smartphones and social media. Various forms of capturing the moment—via postings, comments on others' postings, timelines, profiles, links, and photos shared through communication apps—serve to capture users' mobile lives. By logging into an app and scrolling down, users can reflect on "who they were, who they are now, and who they want to be in the future" (Lincoln & Robards, 2017, p. 530).

Conclusion

This chapter has examined the role and meaning of communication technologies—the smartphone in particular—among the young adult children of Korean transnational families. By examining cultural forces such as family norms and technological forces such as the particular interface of the smartphone and its apps, this chapter has shown how a new technology may undergo "cultural modification" (Campbell, 2006) by means of which the culture of the user community negotiates the meanings of the technology. The young people's recollections of their use of communication technologies, growing up in Korean transnational families, revealed that the phenomenon of precollege study abroad among middle-class Korean children entailed a new form of "doing family," by means of which mediated, as opposed to face-to-face, communication functions as the default setting for family interaction. The transnationally split family members in the study engaged with "connected" and "conversational" modes of communication through the continuous use of smartphones.

For the Korean middle-class families, the transnational process of transitioning to adulthood illustrates how digital media technologies have been deeply integrated into young people's identity formation. Most research participants were not certain how long they would remain in Canada. Due to several factors, such as visa status (as international students or permanent residents) and difficulty finding ideal jobs in Canada, the young adults of Korean transnational families were uncertain whether they could remain in Canada or would have to return Korea, where their parent(s) lived and their family's financial resources were based.[8] For several male interviewees who hold Korean citizenship, the mandatory two-year military service that should typically be completed in their early- or mid-twenties increased their feelings of uncertainty about their future in Canada.

By being online and connected to their left-behind parent(s) through various media forms, young Koreans seek "ontological security" (Giddens, 1991) and a sense of belonging. The technological features of the smartphone, such as its enhanced mobility, connectivity, and storytelling functions, allow transnational family members to negotiate not only their distant relatives and friends in the home country but also different options for being connected. The smartphone's role as a platform on which numerous communication apps converge seemed to play a significant role in redefining family communication in the transnational context, allowing users to switch easily between different communication media and methods (e.g., visual, iconic, and textual). Among the various forms of communication technology and smartphone apps, the Korean-developed Kakao app was commonly used by the Korean transnational families; the app was extensively used for Internet-mediated voice-calling, text-messaging, group-chat, and journal-keeping. The app also contributed to the extensive use of smartphones by not only the young people but also their parents. Of course, the technological features of the smartphone do not determine the actual use of the technology. Rather, its user culture, which comprises factors such as family norms and everyday contexts, deeply influences how a new technology is domesticated and localized.

The growing transnational family phenomenon challenges the significance of the physical boundary of the home as the everyday place of technology appropriation. For some respondents who spent their adolescence at homestay families' houses or rented condominiums with their mothers, who relied on the breadwinning fathers' remittances from Korea, their physical and emotional attachment to the household in Canada seemed tenuous. Due in part to the temporality of the home, the transnational young people in this study—especially those who had been separated from both parents—tended not to own and use many sedentary, household technologies, such as big-screen satellite televisions, at their residences in Canada; rather, they heavily utilized personal and portable technologies, such as smartphones. The young people's fragile attachment to the overseas households and their extensive use of mobile technologies imply a complex process of technology appropriation in the transnational context. The phenomenon of transnational families involves the highly individualized management of family time, space, and norms, while the members' desires for physical togetherness and conventional family relationships, such as gendered parenting, are not replaced by virtual togetherness. However, with the emergence of the smartphone as a gateway to various types of communication apps, the individualized mode of overseas living and the nostalgic desire for home seem to coexist.

As communication technologies have become increasingly affordable, the virtual togetherness of the family is no longer an exceptional phenomenon (Bakardjieva, 2003; Wilding, 2006). Transnational communication via media technologies has been an essential mode of interaction among transnational family members. Given that the family and household have been considered a foundational unit of the appropriation of new technologies (Silverstone & Hirsch, 1992), the transnational reformation of family interaction requires media researchers to rethink the process of technology appropriation. Media technology may no longer be simply domesticated in the family as a locality-based unit but, rather, may be integrated into the process in which the family is reorganized beyond locality.

Notes

1 The term *gireogi gajok* (or romanized as *kirogi kajok*), which is a literal translation of "geese family," is a metaphorical reference to the family that is sustained by seasonal reunions between parents and children who otherwise maintain a long-distance relationship (Finch & Kim, 2012).

2 These young people's acquisition of permanent residency was enabled by their parents being awarded Canadian residency through immigration programs, such as the Immigrant Investor Program or Skilled Worker Program.

3 Ara's mother was an exceptional case because most parents of the young people interviewed for this chapter at least owned a smartphone at the time of the interviews (2014). In the young adult children's recollection, their parents adopted the smartphone in the late 2000s or early 2010s, and yet some

parents were not entirely comfortable with the new technology. Although Korea has been known for its high smartphone user rate, it is important to remember that the device was not introduced until 2007. Thus, it is not surprising that most interviewees did not own their first smartphone prior to arriving in Canada.

4 In 2015, one year after the first field study for this chapter was conducted, the KakaoTalk app was updated to introduce a free video chat function. Thus, it is probable that young transnational Koreans increasingly rely on the Kakao platform without the need to use other platforms, such as Skype, for video calls.

5 While KakaoTalk was initially a smartphone-only app, it became available on personal computers in 2013.

6 According to ethnographic studies of the Korean "geese family," some stay-at-home mothers overseas tend to feel free, as they are less obliged to fulfill gendered responsibilities (such as the roles of wives and daughters-in-law) and, thus, feel empowered to some extent. Jeong, You, and Kwon (2014) observed that the mothers in "geese families" perceived their separation from their husbands and extended families "as an opportunity for personal growth and actively sought and acquired new roles" (p. 1556).

7 In terms of Facebook usage, assessed by the percentage of active daily users, especially in its early period, Canada was the first worldwide. Its 74% usage rate is far higher than the global average of 61% and even higher than the US rate of 70%, despite the US being the birthplace of Facebook (The Canadian Press, 2013).

8 Typically, the transnational family structure is readjusted after the children enter university. For example, for "geese families," the homemaker mother might return to Korea to be reunited with her husband or might remain in Canada until the child's university graduation. Some Korean transnational families own property in Canada for their children studying abroad in Canada. Otherwise, the father in Korea might decide to move to Canada permanently to reside with his other family members.

References

Abelmann, N., Newendorp, N., & Lee-Chung, S. (2014). East Asia's astronaut and geese families: Hong Kong and South Korean cosmopolitanisms. *Critical Asian Studies, 46*(2), 259–286.

Bakardjieva, M. (2003). Virtual togetherness: An everyday-life perspective. *Media, Culture & Society, 25*(3), 291–313.

Bolter, J. D., & Grusin, R. (1998). *Remediation: Understanding new media.* Cambridge, MA: MIT Press.

Bonini, T. (2011). The media as "home-making" tools: Life story of a Filipino migrant in Milan. *Media, Culture & Society, 33*(6), 869–883.

Cabanes, J. V. A., & Acedera, K. A. F. (2012). Of mobile phones and mother-fathers: Calls, text messages, and conjugal power relations in mother-away Filipino families. *New Media & Society, 14*(6), 916–930.

Campbell, H. (2006). Texting the faith: Religious users and cell phone culture. In A. P. Kavoori & N. Arceneaux (Eds.), *The cell phone reader: Essays in social transformation* (pp. 139–154). New York, NY: Peter Lang.

Chib, A., Malik, S., Aricat, R. G., & Kadir, S. Z. (2014). Migrant mothering and mobile phones: Negotiations of transnational identity. *Mobile Media & Communication, 2*(1), 73–93.

Clark, L. S. (2012). *The parent app: Understanding families in a digital age.* Oxford: Oxford University Press.

Clark, L. S., & Sywyj, L. (2012). Mobile intimacies in the USA among refugee and recent immigrant teens and their parents. *Feminist Media Studies, 12*(4), 485–495.

Clayton, T. (2013). Why the largest social network in 2015 won't be Facebook, and will be from Asia. Retrieved from http://insights.wired.com/profiles/blogs/why-the-largest-social-network-in-2015-won-t-be-facebook-and-will?xg_source=activity#axzz3CCLYzO8A

Elias, N., & Lemish, D. (2008). Media uses in immigrant families: Torn between "inward" and "outward" paths of integration. *International Communication Gazette, 70*(1), 21–40.

Finch, J., & Kim, S. K. (2012). Kirŏgi families in the US: Transnational migration and education. *Journal of Ethnic and Migration Studies, 38*(3), 485–506.

Fortunati, L., Pertierra, R., & Vincent, J. (2013). Introduction: Migrations and diasporas—Making their world elsewhere. In L. Fortunati, R., Pertierra, & J. Vincent (Eds.), *Migration, diaspora and information technology in global societies* (pp. 1–17). New York, NY: Routledge.

Francisco, V. (2015). "The Internet is magic": Technology, intimacy and transnational families. *Critical Sociology, 41*(1), 173–190.

Gardner, H., & Davis, K. (2013). *The app generation: How today's youth navigate identity, intimacy, and imagination in a digital world.* New Haven, CT: Yale University Press.

Giddens, A. (1991). *Modernity and self-identity: Self and society in the late modern age.* Stanford, CA: Stanford University Press.

Hoang, L. A., & Yeoh, B. S. (2012). Sustaining families across transnational spaces: Vietnamese migrant parents and their left-behind children. *Asian Studies Review, 36*(3), 307–325.

Horst, H., & Miller, D. (2005). From kinship to link-up: The cell phone and social networking in Jamaica. *Current Anthropology, 46*(5), 755–778.

Horst, H., & Miller, D. (2006). *The cell phone: An anthropology of communication.* Oxford: Berg.

Hjorth, L. (2009). *Mobile media in the Asia-Pacific: Gender and the art of being mobile.* London: Routledge.

Jeong, Y. J., You, H. K., & Kwon, Y. I. (2014). One family in two countries: Mothers in Korean transnational families. *Ethnic and Racial Studies, 37*(9), 1546–1564.

Kakao. (2018). Kakao investor relations. Retrieved from https://t1.kakaocdn.net/kakaocorp/operating/ir/results-announcement/3308.pdf

Kaur, R., & Shruti, I. (2016). Mobile technology and "doing family" in a global world: Indian migrants in Cambodia. In S. S. Lim (Ed.), *Mobile communication and the family: Asian experiences in technology domestication* (pp. 73–91). New York, NY: Springer.

Kim, Y. H., & Shin, S. (2013). SNS user demographics. *KISDI Report.* December 26, 2013.

Korean Educational Development Institute. (2013). Korean educational statistics services. Retrieved from http://kess.kedi.re.kr/

Lan, P. C. (2003). Maid or madam? Filipina migrant workers and the continuity of domestic labor. *Gender & Society, 17*(2), 187–208.

Law, P. L., & Peng, Y. (2008). Mobile networks: Migrant workers in southern China. In J. E. Katz (Ed.), *Handbook of mobile communication studies* (pp. 55–64). Cambridge, MA: MIT Press.

Licoppe, C. (2004). Connected presence: The emergence of a new repertoire for managing social relationships in a changing communication technoscape. *Environment and Planning D, 22*(1), 135–156.

Lim, S. S. (2005). From cultural to information revolution: ICT domestication by middle-class Chinese families. In T. Berker, M. Hartmann, Y. Punie, & K. Ward (Eds.), *Domestication of media and technologies* (pp. 185–204). Maidenhead: Open University Press.

Lim, S. S. (2008). Technology domestication in the Asian homestead: Comparing the experiences of middle class families in China and South Korea. *East Asian Science, Technology and Society: An International Journal, 2,* 189–209.

Lim, S. S., & Soon, C. (2010). The influence of social and cultural factors on mothers' domestication of household ICTs: Experiences of Chinese and Korean women. *Telematics and Informatics, 27*(3), 205–216.

Lincoln, S., & Robards, B. (2017). Editing the project of the self: Sustained Facebook use and growing up online. *Journal of Youth Studies, 20*(4), 518–531.

Ling, R., & Yttri, B. (2006). Control, emancipation, and status: The mobile telephone in teens' parental and peer relationship. In R. Kraut, M. Brynin, & S. Kiesler (Eds.), *Computer, phones, and the Internet: Domesticating information technology* (pp. 219–234). Oxford: Oxford University Press.

Madianou, M. (2014). Smartphone as polymedia. *Journal of Computer-Mediated Communication, 19*(3), 667–680.

Madianou, M., & Miller, D. (2012). *Migration and new media: Transnational families and polymedia*. London: Routledge.

Park, J. S. Y. (2011). The promise of English: Linguistic capital and the neoliberal worker in the South Korean job market. *International Journal of Bilingual Education and Bilingualism, 14*(4), 443–455.

Park, S. J., & Abelmann, N. (2004). Class and cosmopolitan striving: Mothers' management of English education in South Korea. *Anthropological Quarterly, 77*(4), 645–672.

Parreñas, R. (2005). Long distance intimacy: Class, gender and intergenerational relations between mothers and children in Filipino transnational families. *Global Networks, 5*(4), 317–336.

Pearce, K. E., Slaker, J. S., & Ahmad, N. (2013). Transnational families in Armenia and information communication technology use. *International Journal of Communication, 7,* 2128–2156.

Ramirez, E. (2017, January 31). Nearly 100% of households In South Korea now have Internet access, thanks to seniors. *Forbes*. Retrieved from https://www.forbes.com/sites/elaineramirez/2017/01/31/nearly-100-of-households-in-south-korea-now-have-internet-access-thanks-to-seniors/#26384c585572

Seo, D. (2011). The will to self-managing, the will to freedom: The self-managing ethic and the spirit of flexible capitalism in South Korea. In J. Song (Ed.), *New millennium South Korea: Neoliberal capitalism and transnational movements* (pp. 84–100). London: Routledge.

Seth, M. J. (2002). *Education fever: Society, politics, and the pursuit of schooling in South Korea*. Honolulu, HI: University of Hawai'i Press.

Silverstone, R., & Hirsch, E. (Eds.). (1992). *Consuming technologies: Media and information in domestic spaces*. London: Routledge.

The Canadian Press. (2013). Facebook releases stats about Canadian usage; 14 million daily users. Retrieved from http://www.macleans.ca/news/facebook-releases-stats-about-canadian-usage-14-million-daily-users/

Uy-Tioco, C. (2007). Overseas Filipino workers and text messaging: Reinventing transnational mothering. *Continuum: Journal of Media & Cultural Studies, 21*(2), 253–265.

Vancea, M., & Olivera, N. (2013). E-migrant women in Catalonia: Mobile phone use and maintenance of family relationships. *Gender, Technology and Development, 17*(2), 179–203.

Wallis, C. (2013). *Technomobility in China: Young migrant women and mobile phones*. New York, NY: New York University Press.

Wilding, R. (2006). "Virtual" intimacies? Families communicating across transnational contexts. *Global Networks, 6*(2), 125–142.

Yonhap News. (2013). S. Korea tops smartphone penetration rate in 2012. Retrieved from http://english.yonhapnews.co.kr/news/2013/06/25/90/0200000000AEN20130625003000320F.HTML

Yoon, K. (2003). Retraditionalizing the mobile: Young people's sociality and mobile phone use in Seoul, South Korea. *European Journal of Cultural Studies, 6*(3), 327–343.

6 Digital Mediascape of Diasporas

Chapters 4 and 5 addressed transnational Korean youth in a transient phase of transnational migration. While desiring transnational mobility, the young people tended to be uncertain about their future locations of residence, and their status was often transient. For example, the young sojourners discussed in Chapter 4 had difficulty extending their overseas stays due to visa restrictions; thus, with a few exceptions, their overseas experiences involved a rather temporary and transient way of life. In comparison, as discussed in Chapter 5, the young people of middle-class transnational families, who stayed in Canada for several years for study, were relatively flexible in their visa status, partly due to their family resources allowing their extended stay. For some young people, transnational mobility involves a significant degree of precariousness and uncertainty, whereas others have more options regarding their transnational mobility and lifestyle choices. These different implications of mobility reveal how family background and resources may contribute to reproducing "mobility capital" (Jensen, 2011)—that is, the way in which one's overseas education and work–life experiences contribute to one's social and cultural status.

This chapter focuses on young Koreans who left Korea and settled in Canada during childhood or adolescence. Compared with young sojourners and young people of transnational families, young migrants discussed in this chapter are not categorically transient migrants, because they left their birthplace, and do not consider return migration to their homeland. In terms of the sense of belonging and identity, young migrants discussed in this chapter are comparable with the young people of transnational families. Both groups share the experiences of transnational mobility in that they left their homeland during childhood or adolescence. However, the young migrants discussed in this chapter are relatively *diasporic* subjects as their resources and social networks are primarily based in the host land, whereas young people of transnational families are strongly attached to their homeland because families and their financial/social resources are based in the homeland.

In this chapter, the Korean-born young people who left their homeland and "permanently" relocated to Canada with their family members are referred to as "young diasporic Koreans." The term *diaspora* has widely referred to the same ethnic group and community in different regions of the world—outside their ancestral homeland (I. J. Yoon, 2012), whereas it can more specifically mean "the voluntary or forcible movement of people from their homelands into new regions," often in relation to histories of colonialization (Ashcroft, Griffiths, & Tiffin, 1998, pp. 68–69). Korea has been recognized for its widespread diasporic communities. As of 2009, 6.8 million Koreans were estimated to reside abroad (I. J. Yoon, 2012)—which was a significantly large number given the Korean population (approximately 51 million in South Korea and 25 million in North Korea). Due to the poverty and export-oriented economy during the early post-Korean War period, a large number of Koreans relocated overseas, whether willingly or unwillingly (I. J. Yoon, 2012). While the United States (US) has been the most popular destination for Korean migrants outside Asia, Canada has gradually been recognized for its increasing number of Korean migrants, especially since the 1990s. Korea has been consistently ranked as one of the largest sources of immigrants to Canada (Kwak & Hiebert, 2010). In comparison with the larger and older Korean community in the US, the Canada-based Korean community constitutes a relatively young cohort of the Korean diaspora on a global scale. Indeed, the population of people of Korean origin in Canada has visibly increased between the 1990s and the 2000s. According to the latest census in 2016, Korea was ranked among the top birthplaces of immigrants and recent immigrants to Canada (2011–2016); the number during the five-year period was 21,710. In 2016, Koreans were the ninth largest visible minority group in Canada, as 188,710 people of Korean origin, constituting 0.5% of the Canadian population, were identified (Statistics Canada, 2019).

This chapter addresses the roles and meanings of digital media in diasporic life by examining young diasporic Koreans' use of different digital media forms. Digital media technologies have increasingly influenced the processes and experiences of transnational migration. Migrants make use of various forms of digital media technologies for multiple purposes, such as connecting with their countries of origin, adapting to destination countries, and reworking their identities. Communication technologies have moved from background to foreground in migrants' lives since the introduction of low-cost, ubiquitous, personal technologies, such as mobile phones (Miller, 2012). The tendency toward media-saturated migrant lives might be evident, especially among young migrants who have grown up, and are familiar, with digital media (Nedelcu, 2012). In this respect, this chapter examines Korean-born young migrants' appropriation of digital technologies in their transnational transition to adulthood. It focuses on Korean "digital generation" migrants, who grew up during the rapid development of the information and technology (IT) industry in their country of origin. Compared with older migrants, this specific demographic of diasporic youth is deeply immersed in emerging media technologies.

Despite the increasing number of Korean migrants in Canada, their media practices during the processes of migration and cultural negotiation have rarely been addressed. This chapter focuses on young Koreans who were already immersed in the new media environment during their premigration period. It explores their memories of earlier digital media use and their adoption of newer media forms (such as social media and smartphones) during the post-migration period. Diasporic youth embrace transnational mobility as an important component of their transition to adulthood and appropriate digital media technologies. This chapter illustrates how they use digital media during their post-migration period. In the sections following the literature review, three themes are discussed, tracing chronologically how the young diasporic Koreans utilized digital media in their transnational life trajectories. First, this chapter explores how the young people recall their migration to Canada, along with their memories and literacies of the earlier digital media they used in their homeland. Second, it explores how the young people use and think about different digital media forms in their negotiation of different human networks during their diasporic transition to adulthood. For most young people in the study, digital media were effective tools for bonding with their diasporic, ethnic communities. Third, the chapter examines how the diasporic youth engage with their homeland through particular media platforms and content. Drawing on these empirical data, this chapter concludes that diasporic young people's lives involve continuous reengagement with their memories and imagination of the homeland, as well as their cultural adjustment to and negotiation of the new environment of the host land.

Studying Digital Diaspora

How do digital media change the landscape of migration and diaspora? Until the early 2000s, studies of migration and media tended to focus on how migrants consume media content or how they are represented in mainstream media (e.g., Cottle, 2000; King & Wood, 2001), with some exceptions addressing migrants' grassroots media production (Mayer, 2003). These earlier studies primarily examined mass media forms; thus, their findings appear too outdated to enable the effective exploration of recent media use patterns and dynamics, such as ubiquity, mobility, and interactivity. As the Internet, mobile media, and social media are popularly adopted in diasporic contexts, researchers have increasingly explored how various media forms are utilized in different areas of diasporic life. Due to the mundane use of low-cost communication technologies across national borders, migration has been reconsidered as a continuous process involving mediated or physical homecomings, rather than a rupture between the origin and the destination. Thus, in the era of ubiquitous, mediated communication, media research has increasingly engaged with the question of how migrants' lived experiences are interwoven with technologically mediated everyday contexts (Hjorth, 2007; Madianou & Miller, 2012; Nedelcu, 2012; Wilding, 2006).

The existing studies of diasporic media use tend to situate media practices in a spectrum from being homeland-oriented to being host land-oriented (e.g., Elias & Lemish, 2008). The studies have analyzed the role of media in diasporas as either a facilitator in ethnic networking with the homeland (or ethnic communities) or an explorer of new networks in the host society. Through different media practices, diasporic populations can maintain their "bonding" with their homeland and ethnic communities, on the one hand, and/or engage in "bridging" with a wide range of host-country individuals and social groups, on the other (Peeters & d'Haenens, 2005). The ongoing evolution of digital media further facilitates media's bilateral role of "bonding" and "bridging" by "maintaining connections with the country of origin and the ethnic–cultural community, while also establishing connections with the country of residence and its culture" (Dhoest, 2015, p. 278). Overall, the existing studies show that the two orientations—toward the homeland or host land—are relatively common in diasporic media practices. However, this framework may be open to further questions.

First, the two orientations are not necessarily mutually exclusive. Especially in the digital media era, "bonding" and "bridging" can occur simultaneously. Depending on several factors—such as the availability and design of media technologies, as well as the user's media literacy and sociocultural contexts—diasporic individuals may choose and appropriate different forms of media for bonding and/or bridging (Madianou & Miller, 2012). The ever-increasing transnational mobility and media practices may allow groups of migrants who have plural (if not multiple) senses of belonging and identity to engage with omnivorous forms of media across national borders. Bailey (2011) suggested that digital media-equipped diasporic groups are "simultaneously engaging in discursive events with the homeland, the 'local' new home, and transnational home of the web," and thus, the online territory becomes a "comfort zone" in which "multiple identity narratives can be performed while simultaneously engaging in discursive practices and emotional bond maintenance" (p. 268).

Empirical research has revealed that diasporic youth may explore new weak ties with a wider range of people outside of ethnic boundaries; this group may be contrasted with the first-generation immigrants, who may be more reliant on ethnic language media and seek "bonding," due to linguistic and cultural barriers (Elias & Lemish, 2008). The generational differences in immigrants' digital media use imply the significance of the "time variable" in media practices, which consist of the age when an individual's migration path began and the length of time in the host country (Green & Kabir, 2012; Vittadini, Reifova, Siibak, & Bilandzic, 2014). Through their versatile media practices, diasporic youth who have bicultural or bilingual literacies may engage with the homeland *and* host land in almost equal measure through their versatile appropriations of various media forms.

Second, it is noteworthy that neither the homeland nor the host land is a fixed entity, as both are imagined communities that are maintained through media practices and mediated rituals. As Georgiou (2006) aptly stated, "The meanings of the diasporic space are shaped in contexts of continuities, links and conflicts" (p. 5). The diasporic individuals' sense of belonging and affiliation with the homeland and host land may be influenced by how they engage with different media forms and content. For some diasporic individuals, the homeland may remain a nostalgic community partly due to their limited access to up-to-date media from the homeland. In contrast, in the digital era, extensive access to homeland media may allow diasporic audiences to engage with the homeland almost in real time and, thus, to constantly reimagine it from an up-to-date perspective. For example, young diasporic Koreans' increasing exposure to highly hybrid Korean pop music (K-pop) on the Internet may contribute to the de-essentialization of their homeland as a fixed entity that is frozen in their past memories (K. Yoon, 2019).

Third, there is a lack of transnational young media users' voices in existing media and migration studies. While diasporic youth, whose technology-mediated and lived experiences with the homeland and host land coexist, are an interesting demographic, they have been addressed insufficiently in media studies. Moreover, although diasporic young people's media literacy may be influenced by their premigration experiences, the existing literature has not fully addressed migrants' premigration use of media technologies (Mattelart, 2010). Given that migration is not necessarily a discontinuation of life in the country of origin, but rather a continuous process of growing up, especially for diasporic youth, the history and context of migrants' use of media technologies requires attention. It is important to understand media as not simply a tool but, rather, an *environment* in which social and cultural relations are negotiated and online and offline contexts are interwoven.

To explore young diasporic Koreans' digital media practices, 62 semistructured interviews with young Korean migrants in their late teens or twenties were conducted in three Canadian cities—Toronto, Vancouver, and Kelowna—between 2014 and 2018. The interviewees were young people who immigrated to Canada in their teens or preteens. The participants, presented under pseudonyms, were Korean-born, and the period of their residency in Canada varied between 2 and 15 years. They were undergraduate students, recent graduates/job seekers, young professionals (employed at a corporation or small business), or homemakers. With the exception of those who immigrated to Canada relatively recently (i.e., in their late teens or early twenties), the participants considered themselves bilingual and, thus, faced no linguistic barriers in regard to understanding either Korean or Canadian media content. Of course, individual linguistic abilities varied, as those who immigrated at an early (preteen) age were more familiar with English, while later immigrants were more familiar with Korean.

Most interviewees recalled that their and their family's migration was motivated by better education and lifestyle opportunities. Several recalled Korea's highly competitive education system and high social pressure on young people, whereas Canada was considered a destination for self-actualization and individual freedom. In particular, several interviewees who immigrated in their mid- or late teens—relatively later than other interviewees—recalled that they had hoped to avoid the sociocultural pressure that they had constantly faced in Korea. Bobae, who immigrated to Canada 10 years ago and was now in her mid-twenties, noted, "I expected my life to be so free here. Well, this is a new place, and so I thought I didn't have to care how others thought about me. I expected that sort of thing a lot at first." The young diasporic Koreans whose families decide to migrate to improve their children's education and lifestyle can be compared to the earlier generation of Korean immigrants whose mobility decisions were largely driven by economic "push" factors in the form of the home country's poverty (I. J. Yoon, 2012).

The individual interviews, conducted in Korean–the participants' first language– in most cases, centered on questions about the young people's use of media technologies in the origin and host countries during the pre- and post-migration periods. The participants were asked how they used different digital media forms, especially since they had begun using the Internet. This oral history method allowed them to situate their use of new digital media in the temporal and spatial dynamics of transnational migration. This methodology, which often draws on personal and/or collective memories through in-depth interviews, is considered to provide "a 'voice' to those whose experiences might otherwise go unrecorded" (Bornat, 2004, p. 771). By encouraging the young people to recall and discuss their childhood memories of media use, as well as their recent media uses, the research aimed to enable them to reflect on their diasporic trajectories through their memories related to media use. Through the oral history method, this research aimed to trace how diasporic youth grow up in relation to digital media, memories of the homeland, and ethnic networks. In so doing, the research proposes to move beyond the existing studies of digital media and migration, in which digital media practices are not sufficiently examined as an articulation of transitional and transnational processes.

Of course, the young diasporic Koreans in Canada interviewed for this chapter do not represent all diasporic youth in Canada. This chapter draws on qualitative in-depth interviews with a limited number of young Korean migrants, who were recruited via snowballing in Korean ethnic communities, such as Korean Canadian student associations. Thus, it is likely that the research participants might be young Korean Canadians who are relatively involved in Korean ethnic activities and communities, rather than those who are referred to as "bananas" (i.e., "yellow outside but white inside").[1] Despite the limited representativeness of the participants, the findings of this chapter facilitate discussion of how diasporic youth undergo the transnational transition to adulthood through their digital media practices.

Migrating with Digital Media

Transnational migration involves the significant reorganization of the physical and cultural resources available for diasporic youth transitioning to adulthood. The young people in the study were exposed to a new media environment during their early post-migration period, when temporal and spatial adjustments occurred. Their adjusted pattern of media use implies that diaspora involves the migration of not only people but also media—that is, users carrying their literacy and memories of the earlier digital media they used in the homeland. Given that "[p]eople's ability to absorb information is largely dependent on their past experience" (Park, 2017, p. 26), the young migrants' premigration media experiences need to be considered for a better understanding of their post-migration media practices.

Whether by force or by choice, being an immigrant changes one's everyday routines and causes one to question various taken-for-granted assumptions (Bailey, 2008). The young Korean migrants in this chapter who relocated to Canada during their childhood or adolescence recalled encountering emotional difficulties, such as loneliness, insecurity, and uncertainty, especially during the early post-migration phase. While digital media were adopted to meet the migrants' communicative needs following migration, they also carried diverse meanings and memories that were attached to the users. Given that migration involves not only the people on the move but also the relocation of the digital media accompanying them, it is not surprising that the respondents' stories of migration often included their recollections of which digital media were appropriated in the process and how. For example, Sangmi, a 22-year-old woman who initially came to Vancouver as an international student at the age of 15 and whose family later immigrated to Canada, recalled how she realized that her laptop was an integral part of her migrant life:

> At first, I didn't bring my laptop with me [from Korea]. Well, I thought I would be fine without the laptop [laughs]. I expected something fancier to be here [in Canada] . . . but [there was] nothing really [laughs]. Well, so, I struggled a while . . . It was a kind of devastating period, and so after my first semester, I went back to Korea and brought my laptop [back to Canada].

In addition to hardware technology, such as laptops, the media literacy acquired during the premigration period tended to be carried over throughout the migration process. For example, several respondents recalled that even after migration, they continued logging into Korean online communities and playing the same online games they had played in Korea. A certain continuity in media use seemed to reduce their feelings of unfamiliarity caused by their physical relocation.

During the post-migration period, the young people tended to develop certain strategies for appropriating digital media. In particular, while negotiating the new media environment in Canada, the young people adjusted themselves to the spatial and temporal differences between Korea and Canada. Migration was often recalled as a transition from a fast to a slow time zone. Korea was described as "highly wired" and "fast," while Canada was characterized by its relatively relaxed pace. For example, Soha, a 22-year-old woman in Toronto, contrasted Internet speeds in Canada and Korea: "The Internet here is so slow. Whenever I go back to Korea, I feel like I am in paradise. The Internet is kind of slow everywhere here, whether at the coffee shop or on campus." This perception of slow Internet speed in the host country may not be exclusive to young Korean migrants in Canada, as the findings of some previous studies suggest. For example, according to Hjorth's (2007) study, young Koreans in Australia depicted the Internet infrastructure in the host country as "slow and frustrating."

Indeed, Canada has been behind countries such as Korea in terms of IT infrastructure and resources (Middleton, 2011). For the past 15 years, Korea has far exceeded Canada in numerous IT indicators; one 2014 comparison revealed that the average Internet upload speed in Korea (45 Mbps) was far faster than in Canada (5.67 Mbps), which was ranked fifty-third in the world (Nowak, 2014). Owing to Canada's relatively slow Internet speed and limited digital infrastructure, some young migrants had adjusted their Internet use patterns, especially in the initial post-migration phase. Nahyun, a 22-year-old woman in Toronto, noted the following:

> My time on the Internet has decreased since I came to Canada. In Korea, I was on the Internet almost all day. I use the Internet here as well, but . . . well, here, I don't use it as much as in Korea. That's partly because it's quite slow here, and the connection is often unstable. It's irritating.

The interviewees' experiences of slower Internet speed in Canada might partly reflect the two countries' Internet regulation and business models. As the capacity-based billing system is dominant in Canada, users have limited connection speed and downloading capacity, unless they subscribe to a top package; in contrast, most telecommunication providers in Korea offer unlimited, flat-rate monthly plans, thereby giving users more freedom and speed.

The young people's relocation to Canada not only involved a new sense of time and speed, as evidenced by the adjustment to slower Internet, but also required spatial adjustment. In contrast to their descriptions of limited personal space due to the compact sizes of the urban dwellings in their homeland, Canada was described as a spacious location where more outdoor activities are available and individuals are not as deeply immersed in digital media. Junha, a 29-year-old man who immigrated at the age of 13 and had been a heavy player of online games in Korea, recalled, "I got to play online games less and less here. Here in Canada, I hung out with guys, having fun and going camping, so it's like I didn't have time for online gaming." For Minwoo, a 20-year-old undergraduate who had played online games extensively in Korea, online gaming was no longer an option, as he could not find many enthusiastic players among his peers nor physical spaces in which to play online games together (e.g., an Internet café). According to Minwoo,

> There was no PC *bang* [i.e., the Korean style Internet café for playing online games] here in Canada. It's not like in Korea. I couldn't find many Korean buddies to play online games with at my high school in Vancouver at that time [i.e. the early 2010s]. Also, a few Canadian friends who played games tended to play console games rather than online games.

Consequently, for some interviewees, their increased participation in outdoor school-related and extracurricular activities reduced the amount of time they spent on the Internet since their migration to Canada. However, the young people's post-migration life cannot simply be summarized as the spatial experiences of a flexible lifestyle and an abundance of outdoor activities. For example, Chanmi, a 28-year-old homemaker, recalled how and why she spent time outside. After immigration, her parents had to work hard six to seven days per week to make ends meet. They ran a small business and were, thus, unable to have daily family time. Being outdoors enabled Chanmi to escape the tensions between her family members during her early post-migration period: "After migration, my parents were often stressed out [due to struggles in the workplace]. I felt bad. My solution was to go home late so my parents could have more free time." Alternatively, for Chanmi, accessing particular virtual Internet "rooms", such as social media and blogs, was a way to cope with the struggle of growing up in an immigrant family and to negotiate the frustrating atmosphere of the family home.

Several interviewees recalled their earlier Internet use in Korea as an intimate activity involving close friends. In describing their media practices in Korea with Korean peers, they sometimes used a spatial metaphor; the Internet was played in a bang (room). Partly echoing the findings of Chapter 5, the young people who spent part of their childhood in Korea associated their digital media experiences in the homeland with the image and feeling of a bang. For example, a few male respondents who used to be heavy online gamers recalled the PC bang as a common venue for spending time with friends during their childhood in Korea. Online gaming (especially role-playing games) and gathering at a PC bang were more common practices among young men; few female respondents had been enthusiastic about online gaming and would go to a PC bang. Some Toronto-based young men would gather at a PC bang in Korea town during the early post-migration period. In comparison, most young men and women used to gather at a Korean-based virtual bang—Cyworld, thereby connecting them with the homeland and diasporic community, especially in the early post-migration period.

The young migrants' media practices were adjusted during the post-migration period. The aforementioned factors, such as Canada's relatively inconvenient IT infrastructure and migrants' increased outdoor/leisure time, influenced particular media practices among the young migrants. For example, file downloading and online gaming activities, by and large, decreased at least for the first few years following migration. In addition, mediated interpersonal communication with separated friends and families during the first few post-migration years was increasingly integrated into the respondents' lives as they sought a sense of continuity and belonging. Furthermore, the emergence of streaming sites and social media, such as YouTube and Netflix, allowed the respondents to enjoy Korea's online media content without downloading it. The shift from downloading to streaming was a strategy for temporal and spatial adjustment in the host society, enabling them to cope temporally with the slow Internet and the aforementioned capacity-based billing system and to engage spatially with the relatively fragmented, individualized pattern of Internet use in Canada.

As the low-cost, high-speed Internet, which had been taken for granted during the premigration period, was not a default media setting in Canada, the young Korean migrants had to use digital media more strategically, especially in the early post-migration period. They adjusted their use of digital media in response to the temporal and spatial media environment in Canada. This tendency does not necessarily mean that diasporic Korean youth always intentionally change their media user experiences in the post-migration period. A few respondents who migrated to Canada at a relatively older age continued their Internet user behaviors with minimal adjustment even after migration. However, most young people in the study had to adjust their digital media use patterns to some extent. This process of adjusted media practices appeared to provide the young people with a sense of continuation between their pre- and post-migration lives via transnational communication—including social networking in ethnic communities and access to media produced in the homeland—which will be addressed in the following sections.

Transnational and/or Ethnic Sociality

Diasporic youth develop sociality strategies to negotiate their transnational identities and networks. The young diasporic Koreans in the study adopted different digital media, such as communication and social media applications (apps), thereby engaging with different or sometimes overlapping groups of people; for some, their social networks were, to a large extent, divided ethnically.

Technologically mediated communication has increasingly enabled migrants to be connected with their countries of origin and to, thus, maintain a sense of continuity and belonging (Madianou & Miller, 2012). The young people sought to remain connected to their left-behind friends and family members via various digital media forms. The particular media that had been used for transnational and interpersonal communication had been rapidly supplemented, if not replaced, by newer ones. Sangmi, the aforementioned 22-year-old woman who had to be separated from her family for the first few years of her life in Canada, described "a really, really big change" in her communication with people in Korea: "I never imagined this before. [. . .] From international telephone cards to Skype, and then to the Internet phone, and then smartphones became popular, and then, recently, [there's been] another shift to KakaoTalk [i.e., a Korean-developed messaging app]."

Notably, the smartphone appeared to contribute to the diasporic young people's negotiation of the new spatial and temporal environment since their entry into Canada during their childhood or adolescence. Yunho, a 27-year-old man, noted, "Without this [pointing to his smartphone], I may not be able to do anything. I may simply be frozen. I cannot do any communication, and I cannot do any work."

The young people used a few communication apps frequently—in particular, the globally popular social networking app Facebook and the Korean-based messaging app KakaoTalk. These two apps were supplementary to each other but seemed unable to replace each other completely. For some respondents, Facebook provided a strategic way to explore a wide range of peers, rather than simply maintain their existing peer networks. For example, when asked how the Internet played a role in her settlement in Canada, Miro, a 22-year-old female undergraduate in Toronto, noted that Facebook was especially helpful in enabling her to meet new friends beyond language and cultural barriers and learn everyday English:

> I would say that, without Facebook, life would have been much tougher. When I first came here, my English wasn't fluent enough; so, I had to think a lot before speaking. On the Internet, I could copy and paste what my friend said and Google it. I could also Google what I was trying to say [before speaking on Facebook] . . . Using Facebook helped me learn how to speak English.

In comparison, KakaoTalk, which offers services such as instant messaging, group chats, and free calls, was used frequently, especially among Korean peers and small groups. The app was considered more "personal" and "intimate," especially compared to Facebook's highly public interface. In addition to Facebook, the aforementioned Miro recently began to use WeChat, a Chinese-developed app recommended by her Chinese-Canadian friends, with whom she often socialized and studied. Consequently, Miro adopted various digital apps to engage with different ethnically divided user networks. Of course, access to different media platforms is not fully determined by ethnic orientation. For some respondents who migrated to Canada at an early age and considered themselves fully bilingual, access to Korean or Canadian digital platform was described as a code-switching process. For example, Hyunsoo, a 25-year-old man who immigrated at the age of eight, noted that people can "learn cultural cues" using different media outlets, which, for him, involved code switching across two or more cultures.

Some young migrants contrasted the earlier, Korean-based social media site Cyworld with recent social media, such as Facebook. The respondents' recollections reflected the "Cyworld phenomenon" that arose among Korean youth in the early and mid-2000s (Choi, 2006). Based on the respondents' recollections, the Cyworld technology enhances a sense of belonging and sharing, despite being outdated. The respondents, most of whom had used Cyworld enthusiastically for at least a few years (in Korea and/or Canada), were no longer active Cyworld users; they had begun utilizing other social networking sites—Facebook in particular. In fact, the Cyworld phenomenon has ceased in recent years due to the site's failure to respond to the rapidly changing mobile environment (Hjorth, 2014). A few young people still logged into Cyworld to revisit their past diaries, pictures, and peers' comments; however, as of 2014, only one respondent still used the site regularly.[2] Despite the young people's rapid transition to Facebook and other newer social networking tools, such as Instagram, their unique user experiences with Cyworld were not replaced by those of newer social networking sites and apps, as pointed out by Hongshin, a 23-year-old woman who migrated to Canada at the age of 15:

> Facebook does not have a space for keeping journals. On Cyworld, I kept diaries. I also kept [offline] diaries. [Now that I no longer use Cyworld,] I put general information on Facebook while writing my feelings in my diary. Facebook is mainly used to post photos.

In addition, Hongshin considered Facebook a "convenient" tool for organizing events, grouping, and sharing information, while she described Cyworld as a "nest." She noted that Facebook is "too open, and so there is no privacy." The user experiences with Cyworld were often recalled in emotional and intimate terms, as some respondents distinguished its intimate and attractive icons and design from those of Facebook. "I think Facebook is quite dry, but maybe Koreans want a variety of emotional expressions," noted Dami, a 24-year-old woman in Toronto. Such comments seemed to resonate with Hjorth's (2009) observation of young Koreans' use of Cyworld in a highly affective way. The diasporic young people's increasing engagement with Facebook did not necessarily imply that new friend networks were initiated by a digital media form. While several respondents used Facebook to explore new ties, moving beyond ethnically bound and often offline-based friendship circles, most respondents' Facebook friends were largely Koreans in Canada or in Korea, rather than non-Korean Canadians. This finding suggests that, in general, social networking tools may not operate beyond the user's offline networks. This tendency resonates with the findings of a recent American survey, the results of which indicated that young people tend to appropriate social media apps to communicate with peers whom they already know offline (Madden et al., 2013). In the interviewees' recollection, Cyworld was recalled as not only a social networking site but also an archive of personal diaries. By occasionally revisiting Cyworld, which had their notes, postings, and photos, some young people became nostalgic about their childhood and homeland.

The young people's use and perception of Cyworld implies that digital media are culturally appropriated artifacts. Of course, this does not necessarily imply that a particular digital media form has an inherent affinity with a particular cultural or ethnic user group. While culturally specific media design components contribute to attracting a particular user group, a media form's local user base may be significant in its diasporic circulation among user communities that share the same language and culture. That is, a new media form's initial user base (by language and culture), sometimes in combination with a culturally unique design, leads to particular user expansion on a global scale.

Many young people in the study were largely reliant on ethnic (Korean Canadian or Asian Canadian) networks in their everyday lives while acknowledging the obstacles they encountered as ethnic minorities. Regardless of the number of years they had lived in Canada, most young Korean migrants' offline and online social networks largely comprised a substantial number of ethnic Koreans. With the passage of time, the respondents appeared to have become increasingly aware of their ethnic identity. This awareness was evident in the narratives of the older respondents who had experienced discrimination at their workplaces or universities. For example, Bona, a 25-year-old teachers' college student who immigrated to Toronto with her family at the age of 15, commented on the marginalized position of ethnic minorities in the workplace:

> This may be my prejudice, but, you know, when you are looking for a job, whom you know does matter. It seems Asians and Koreans have a limit when it comes to promotions. The top of the ladder is

filled by White people. All White! For example, at my school [i.e., the school where I work as a trainee], the students are mostly immigrants [or ethnic minorities], but more than half of the teachers are White. [. . .] People often say this country is multicultural, but its mainstream is all White.

In this manner, while growing up in Canada, some young migrants gradually discovered the ethnic "glass ceiling" above them. Bomin, a 25-year-old woman who had lived in Toronto for 11 years, recalled,

At college, those whom I can really get along with were Korean [i.e., Korean Canadian] friends. Regarding Canadian [i.e., Canadian-born White] friends, I felt like they're only my colleagues, but not like my friends . . . There was a sort of distance.[3]

Several young people who had lived in Canada longer than in Korea expressed their limited sense of belonging to Canada, which was reflected in their social media use—that is, their ethnically divided online networks. The ethnic enclaves in the digital mediascape may illustrate Canada's ethnically and racially divided social landscape (Henry & Tator, 2009). Thus, the findings in this chapter raise questions about the recent claims that digital media—social media in particular—provide migrant populations with opportunities to explore different levels of social networks, including new networks in the host society (Dekker & Engbersen, 2014). Even for the young cohorts of immigrants, social media enables "bonding" between families and ethnic communities, rather than "bridging" with a wide range of new ties. It can be argued that digital media may not necessarily contribute to building the public sphere but, rather, are appropriated for strengthening homophily—that is, a tendency for people to form ties with others who are similar to themselves. Young diasporic Koreans' digital media practices regarding ethnic bonding are not limited to the media-assisted maintenance of family-like ties. The young people also desire digital homecomings through frequent access to Korean-produced digital media forms and content, as discussed in the following section.

Digital Homeland

In the rapidly evolving media environments, media not only serve to express and construct nostalgia but also function as nostalgic objects; people become nostalgic by engaging with earlier, older media forms and content. Thus, Niemeyer (2014) claimed that "media practice becomes an essential element of nostalgia" (p. 7). Access to the homeland through media content may not be limited to older, first-generation immigrants but also be observed among some young migrants who are fully bilingual (Korean and English) and thus extensively exposed to global media content. Interestingly, though, these young people's engagement with Korean media might involve not only looking back but also exploring who they are through their physical or mediated homecomings.

Accessing Korean media was an important part of the young Korean migrants' media practices, as it kept them updated about their home country and helped them explore their cultural identity. Most respondents often accessed Korean media content via various mobile media, including Korean-based portal sites and video-streaming sites, often in combination with social media—YouTube in particular. Diasporic individuals' efforts to engage in mediated communication with their countries of origin have been observed in the previous literature (e.g., Georgious, 2006; Gillespie, 1995; Kim, 2018; Madianou & Miller, 2012; Wilding, 2006) and are, thus, not unique to the case of young Korean migrants. However, these previous studies focused on conventional media outlets, such as Television (TV), videocassette recorders, and films, without fully exploring how media literacy, experience, and memories of the premigration period might be involved in post-migration media practices. For the young people in the study, older and conventional media forms were often remediated through newer media outlets—for example, watching Korean TV via online streaming services. Moreover, Korean media content was circulated through Korean-based platforms (such as Kakao) and global platforms (YouTube and Netflix).

First, some young migrants favored Korean-based digital platforms. Notably, for several interviewees, a Korean-based media platform was set as the default page for information seeking. While many interviewees identified Google as a popular start-up page on Internet browsers, some had Korean portal sites, such as Naver.com, Nate.com, and Daum.net, as their start-up pages; these were the sites with which they had been familiar during the premigration period. Major Korean portal sites have offered a wide range of services—such as email, news updates, user-generated content, personal blogs, web-based comics (also known as "webtoons" in Korea), and questions and answers (Q&A) sections—and have, thus, created a unique cyberspace in which users can enjoy different forms of media content simultaneously and across genres while communicating with other users.

Nami, a 19-year-old woman who migrated to Canada at the age of 14, recalled how frequently she had used Junior Naver, a sub-portal service for children, offered by the Korean portal site Naver, during her childhood in Korea:

> My first memory of using the Internet was in Grade 1 [in Korea]. I began using the Internet, and at first, I played flash games on Junior Naver. I played them a lot . . . really . . . a lot.

Due to their earlier immersion in Korean portal sites, some respondents seemed to continue using these portals even after migrating to Canada. Sangmi, the aforementioned 22-year-old undergraduate, noted,

> I have been using those portal sites for a while . . . Well . . . they have become a part of my daily life. Through those sites, I figure out what's going on in the world, how others are living, and what's going on in Korea.

In a similar vein, Dami, the aforementioned 24-year-old woman who migrated to Canada at the age of 10, explained what it meant for her to keep track of Korean news on portal sites:

> For me, keeping track of Korean news is kind of the only way I can believe I am Korean. I don't feel I belong to Canada or Korea, and I am desperate to be connected to Korea by catching up with Korean news. [. . .] I don't feel like I understand Canadian culture 100%, because it's a mixed culture.

The respondents who migrated to Canada at a relatively late stage of their adolescence often noted the extensive use of Korean-based portal sites as common mobile platforms. Hyeji, a 20-year-old woman who migrated to Canada at the age of 17, was one such respondent:

> As soon as I get up, I read Naver News [i.e., news available on the Korean portal site Naver] and webtoons. Since it takes one and a half hours to commute, I read Korean news on my smartphone. Mostly news on entertainment or current affairs. Not interested in sports news at all. I read news on politics as well. That's because my dad and mom often talk about [Korean] politics.

As Georgious (2011) argued, diasporic populations' consumption of news from their countries of origin reveals "the desire to keep in touch with the mundane nature of news that can then be shared within familial, domestic, and transnational contexts" (p. 212). Several young Koreans in the study consumed Korean news daily so that their sense of belonging to the homeland might be maintained. Regardless of their citizenship status, several interviewees who had moved to Canada in their early or mid-teens did not self-identify as members of Canada as an imagined community. For example, Misun, a homemaker who had lived in Vancouver for over four years, noted the following:

> Even if I come across news on a big accident that happened in Canada, I don't feel involved. It seems like just an accident—not

much to do with me. But if a similar thing happened in Korea, I would feel much involved. I feel it would be much more important to me, even if I don't live there.

Indeed, some interviewees, regardless of the length of their residency in Canada, expressed their interest in Korean current affairs. When asked what news she followed most at the time of interview (July 2014), Sarang, who immigrated at 14, commented on the sinking of the Sewol ferry in Korea's south sea (April 2014), which resulted in the deaths or missing of 304 passengers, most of whom were minors:

> I follow news about the Sewol ferry incident. I follow things happening in Korea. I used to have fun without following those current affairs, but I am interested in things like Korean politics, as I am away from home. However, I have no interest in Canadian politics. I don't even know who the prime minister is. That's weird, isn't it?

Few interviewees expressed an interest in Canada's provincial or federal politics. Of course, this attitude may not be unique to Korean immigrants, given that the decreasing interest and participation of Canadians in public agendas have been observed in several national surveys (Taras, 2015). However, it seemed evident among several Korean immigrants in the study that Canada was perceived as a place of physical residence rather than one of cultural citizenship. As Lee and Ahn (2019) found in their interview-based study of Korean students in the US, imaginative dwelling on home news and home-country portal sites may adversely affect migrants' interest in news about the host country.

Unlike Canadian or American news portal sites, Korean portals provide various forms of user-generated content and invite users to comment on others' content. In this regard, Korean portal sites have been referred to as commercial "playgrounds for netizens" (Chae & Lee, 2005). However, while most respondents frequently accessed Korean portal sites, these sites were not necessarily their sole or final destinations when using mobile media. The young migrants in the study tended to use different sites and apps omnivorously. While most respondents accessed Korean portal sites frequently, these were not necessarily their sole sources of Korean news and media content. As evidenced by Jimi, a 19-year-old woman who immigrated to Canada at the age of 15, the young migrants tended to use different sites and apps:

> I don't go to any particular news sites anymore. On my Facebook, people link news, video clips, or pictures. When I come across any of those links, and I feel they are important matters, I go to search for them on Naver or Daum [i.e., Korean portal sites].

Despite the geographical distance between Korea and Canada, the young people in the study were frequent or occasional users of Korean-based platforms, such as portal sites and communication apps. By appropriating Korean digital media platforms, they remained exposed to their homeland's current affairs and popular culture.

In addition to the Korean-based portal sites, Korean-produced content itself was deeply incorporated into the diasporic young people's everyday lives. Watching Korean variety shows, reality TV shows, and TV dramas via streaming or file-sharing sites was a common pastime among most respondents. By consuming Korean media content, the young migrants felt the sameness with other diasporic Koreans, on the one hand, and with Koreans in the homeland, on the other. Bona, the aforementioned 25-year-old woman in Toronto, explained, "Watching Korean TV is such a pleasure and a big comfort in the middle of tough migrant life." It is also a nostalgic and emotional activity. Donghyun, a 22-year-old man who immigrated at the age of eight, noted,

> It's [Korean TV viewing] about nostalgia . . . memories . . . It's hard to explain. I mean, I did live in Canada for more than half of my life . . . Korea is where I was born, and I just miss it.

Constant consumption of Korean media content was especially common for a few young homemakers whose daily routines were relatively domestic or whose English language skills were limited. They watched Korean TV dramas as a way to cope with their homesickness, loneliness, and marginality in Canada. Being immersed in Korean TV dramas from time to time seemed to enable the diasporic Korean homemakers to feel as if they were in the homeland. Misun, the aforementioned mother of one, described how habitual her drama watching had been since her immigration.

> I have just kept watching Korean dramas. I watch them more regularly than when I was in Korea. If I visit Korea, I don't watch the dramas. I probably go out or do something else. However, here, I watch them regularly. I feel like I have to watch this show today or that show tomorrow. [. . .] Actually, the dramas seem similar to each other, but the stories are interesting [Interviewer: What aspect of the stories are particularly interesting?] The stories are *makjang* [extreme], but I am still curious about what is going to happen in the next episode.

A few young homemakers frequently accessed other Korean homemakers' blogs or web forums (often called "cafés" or "communities" among Korean Internet users). Among them, three homemakers also had their own blogs to host their diaries in Korean and post pictures through the free blog services available on the aforementioned Korean portal services. Major Korean portal sites offer their subscribers free blog spaces, templates, and visitor statistics, along with many associated services, such as email, networking with other blogs, and Q&A sections. Given the popularity of Korean-based portal services among diasporic Koreans, it was not surprising that some interviewees had personal blogs that were associated with Korean portal services. While only a few respondents, including the aforementioned three homemakers, updated their personal blogs consistently, several more respondents had blogs, whether or not they kept them updated. Blogs seemed to be a means of communicating with their families and friends in the homeland, as well as other Koreans in their current location and in Canada more widely. For these diasporic homemakers, accessing and reading other homemakers' postings provided emotional support and enabled information sharing.

Korean media content, including several Korean variety shows, such as *Infinite Challenge* (2005–2018), was popular among the young migrants in the study. The variety shows, wherein a group of celebrities talk, play, and/or compete together, provide diasporic young people with up-to-date jokes, information about fashion trends, and colloquial expressions that might be circulating in the homeland. Some interviewees noted that TV dramas constituted a genre for their parents, while variety and talk shows were more popular among young people. More recently, the young people in the study were interested in amateur YouTube shows that were produced by Koreans or diasporic Koreans. A few respondents regularly viewed fashion-, cosmetic-, or food-related YouTube channels. For example, Nana, a 19-year-old undergraduate who left Korea at the age of seven, recently enjoyed watching Korean YouTubers' videos. She described a fashion-related Korean YouTube channel that she watched regularly:

> They [the YouTubers] are regular people—not celebrities. So, it's much easier to relate to and understand them. And their videos focus on kind of upbeat things, so they have videos like "What if a coordinator styled your clothing?" They'd all start trying on clothes, and Korean stylists would help them.

Some young people in the study had become interested in the Korean programs only recently, owing to the Korean Wave (i.e., the increasing global spread of Korean media content) and the high availability of these programs on social media, while others had viewed Korean TV programs regularly throughout their post-migration period, representing a continuation of their premigration media experiences. At the time of interviewing, most respondents watched at least one Korean TV program on the Internet on a regular basis. The Korean Wave, emerging via YouTube and numerous streaming sites, has allowed young Korean migrants to easily access the home country's popular culture. They were well aware of how to access Korean media content via numerous channels, sometimes illegally or using foregin-based streaming sites to circumvent copyright regulations.

Why are young diasporic Koreans attracted to their homeland media content? Some respondents noted that they were attracted to Korean shows because of their familiar themes and characters, which were compared to their unfamiliar feelings about Canadian or Western media. Korean TV stars were described as more familiar than their Western counterparts. Korean pop culture might represent an alternative way to negotiate the mainstream (Western) media forms, as Hani, a 25-year-old woman, stated:

> When I chat with Canadians, they talk about some movie star and ask me, "You know him?" But I cannot match them up. Unless I am really into them, I cannot match up Western stars' names and faces. They are quite blurry. But I can easily recognize Kwon Sang Woo, Song Seung Hun . . . [i.e., Korean movie stars].

For the young diasporic Koreans, homeland media did not simply fulfill their nostalgic desires but rather address their interests in youthful and diverse cultural expressions, which are different and move beyond conventional Western pop cultural content. A few interviewees who had lost interest in Korean media for a while after immigration recently began to enjoy Korean content, especially through social media-driven flows of Korean popular culture content. Jenna, a 19-year-old woman who immigrated to Canada in her preteen and several years later became enthusiastic about K-pop, noted, "when I was younger I used to listen to more American pop, because a lot of my elementary school friends just listened to the radio, and they would just listen to what's on." She explained why she became more interested in K-pop than in American pop music: "American songs, usually Hip-Hop, are like really chill, and then their music videos are usually dark. For K-pop, it [the music video] can be really bright, red, yellow, black, white, whatever! And then, the idols dance as well." For Jenna, K-pop was a versatile cultural resource with which she can engage from different angles.

Most respondents, including those who identified themselves as fully bilingual, accessed Korean TV and news frequently, while remaining relatively indifferent to Canadian or American media. Few respondents watched Canadian network TV daily or even weekly. It seems that although cultural diversity is one of the main goals of the Canadian television system (Canadian Radio-television and Telecommunications Commission, 2014), ethnic minorities' interests might not be fully reflected in the national mediascape. The increasing availability of home-country media via the Internet seemed to diminish the migrants' needs to engage with Canadian mainstream media. Direct access to the home-country media might also reduce the role of the locally grown ethnic media—that is, the media "produced by ethnic communities in the host country to serve ethnics' cultural, political, economic and everyday needs" (Shi, 2009, p. 599).

As discussed in this section, the young diasporic Koreans used Korean-based portal sites extensively for information seeking and Korean-based streaming/downloading sites to access Korean popular culture materials. In comparison, Canadian media content did not capture the interests of the young people in the study. This tendency of mediated, transnational identification with the country of origin implies that the literacy and memories of earlier media during the premigration period are persistently integrated into post-migrant lives.

Conclusion

Among various types of transnational youth mobility, diasporic flows of young migrants who relocate to, and grow up in, a distant geographical and cultural context interestingly show how digital media are incorporated into young people's transnational reimagination of who they are and who they become. This research has explored how young diasporic Koreans use digital media in their migrant lives in relation to not only their premigration media experiences but also the persistence of ethnic boundaries. The chapter has shown that new digital media forms are consumed and redefined by the ways in which young migrants, equipped with digital technologies and literacies, negotiate their lives. Their diasporic media practices were largely influenced by their memories and literacies of earlier media in Korea and their desires to connect with ethnic networks. For example, the young people's familiarity with Korean-based social networking and portal sites during the premigration period appeared to affect their post-migration appropriation of newer social media forms.

A particular form of digital media might be adopted in relation to larger media environments. A media form's cultural meaning might be constructed in the context of what Gershon (2012) refers to as "media ideology," whereby media users perceive and understand an individual medium in relation to other existing media options. Moreover, users' experiences and knowledge of previous media forms may also affect how an emerging media form is perceived and used. Migrants' memories of the digital media they used during the premigration period were articulated with the ways in which they defined and used the emerging media forms.

This study has found that while the young diasporic Koreans were able to omnivorously access and appropriate different new media forms beyond the language barriers that older migrants may encounter, their media practices were highly affected by homeland media platforms and content as well as ethnically oriented boundaries. For example, despite its popularity among the respondents, Facebook did not seem to fulfill some young people's desires for intimate communication in ethnic networks. In addition, their social network friendships were ethnically organized, resonating with their offline peer networks. The young migrants' media practices were conditioned by ethnic memories and sociality, as evidenced by their regular and direct access to Korean news and popular culture via Korean-based portals and streaming sites, as well as their ethnic use of social media.

The diasporic young people in the study engaged with the homeland via various Korean-based communication tools and the new media's "filter bubbles" (Pariser, 2011), which often overlapped with offline social networks focused on ethnic ties, as well as their previous media literacies and interests. The ethnic enclave observed in the digital mediascape of diasporic youth in this chapter implies the paradoxes and complexities of digital media practices. That is, despite the enhanced capabilities of ubiquity, interactivity, and transnational mobility, digital media may not necessarily facilitate intercultural communication across ethnic and cultural boundaries.

This chapter's findings suggest that, despite their bilingual and media literacy, diasporic youth are not free of the sociocultural context of their current residence (Gomes, 2018). For example, in response to the dominant representation of Canada as a "cultural mosaic," in which different ethnic groups coexist harmoniously and in a mutually beneficial way, the diasporic Korean youth in the study seemed to engage in the digital ethnic enclave rather than the digital public sphere. As several young migrants in this chapter noted, the ethno-racial glass ceiling gradually becomes noticeable as they grow up (Kim, 2014), and the realities of ethnic division affect their digital media practices. The experiences of marginalization in the "multicultural" host society may partly explain why some diasporic young people engage with their homeland media rather than Canadian media. Of course, digital media may not simply mirror sociocultural contexts. While diasporic young people's access to and appropriation of digital media are influenced by their sociocultural contexts, digital media offer them resources that enable them to constantly reengage with different forms of affiliation (with the homeland, the host society, and in between) and identity (Bailey, 2011; Green & Kabir, 2012; K. Yoon, 2019). The structural discrimination that young migrants encounter might not necessarily be the primary factor in their particular orientation in media practices. Their diasporic choices may affect how digital media are used in their transnational contexts (Oh, 2015). In his study of Korean Americans' use of digital media, Kim (2018) also suggested that 1.5 or later generation Korean immigrants in the US can choose and negotiate between assimilation to the host society and ethnic identity. Furthermore, partly due to evolving digital media environment, migrants' integration into the host land and diasporic orientation toward the left-behind homeland can coexist more easily than ever before.

This chapter's findings suggest the need for further research. First, given that the young migrants' media use revealed certain ethnic boundaries in the digital mediascape, their media practices may have some similarities with those of older migrants, as both show ethnic orientations rather than immersion in the host society's mainstream media. Thus, it may be hasty to contrast the digital generation migrants with other migrant groups in terms of their digital media use. In fact, several scholars have found that the media practices of the younger generation of immigrants do not necessarily differ significantly from those of their first-generation counterparts, as new media environments allow for the continuous convergence of old and new media forms (Han, 2017). In this regard, while acknowledging the potential importance of generational factors in the studies of media and migration, further empirical and comparative studies may be necessary. It seems important to explore differences in media use not only between younger and older immigrant cohorts but also between first- and second-generation immigrants, even those within the same age group.

Second, as Dhoest (2015) pointed out, the recent literature has tended to frame young migrants as underprivileged, marginalized groups in the context of the digital divide discourse. However, this chapter has implied that some young people may already be highly knowledgeable about digital technologies prior to migration and, thus, carry and use their digital literacies as a way to negotiate the experience of mobility. Furthermore, the media literacy and culture that migrants obtained in their country of origin can increasingly be carried over to the host country. In this respect, the recent global rise of Korean popular cultural flows may benefit from the diasporic mobility of young Koreans and Asians who have brought with them their media literacy and memories of Korean media (Yoon & Jin, 2016). It is necessary to further examine how the digital literacy of young people who are on the move is involved in creating a new transnational mediascape.

Notes

1 Banana is a metaphor referring to an Asian ("Yellow on the outside") who is Westernized ("White on the inside") and does not have a sense of connection with his or her Asian cultural heritage. The term often has a derogatory nuance, as used among the diasporic Korean youth interviewed for this chapter. According to Jenna, a 19-year female participant in the study, who identified herself as a K-pop fan, "there are the Korean kids

who were more Canadian rather than Korean. They don't know about K-pop that much."

2 Cyworld terminated its services in 2015.

3 Such distance was less overtly addressed by a few respondents who immigrated to Canada at a relatively early age and who spoke English more frequently than Korean. However, overall, until their transition to university or the labor market, most respondents were not very aware of the structure of White privilege. They noted that they used to have several, if not many, White friends in high school, yet they became gradually aware of differences. High school was described as a place where they became easily immersed in a variety of peers regardless of race and ethnicity, in comparison with their universities or workplaces, where friendship circles are largely segmented according to cultural and ethnic backgrounds. As found in several previous studies, diasporic youth are affiliated more positively with their ethnic identities while at university, rather than during elementary or secondary school (Kim, 2014).

References

Ashcroft, B., Griffiths, G., & Tiffin, H. (Eds.). (1998). *Key concepts in post-colonial studies*. London: Routledge.

Bailey, O. G. (2008). Diasporic identities and mediated experiences in everyday life. In I. Rydin & U. Sjoberg (Eds.), *Mediated crossroads: Identity, youth culture and ethnicity* (pp. 17–38). Göteborg: Nordicom.

Bailey, O. G. (2011). Reconfiguring diasporic-ethnic identities: The web as technology of representation and resistance. In M. Christensen, A. Jansson, & C. Christensen (Eds.), *Online territories: Globalization, mediated practice and social space* (pp. 256–271). New York, NY: Peter Lang.

Bornat, J. (2004). Oral history. In M. S. Lewis-Beck, A. Bryman, & T. F. Liao (Eds.), *Sage encyclopedia of social science research methods* (pp. 771–772). Thousand Oaks, CA: Sage.

Chae, M., & Lee, B. (2005). Transforming an online portal site into a playground for Netizen. *Journal of Internet Commerce, 4*(2), 95–114.

Choi, J. H. (2006). Living in *Cyworld*: Contextualising Cy-ties in South Korea. In A. Bruns & J. Jacobs (Eds.), *Uses of blogs* (pp. 173–186). New York, NY: Peter Lang.

Cottle, S. (Ed.). (2000). *Ethnic minorities and the media: Changing cultural boundaries*. Buckingham: Open University Press.

Canadian Radio-television and Telecommunications Commission. (2014). Offering cultural diversity on TV and Radio. Retrieved from http://www.crtc.gc.ca/eng/info_sht/b308.htm

Dekker, R., & Engbersen, G. (2014). How social media transform migrant networks and facilitate migration. *Global Networks, 14*(4), 401–418.

Dhoest, A. (2015). Connections that matter: The relative importance of ethnic-cultural origin, age and generation in media uses among diasporic youth in Belgium. *Journal of Children and Media, 9*(3), 277–293.

Elias, N., & Lemish, D. (2008). Media uses in immigrant families: Torn between "inward" and "outward" paths of integration. *International Communication Gazette, 70*(1), 21–40.

Georgiou, M. (2006). *Diaspora, identity and the media: Diasporic transnationalism and mediated spatialities*. Cresskill, NJ: Hampton Press.

Georgiou, M. (2011). Diaspora, mediated communication and space: A transnational framework to study identity. In M. Christensen, A. Jansson & C. Christensen (Eds.), *Online territories: Globalization, mediated practice and social space* (pp. 205–221). New York, NY: Peter Lang.

Gershon, I. (2012). *The break up 2.0: Disconnecting over new media*. Ithaca, NY: Cornell University Press.

Gillespie, M. (1995). *Television, ethnicity and cultural change*. London: Routledge.

Gomes, C. (2018). *Siloed diversity*. New York, NY: Palgrave.

Green, L., & Kabir, N. (2012). Australian migrant children: ICT use and the construction of future lives. In L. Fortunati, R. Pertierra & J. Vincent (Eds.), *Migration, diaspora and information technology in global societies* (pp. 91–103). London: Routledge.

Han, G. S. (2017). Korean immigrant media and identity: Minority media, its contributions and constraints. In J. Budarick & G. S. Han (Eds.), *Minorities and media: Producers, industries, audiences* (pp. 125–145). New York, NY: Palgrave.

Henry, F., & Tator, C. (2009). *The colour of democracy: Racism in Canadian society* (4th ed.). Toronto: Nelson Thomson.

Hjorth, L. (2007). "Home and away": A case study of the use of Cyworld mini-hompy by Korean students studying in Australia. *Asian Studies Review, 31*(4), 397–407.

Hjorth, L. (2009). Gifts of presence: A case study of a South Korean virtual community, Cyworld's Mini-Hompy. In G. Goggin & M. McLelland (Eds.), *Internationalizing internet studies* (pp. 249–263). London: Routledge.

Hjorth, L. (2014). Locating the social and mobile: A case study of women's use of Kakao social mobile media in Seoul. *Asiascape: Digital Asia, 1*(1–2), 39–53.

Jensen, A. (2011). Mobility, space and power: On the multiplicities of seeing mobility. *Mobilities, 6*(2), 255–271.

Kim, D. Y. (2014). Coping with racialization: Second-generation Korean-American responses to racial othering. In P. G. Min & S. Noh (Eds.), *Second-generation Korean experiences in the United States and Canada* (pp. 145–165). Lanham, MD: Lexington Books.

Kim, D. Y. (2018). *Transnational communities in the smartphone age: The Korean community in the nation's capital*. Lanham, MD: Lexington Books.

King, R., & Wood, N. (Eds.). (2001). *Media and migration: Constructions of mobility and difference*. London: Routledge.

Kwak, M. J. & Hiebert, D. (2010). Globalizing Canadian education from below: A case study of transnational immigrant entrepreneurship between Seoul, Korea and Vancouver Canada. *Journal of International Migration and Integration, 11*(2), 131–153.

Lee, C. S., & Ahn, J. H. (2019). Imagining homeland: New media use among Korean international graduate students in the U.S. In A. Atay & M. U. D'Silva (Eds.), *Mediated intercultural communication in digital age* (pp. 185–203). London: Routledge.

Madden, M., Lenhart, A., Cortesi, S., Gasser, U., Duggan, M., Smith, A., … Beaton, M. (2013). Teens, social media, and privacy. *Pew Research Center's*

Internet & American Life Project. Retrieved from https://www.pewinternet. org/2013/05/21/teens-social-media-and-privacy/

Madianou, M., & Miller, D. (2012). *New media and migration.* London: Routledge.

Mattelart, T. (2010). Media, migrations and transnational cultures. In S. Papathanassopoulos (Ed.), *Media perspectives for the 21st century* (pp. 100–114). New York, NY: Routledge.

Mayer, V. (2003). *Producing dreams, consuming youth: Mexican Americans and mass media.* New Brunswick, NJ: Rutgers University Press.

Middleton, C. (2011). From Canada 2.0 to a digital nation: The challenge of creating a digital society in Canada. In M. Moll & L. R. Shade (Eds.), *The Internet tree* (pp. 3–16). Ottawa: Canadian Centre for Policy Alternatives.

Miller, D. (2012). Preface: Mediating a restless world. In L. Fortunati, R. Pertierra, & J. Vincent (Eds.), *Migration, diaspora and information technology in global societies* (pp. xiii–xvi). London: Routledge.

Nedelcu, M. (2012). Migrants' new transnational habitus: Rethinking migration through a cosmopolitan lens in the digital age. *Journal of Ethnic and Migration Studies, 38*(9), 1339–1356.

Niemeyer, K. (2014). Introduction: Media and nostalgia. In N. Niemeyer (Ed.), *Media and nostalgia: Yearning for the past, present and future* (pp. 1–23). New York, NY: Palgrave.

Nowak, P. (2014). Why Internet upload speed in Canada lags behind world average. Retrieved from http://www.cbc.ca/news/technology/why-internet-upload-speed-in-canada-lags-behind-world-average-1.2578682

Oh, D. C. (2015). *Second-generation Korean Americans and transnational media: Diasporic identifications.* Lanham, MD: Lexington Books.

Park, S. (2017). *Digital capital.* New York, NY: Palgrave.

Pariser, E. (2011). *The filter bubble: What the Internet is hiding from us.* New York, NY: Penguin Press.

Peeters, A. L., & d'Haenens, L. (2005). Bridging or bonding? Relationships between integration and media use among ethnic minorities in the Netherlands. *Communications: The European Journal of Communication Research, 30*(2), 201–231.

Shi, Y. (2009). Re-evaluating the alternative role of ethnic media in the U.S.: The Case of Chinese language press and working-class women readers. *Media, Culture and Society, 31*(4), 597–606.

Statistics Canada (2019). Focus on geography series: 2016 Census. Retrieved from https://www12.statcan.gc.ca/census-recensement/2016/as-sa/fogs-spg/Facts-can-eng.cfm?Lang=Eng&GK=CAN&GC=01&TOPIC=7

Taras, D. (2015). *Digital mosaic: Media, power, and identity in Canada.* Toronto: University of Toronto Press.

Vittadini, N., Reifova, I. C., Siibak, A., & Bilandzic, H. (2014). Generations and media: The social construction of generational identities and differences. In N. Carpentier, K. Schroder & L. Hallet (Eds.), *Audience transformations. Shifting audience positions in late modernity* (pp. 65–81). London: Routledge.

Wilding, R. (2006). "Virtual" intimacies? Families communicating across transnational contexts. *Global Networks: A Journal of Transnational Affairs, 6*(2), 125—142.

Yoon, I. J. (2012). The Korean diaspora from global perspectives. In S. Noh, A. H. Kim & M. S. Noh (Eds.), *Korean immigrants in Canada: Perspectives on migration, integration, and the family* (pp. 37–52). Toronto: Toronto University Press.

Yoon, K. (2019). Diasporic youth culture of K-pop. *Journal of Youth Studies*, 22(1), 138–152.

Yoon, K., & Jin, D. Y. (2016). The Korean wave phenomenon in Asian diasporas in Canada. *The Journal of Intercultural Studies*, 37(1), 69–83.

7 Conclusion
Youth as Cultural Translators

This book has examined how young people engage transnationally with digital media. Drawing on an ethnographic analysis of different groups of young people who are physically or virtually on the transnational move, the book has discussed how digital media are incorporated into transnational flows of popular culture and young people. It has sought a nuanced understanding of the user agency and context of digital mediascapes. The young people examined in this book engaged with transnational popular culture and media forms while negotiating everyday life and imagining different ways of life. They developed their own strategies for using digital media as a method of coping with different forces that affected their cultural consumption, communication, sense of belonging, and future prospects.

To examine the transnational mediascapes of young people in relation to Korean media and popular culture, this book has explored two approaches. The first draws on audience studies of young media fans in Korea and Canada who consume popular cultures other than their own. Through this approach, Chapters 2 and 3 have illustrated how Japanese popular culture was incorporated into Korean youth culture in the early digital era and how K-pop has recently emerged as a digital media-driven, global youth cultural trend. Audience studies have shown how media are not simply the objects of consumption; media are incorporated into everyday lives and create different meanings depending on audience members' subject positions and cultural contexts (Athique, 2017; Liebes & Katz, 1994). In particular, recent studies of fan audiences have engaged with the transnational dimension of cultural consumption and production among media fans (e.g., Chen, 2018; Chin & Morimoto, 2013; Min, Jin, & Han, 2018; Yoon, 2019). While transnational fan studies explore how and why fans engage with cultural materials produced in different cultural and linguistic contexts, they do not always effectively address the structural forces that may affect fans' responses to media. To move beyond this limitation, Chapters 2 and 3, the two empirical chapters that drew on media fan studies, paid due attention to the structural factors that may condition young people's media practices. Chapter 2 addressed national regulation and gatekeeping regarding the consumption of Japanese media in Korea, and Chapter 3 considered the technological affordance and corporate power involved in digital and social media that seemingly enable a participatory culture.

The second approach draws on technology domestication studies to explore how media technology finds a place and is contextualized in the lives of young people who are physically on the transnational move. The technology domestication approach provided an effective framework for understanding media practices in context. While early empirical studies focused in particular on exploring the meanings and uses of media technology in the home and household, recent studies have widened the scope to include transnational contexts beyond the domestic surroundings. Domestication studies have strengthened their holistic, context-oriented approach, by examining wider social contexts in which media practices occur and thus gain meaning (Lim, 2016). The second half of this book—Chapters 4–6 in particular—contributes to expanding the scope of technology domestication analysis to transnational contexts. It informs how digital media are contextualized and appropriated in relation to other daily activities and human networks. However, given the inherent limitations of the domestication approach as a microanalysis, it can be supplemented by a macro-level analysis that examines media use trends over time (Haddon, 2011).

By combining audience studies and technology domestication studies, this book contributes to a better understanding of transnational media practices in context from the users' perspectives. The young people in the study seemed to function as foot soldiers of "transnationalism from below" (Smith & Guarnizo, 1998). The diverse groups of young people in the study were exposed to a wide range of available media and were equipped with the media literacy to use them. However, digitally equipped youth are not inherently empowered. As both audience studies and technology domestication studies suggest, media users are required to negotiate contextual and structural forces. The young people's media practices seemed not to be based solely on their user agency to choose particular media options; rather, their use implied that media were always practiced in context.

Media practices need to be examined in context, especially in relation to other activities and forces in the offline environment, as well as previous media experiences. For example, the same smartphone and its apps can have different meanings and usages for young people in diverse situations. Through their interactions with their sociocultural resources, young people make choices and develop media strategies (Madianou & Miller, 2012). For example, the young sojourners, whose lifestyles are transient, restricted their media use at least temporarily to cope with their limited material resources and/or to enable them to imagine themselves as authentic overseas sojourners. In comparison, due to their bicultural and bi-linguistic literacy, the young permanent migrants discussed in this book were more flexible with regard to accessing different media forms. However, they chose to engage extensively with ethnic language or homeland-produced media due to strong offline ethnic networks and existing racial discrimination in the host society.

While digital media contribute to young people's transnational mobility, the shape, scope, and speed of transnationality are not free of the national and local contexts in which they access, explore, utilize, and negotiate particular digital media. For example, young Korean *otaku*'s media consumption relates to how to negotiate the national regulations and sentiments toward the ex-colonizer. In comparison, young K-pop fans in Canada access Korean popular culture through digital media, which are partly affected by the ways in which they translate the national signifier "K" in K-pop in relation to their own ethnic and cultural backgrounds. Young people in transnational families adopt and resignify different digital communication technologies to maintain a sense of familial connection. The premigration media experiences of young Korean migrants in Canada may influence how they understand and use emerging media forms in their current location.

In the digitally saturated world, it is difficult to demarcate context from text (e.g., media form from content). Digital media have been seamlessly integrated into young people's everyday lives and, thus, reveal the importance of the context of media practices. Due to the increasing incorporation of digital technologies into daily rhythms, a clear demarcation between media-related and others types of activities no longer seems to exist. For example, according to the descriptions provided by many of the young people who were interviewed for this book, their daily routines both began and ended with their smartphones. Some held their smartphones and/or habitually viewed the screens during the interviews. Indeed, as young people's daily lives become more media-saturated than ever before, it may be difficult to demarcate media practices from other daily rituals, interactions, and activities. Digital media are incorporated into various areas of young people's everyday lives; thus, it would be difficult to examine youth and their culture without addressing how media are synergistically converged to generate diverse meanings for different moments in life.

The increasing time and space saturated by various forms of digital media appear to call for "non-media centric media studies," which address media users' "everyday environmental experiences, including their practical, embodied and sensuous involvements with media of communication" (Moores, 2012, p. 109). As McMillin (2009) suggested, despite their important roles, "media are only a part of people's daily rituals" because media constitute "one element in the many practices that flow through an individual's daily routine" (p. 184). A closer look at the context of media practices, as proposed by the advocates of non-media-centric media studies, offers insights into how digital media can contribute to better understanding transnational youth and their cultures. A contextual analysis of transnational media use reveals the diversity and complexity of the digital mediascapes with which young people engage.

The research's findings suggest further investigation of digital contexts in which young people's media literacies and practices influence, and are influenced by, the uneven distribution of "digital capital"—a particular ecosystem that "shapes and guides how the user engages with digital technologies" (Park, 2017, p. 1). That is, despite the seemingly abundant digital media resources, digital media literacies are unevenly distributed, and thus, digital mediascapes may not necessarily be the public sphere open to every media user. Young people today are undeniably exposed to and have access to digital media, compared with their predecessors. Globally, a higher proportion of the young demographic (71% of those aged 15–24 years), in comparison with the general population (48%), have regular access to the Internet (ITU, 2017). However, the flourishing digital media environment and accessibility may not necessarily guarantee the empowerment of young people. Noticeable divides and inequality continue to exist in regard to digital media resources. While an increasing number of young people access the Internet, this alone cannot explain the uneven distribution of digital resources. As recent studies have revealed, what is increasingly important is the "second-level digital divide" (i.e., the disparity in Internet use skills), rather than the rate of access to digital media (Hargittai, 2002). This nuanced understanding of the digital divide helps to avoid the technological determinist perspective that is pervasive in discussions about youth and digital media (Selwyn, 2004; Warschauer, 2003). Moreover, it is important to consider which type of digital literacy is more valued than others and thus transferred to a form of sociocultural capital. For example, it is interesting to examine how young migrants' digital media literacies and experiences in their past—in their left-behind homeland—would be recognized in the host society. There may be some obstacles for transnational media users to transfer and develop their media literacy in negotiation of structural forces, such as national regulations (as shown in the Korean government's ban on Japanese popular culture) and racial discrimination (as shown in the case of young migrants and K-pop fans in Canada).

It is true that, compared to conventional, earlier media forms such as television, radio, and landline telephone, digital media offer further room for user engagement. In particular, digital advocates have emphasized that it is not the platform provider but the user that curates information in the digital media environments (Rheingold, 2012). However, given that the user is not fully informed of how the platform's algorithm operates, the user's agency and influences may not be as substantial as the digital advocates claim. Indeed, regardless of several factors, such as users' geographic locations and sociocultural positions, the digital mediascape appears to be standardized to some extent, due to similarity in the technological design of major digital media platforms. In particular, as Kellerman (2006) claimed, technologies that enhance transnational mobility seem to be more and more standardized. The standardization of technology in terms of design and user interface has also been observed since the early period of the Internet (Bowers, Vasquez, & Roaf, 2000). Digital media's technological affordances may reinforce the seamlessness between media practices and other daily practices and, thus, often conceal the ongoing structural forces of global capitalism and its endless commodification of culture through exploitation of free labor of media users (Terranova, 2000). A contextualized and comprehensive analysis can reveal the complexity of digital media culture and, thus, critically reexamine the celebrated tone of the proponents of digital media-driven and user-oriented participatory culture.

This book began with appropriating Appadurai's (1996) notion of mediascape to address the emergence of complex, multicentric, and multidirectional flows of media and popular culture and people. In increasingly transnationalized worlds, digital mediascapes are evolving, negotiated, and redefined by different stakeholders. In particular, young people participate in digital mediascapes not only as consumers but also as producers. Furthermore, they are rather cultural translators—"in both literal and metaphorical ways" (Kustritz, 2016, para. 1). Some are literally translators, as exemplified by fansubbers who translate texts into different languages and contribute to transnationally disseminating particular cultural forms; others metaphorically translate (i.e., reinterpret and rework) cultural texts produced in a linguistic and cultural context into content relevant to another context. The literal and metaphorical modes of translation in transnational digital mediascapes are ongoing rather than complete at one point. Young people continuously generate new meanings of digital media in transnational contexts. For example, fan subs can continuously be revised and updated, without necessarily resulting in authoritative, final versions of translation. As another example, a locally produced app, such as KakaoTalk, can be appropriated in a different cultural contexts and thus continuously generate new meanings. By engaging with different forms of digital media from their own perspectives and negotiating structural forces through their own strategies, young people translate digital mediascapes.

References

Appadurai, A. (1996). *Modernity at large: Cultural dimensions of globalization.* Minneapolis, MN: University of Minnesota Press.

Athique, A. (2017). *Transnational audiences: Media reception on a global scale.* Oxford: Polity.

Bowers, C. A., Vasquez, M., & Roaf, M. (2000). Native people and the challenge of computers: Reservation schools, individualism, and consumerism. *American Indian Quarterly, 24*(2), 182–199.

Chen, L. (2018). *Chinese fans of Japanese and Korean pop culture: Nationalistic narratives and international fandom.* London: Routledge.

Chin, B., & Morimoto, L. (2013). Towards a theory of transcultural fandom. *Participations: Journal of Audience and Reception Studies, 10*(1), 92–108.

Haddon, L. (2011). Domestication analysis, objects of study, and the centrality of technologies in everyday life. *Canadian Journal of Communication, 36*(2), 311–323.

Hargittai, E. (2002). Second-level digital divide: Differences in people's online skills. *First Monday, 7*(4). Retrieved from https://firstmonday.org/ojs/index.php/fm/article/view/942

ITU (International Telecommunication Union). (2017). ICT facts and figures. Retrieved from https://www.itu.int/en/ITU-D/Statistics/Pages/facts/default.aspx

Kellerman, A. (2006). *Personal mobilities.* London: Routledge.

Kustritz, A. (2016). Transnational fan works as popular translation. Retrieved from http://mediacommons.org/fieldguide/question/what-ways-do-internet-tools-and-culture-recursively-affect-both-international-and-localiz-8

Liebes, T., & Katz, E. (1994). *The export of meaning: Cross-cultural readings of Dallas.* Oxford: Polity Press.

Lim, S. S. (Ed.). (2016). *Communication and the family: Asian experiences in technology domestication.* New York, NY: Springer.

Madianou, M., & Miller, D. (2012). *Migration and new media: Transnational families and polymedia.* New York, NY: Routledge.

McMillin, D. (2009). *Mediated identities: Youth, agency, & globalization.* New York, NY: Peter Lang.

Min, W. J., Jin, D. Y., & Han, B. (2019). Transcultural fandom of the Korean Wave in Latin America: Through the lens of cultural intimacy and affinity space. *Media, Culture & Society, 41*(5), 604–619.

Moores, S. (2012). *Media, place and mobility.* New York, NY: Palgrave.

Park, S. (2017). *Digital capital.* New York, NY: Palgrave.

Rheingold, H. (2012). *Net smart: How to thrive online.* Cambridge, MA: MIT Press.

Selwyn, N. (2004). Reconsidering political and popular understandings of the digital divide. *New Media & Society, 6*(3), 341–362.

Smith, M. P., & Guarnizo, L. (Eds.). (1998). *Transnationalism from below.* New Brunswick, NJ: Transaction Books.

Terranova, T. (2000). Free labor: Producing culture for the digital economy. *Social Text, 18*(2), 33–58.

Warschauer, M. (2003). *Technology and social inclusion: Rethinking the digital divide.* Cambridge, MA: MIT Press.

Yoon, K. (2019). Transnational fandom in the making: K-pop fans in Vancouver. *International Communication Gazette, 81*(2), 176–192.

Index

Note: Page numbers followed by "n" denote endnotes.

Printed in the United States
by Baker & Taylor Publisher Services